ETHICAL LEADERSHIP

"*Ethical Leadership* is a vital contribution as a new generation prepares to enter a world of unscripted moral challenges. Drawing on theorists from a broad spectrum of disciplines, *Ethical Leadership* delivers a persuasive appeal for compassion and courage: compassion to listen to our own stories and the stories of others and courage to lead in community despite difficult differences. Heir to a tradition of extraordinary leaders at Morehouse College, Fluker challenges us to lead in service of the common good. For all seeking practical wisdom on the road to change, *Ethical Leadership* will serve as a remarkable and inspiring resource."

—Carol Geary Schneider
   President, Association of American Colleges and Universities

"I applaud Dr. Fluker for bringing Howard Thurman to life in this volume. He was one of the most powerful, but probably least known, of the great teachers and mentors who influenced Martin Luther King."

—Ambassador James A. Joseph
   Duke University

ETHICAL LEADERSHIP

The Quest for Character, Civility, and Community

Walter Earl Fluker

Fortress Press
MINNEAPOLIS

For Sharon

ETHICAL LEADERSHIP
The Quest for Character, Civility, and Community®

Cover image: © Ryan McVay / Photodisc / Getty Images
Cover design: Glennon Design Group
Author photo: Phillip McCollum
Book design: James Korsmo

Library of Congress Cataloging-in-Publication Data
Fluker, Walter E., 1951-
  Ethical leadership : the quest for character, civility, and community / Walter Earl Fluker.
    p. cm.
  Includes bibliographical references and index.
  ISBN 978-0-8006-6349-0 (alk. paper)
  1. Leadership—Religious aspects—Christianity. 2. Leadership. 3. Christian ethics. 4. Ethics. I. Title.
  BV4597.53.L43F58 2008
  241'.641—dc22   2008040729

Manufactured in the U.S.A.

13   12   11   10   09   1   2   3   4   5   6   7   8   9   10

Contents

PREFACE

A public conversation on the role of ethical leadership is escalating in our society. As I write this preface, our nation is involved in two costly wars; struggling with a financial crisis precipitated by unscrupulous ethical practices on Wall Street; recovering from a presidential campaign that degenerated into character assassination based on race, religion, and unresolved cultural wars; and hearing a confused and frightened citizenry that is asking, "Which way is north?" Leadership studies abound with various approaches to this question. Among the most popular are theories of adaptive strategies, authenticity, personal efficacy, character development, and more recently, a growing literature on emotional and social intelligence, connectivity, and resonance.[1] Absent from many of these approaches is attention to the relationship between spirituality and ethics and how it informs and shapes human consciousness so that leaders are predisposed to make fitting decisions and are enabled to carry out appropriate ethical actions among competing claims and a cacophony of voices and visions.

A major assumption of this book is that leaders of the new century must not only be aware of environmental realities that shape the challenges and issues that they must confront. They must also be aware of the inner environments that shape character, civility, and a sense of community. Leaders who are not awake, that is, aware of the interiority of experience, the subconscious elements that often drive behavior and action, are increasingly in very vulnerable circumstances and can endanger the mission of a team, organization and, as we have witnessed too many times to ignore, very large numbers of people. Therefore, we ask, what are the critical resources and methodologies at our disposal to develop a new generation of emerging leaders who are *awake*—physically and emotionally

viii   ETHICAL LEADERSHIP

whole, spiritually disciplined, intellectually astute, and morally anchored? In this book, I attempt to answer this question and to address the challenges and issues attendant to ethical leadership by using a model that I developed as part of a research project funded by the W. K. Kellogg Foundation in the early 1990s, my continuing editorial work on the Howard Thurman Papers Project, and my work with the Morehouse College Martin Luther King Jr. Collection at Morehouse College in Atlanta, Georgia.

Basically, the model revolves around three ethical practices: character, civility, and community. Each practice represents a corresponding dimension of the personal (character), societal (civility) and spiritual (community). In the research funded by the Kellogg Foundation project, which examined the development of ethical leadership from the black church tradition, we discovered that narrative-based ethics was the most appropriate way to understand how character, civility, and community were formed among leaders in that tradition.[2] After four years of work with "at-risk youth" in the poverty-stricken areas of Rochester, New York, we developed a curriculum for training emerging leaders that has resulted in my work at the Leadership Center at Morehouse College and VisionQuest International at colleges and universities, and with private and public leaders, here and abroad.

The audience for this book is primarily the intelligent lay reader. It is not limited to academics, theologians, leadership scholars and practitioners, but to a large spectrum of individuals who are interested in the relation between spirituality, ethics, personal development, calling, and a deep sense of justice. I introduce, to some, the legacy of Howard Washington Thurman (1899-1981) and the better-known work of Martin Luther King Jr. (1929-1968) as critical resources in the development of a model of ethical leadership that promotes the relationship between spirituality and social transformation. My work on Thurman and King, published as *They Looked for a City: A Comparative Analysis of the Thought of Howard Thurman and Martin Luther King Jr.* (University Press of America, 1989), is the early blueprint that led me to further investigate the black church tradition as a source for the development of ethical leadership. A basic premise that informs their place in this earlier publication is that out of their particularized social historical locations, they provide a larger vision for the place of ethical leadership in America and the world. King's description of leaders as *transformed nonconformists* and Thurman's idea of *apostles of sensitiveness* describe in part what I have in mind when I speak of ethical leadership.

The underlying theme that runs through the manuscript is the need for spirituality, ethics, and leadership that will require a new way of looking at all three components—especially around issues of difference. In the Intro-duction, "At the Intersection Where Worlds Collide," I offer a personal story which contextualizes the language of "lifeworlds" and "systems," liberally borrowed from Husserl, Heiddeger, Arendt and Habermas, but without a lot of chatter about the history of the terms. I am most inter-ested in helping readers to understand that fragile lifeworlds, as described, are under assault by vast and often impersonal systems that place leaders in very dangerous, vulnerable, and practically impossible situations (the intersection). Leaders, therefore, who aspire to ethical life and practice, need to cultivate certain habits and practices that allow them to negotiate and hopefully transform the intersection. I am not all convinced that the proliferation of rules, laws, and penalties that promote governance, trans-parency, and accountability among public leaders—though necessary—are adequate. I believe we need to look at the question of ethics and leadership differently in order to address the challenges of the intersection.

Often when we use terms like "ethical leadership," it is done without any critical or reflective thought. The words *ethical* and *leader* are so well entrenched in everyday speech that it is difficult to dislodge them from their popular, though largely unexamined, meanings. When most people think of ethical leadership, they tend to imbue leadership with values or a certain kind of moral character that we have witnessed in particular indi-viduals. These associations are correct, but ethics and leadership are a lot like love and war: all is fair, but underneath their common employment lie a multitude of sins and methodological errors.[3] The philosopher Ludwig Wittgenstein challenged his listeners to really "look" at a phenomenon beyond its accepted linguistic configurations and to ask the harder ques-tion of "What do I mean when I say *x, y,* and *z?*" For instance, *ethical* in certain contexts does not properly apply in others. Clearly, the moral quag-mires of same-sex marriage, euthanasia, stem cell research, and abortion are testaments of what is at stake for ethical questions raised in public life. Moral norms and customs that are so easily accepted within certain com-munities of discourse and practice run into complex conundrums when placed in a larger public debate where a diversity of views prevails.

The question of leadership is just as difficult to address when we are forced to look at it. For instance, are all leaders, by virtue of the label, good leaders? Can one be a leader and not be good? Is there something inherent in the definition of *leader* that suggests some moral obligation? When lead-ers fail to be "good," what are we implying about the definition of *leader*? Is leadership tied to position only, or are other assumptions being made about "leadership" and "good"? If all leaders are not "good," and if position is not the defining variable of leadership, then what is? What do we mean by a "good leader" anyway? This book is a call to leaders at the intersection who dare to remember, retell, and relive their stories as a basis for personal and social transformation. I begin by remembering and retelling my own story, and throughout the book I interweave personal memories and meditations that I hope will inspire and challenge others to do the same.

Chapter 1 introduces the ethical leadership practices of Howard Washington Thurman and Martin Luther King Jr. as critical resources in the development of ethical leadership. Their remarkable lives and social witness are not only tributes to the legacies of excellence that they leave for us, but also are rich in explicating the problematic issue of ethical leadership in the twenty-first century. In chapter 2, "What Is Ethical Leadership?" I provide an early working definition of ethical leadership that incorporates the dynamics of spirituality, ethics, and leadership as a way of addressing the challenges of character, civility, and community. It outlines four traditional ways that the modern world has conceived the practices of ethics and how these practices impact leadership at the intersection of *lifeworlds* and *systems*. I present a fifth, non-exclusive way of doing ethics that I describe as the way of the storyteller. Here the emphasis is on narrative-based ethics and the ways in which leaders critically reflecting on collective memory and specific cultural narratives are enabled to reconnect with forgotten practices. These practices form certain kinds of communities of discourse and practice that represent virtues, values, and virtuosities (excellencies) that allow retrieval and appropriation for the present. In chapters 3-5, utilizing the three pivotal practices of character, civility, and community, I discuss the critical virtues, values, and virtuosities that are integral to the practices. I invite the reader to rethink these pivotal practices in respect to race and difference, which are long-standing issues that test the vision of America and its quest for character, civility, and community. Respectively, under chapter 3, "Character at the Intersection," I discuss three virtues: integrity, empathy, and hope; chapter 4, "Civility at the Intersection," the three values or social practices: recognition, respect, and reverence; and chapter 5, "Community at the Intersection," three virtuosities: courage, justice, and compassion.

Chapters 6-8 present practical skills and competencies that emerging leaders need in order to negotiate and transform the traffic at the intersection. These last chapters integrate the proposed model of ethical leadership for the development and training of emerging leaders using the defining concepts and practices of character, civility, and community. Chapter 6, "Staying Awake at the Intersection," addresses the challenge for emerging leaders to become aware of internal and external environments that engender possibility, hope, and vision. Emphasis is placed on the role of spirituality and imagination in public life with specific emphases on character, civility, and community. Chapter 7, "Remembering, Retelling, and Reliving Our Stories" is one of the most practical of the discussions that encourages emerging leaders to return to personal narratives that are connected to larger social historical narratives that form character, civility, and community. Chapter 8 introduces a process for ethical decision-making for leaders involving *looking, listening,* and *learning;* and *discerning, deliberating,* and *deciding* with attendant examinations of specific cases of ethical leadership.

ACKNOWLEDGMENTS

While responsibility for the final product is clearly my own, I am deeply indebted to a large range of institutions, foundations, and people for this book. Morehouse College has provided the space, resources, and intellectual camaraderie for the completion of the basic conceptual model presented here. My day-to-day interaction with some of the brightest and most energetic students I have encountered in my twenty years of teaching have forced me to rethink the practical usages of ideas and materials associated with my role as Coca-Cola Professor of Leadership Studies and Executive Director of the Leadership Center at Morehouse College (LCMC). Scholars-in-Residence at LCMC, Dr. Preston King and Dr. R. Drew Smith, have been steady interlocutors who have challenged basic assumptions about ethics, leadership, and philosophical, political, and religious traditions that I hope are presented with greater clarity in this present work. The LCMC advisory board and LCMC administrative team—Dr. Melvinia Turner King, Ms. Geri Oladuwa, and Ms. Laketha Hudson—have made it possible for me to find time to write and manage the day-to-day operations of the Center's work. Dr. King deserves special mention for her meticulous reading of the manuscript and critical feedback throughout the preparation of the final draft. The final stages of permissions, copyediting, and meeting the publisher's deadlines would have been impossible without the dedication of Dr. Kai Issa-Jackson and the Howard Thurman Papers Project staff, Mr. Jamison Collier and Ms. Michelle Meggs. Dr. Jackson has been a critical liaison between the publisher and me during the hectic process of finalizing the book for publication. I also owe a huge debt of gratitude to Ms. Mae Gentry for her assistance in copyediting the first draft.

A grant from the Louisville Institute under the direction of Dr. James Lewis allowed a semester-long sabbatical at Princeton Theological Seminary in spring 2005 to conduct research and writing. Many thanks to Dr. Peter J. Paris and former President of Princeton Theological Seminary, Dr. Thomas W. Gillespie for the quiet space and access to library holdings and for their earlier invitation to deliver the Dr. Martin Luther King Jr. Lecture on December 1, 2003 in Miller Chapel, "Transformed Nonconformity: Spirituality, Ethics, and Leadership in the Life and Work of Martin Luther King Jr.," which is incorporated in the present work. In fall 2000, I was invited to serve as Visiting Professor of African-American Religious Studies at the Harvard University Divinity School, where I taught seminars on The Development of Ethical Leadership from the Black Church Tradition, The Ethical Leadership of Martin Luther King Jr. and The Religious Thinking of Howard Thurman, which were invaluable opportunities to test ideas presented here. I am also indebted to Dr. Terrence Johnson, now an assistant professor at Haverford College, who quietly and diligently served as my research assistant during that year. During the same year I was a Fellow at the Center for Public Leadership at the John F. Kennedy School of Government at Harvard University, where I presented an earlier version of the ethical leadership model to distinguished leaders and leadership theorists whose critiques and feedback have shaped my methodological approach and discussion on traditions and traditionalism in chapter 2. My friendships and collegial relationships with Professors David Gergen, Warren Bennis, Barbara Kellerman, and Ronald Heifitz evolved into my present membership on the selection panel for U. S. News and World Report's *America's Best Leaders,* where I have had opportunity to explore more deeply the dynamic relation of ethics and leadership in public domains. A special thanks to Warren Bennis, who read an earlier draft of the manuscript and offered important insights and encouragement.

I would like to express my gratitude to Professor Kurt April and Ambassador James Joseph, who were instrumental in my appointment as Visiting Professor at the Graduate School of Business at the University of Cape Town, South Africa, in 2004, where I presented lectures on "Authentic Leadership Practices." This relationship with Kurt April produced two articles: "Somewhere, Sometime, Someplace: The Call to Ethical Leadership" (2005); and "Beware of the Unicorns! Ethical Leadership and the Power of Imagination" (2006),[4] which have been modified and integrated in chapters 5 and 6.

The journey to this final product has been informed mainly by practical implementation of the ideas presented here with emerging leaders. In this regard, I owe a great deal of thanks to Ms. Oprah Winfrey for her generosity of spirit. In February 2004, at the Morehouse College gala, my wife and I sat at dinner with Ms. Winfrey along with former Morehouse president, Walter E. Massey and his wife, Mrs. Shirley Massey. I shared with Ms. Winfrey my vision to develop a new generation of ethical leaders at Morehouse College who would serve as ambassadors and learners in the developing democracy of South Africa. She listened intently and had probing questions about my plans and the meaning of ethical leadership that combined spirituality and ethics in the development of leaders. When she was called to the podium that evening to address a capacity crowd, she announced that she would endow the program. The Oprah Winfrey South African Leadership Program now sponsors an annual study tour to South Africa that allows Morehouse students to study ethical leadership practices in South Africa around issues of poverty and HIV/AIDS and then to return to the Morehouse College campus and initiate projects that promote practices of ethical leadership. Special thanks are extended to Ms. Caren Yanis (Executive Director) and Dr. Sonya Anderson (Education Program Director, the Oprah Winfrey Foundation), who work closely with the Leadership Center at Morehouse College each year in this ongoing effort. Other foundations and corporations that have been instrumental in providing support for our work and have provided opportunities for practical engagement with emerging leaders in the United States and around the globe deserve acknowledgment. Ms. Ingrid Saunders Jones and Mrs. Helen Smith-Price of the Coca-Cola Foundation sponsor an annual pre-college leadership program at Morehouse College where 30 high school students from different regions of the country are trained by VisionQuest International facilitators in ethical leadership utilizing curriculum developed from the model discussed in this book. Dr. Carol Schneider, President, and Dr. Caryn McTighe Musil, Senior Vice President, Office of Diversity, Equity, and Global Initiatives of the Association of American Colleges and Universities, have been great supporters of this work in liberal arts colleges and universities. I wish to extend my appreciation to Ms. Stephanie Bell-Rose (President of the Goldman Sachs Foundation) and Dr. Allan E. Goodman (President and CEO of the Institute of International Education), sponsors of the Goldman Sachs Global Leaders Program; Ambassador Charles Stith, Director of the African Presidential Archives and Research Center at Boston University, which sponsors an annual teach-in on ethical leadership for emerging U.S. and African leaders taught by LCMC staff; and the U.S. State Department, which has invited me to lecture and teach ethical leadership in India, China, Nigeria, and South Africa. Mr. Peter J. Vedro, Dr. Howard Rossman, Mr. Tommy Brewer, Mr. Melvin Watson III, and Clinton Fluker of VisionQuest International (a nonprofit I founded in 1996 dedicated to the development of ethical leadership practices in education and other public venues) continue to provide opportunities for the model presented here to find creative and practical engagement.

Finally, I would like to thank my family: Dr. Sharon Watson Fluker, my fellow traveler to whom this book is dedicated; Clinton and Hampton, my "sons of thunder"; Melvin "Tres" Watson: nephew, visionary, and leader extraordinaire; Wendy Deneen Whitley and Tiffany Marie Henderson: my daughters; and five grandchildren: Nia, Tyrone, Jeremiah, Genesis, and Mason.

INTRODUCTION

AT THE INTERSECTION
WHERE WORLDS COLLIDE

Sierra Leone is a small West African nation on the Atlantic Ocean tucked between Guinea and Liberia. Its name means "Lion Mountains." Like most African nations, it has a long history of European exploitation dating back as far as 1652, when the first slaves were taken from its shores and shipped to the Sea Islands in what is now the United States. Sierra Leone was founded as a British colony in 1792 as a settlement for freed slaves from the United States and Nova Scotia. Its capital, Freetown, was originally called "the Province of Freedom." From 1991 to 2002, Sierra Leone was engaged in a bloody civil war that resulted in tens of thousands of deaths and the displacement of more than two million people (about one-third of the population).

In 1998 I visited Freetown with a colleague to interview people who had been affected by the political turmoil wrought by the war. Young rebels, drugged and coerced into militias by powerful chieftains, were being used to disrupt the fragile political order of this poverty-stricken nation. The chieftains created the disorder in order to smuggle diamonds to rich, clandestine actors who profited from Sierra Leone's misery. We heard the stories of many of the youth and their elders who had been displaced by the invasion of rebel gangs. We met with women and families that had been torn apart and with local religious leaders who had been hiding for days in the bush to escape marauding rebel militias. Late one evening, ensconced in our temporary abode, the deserted Solar Hotel in the heart of Freetown, I made a journal entry:

> The effects of the recent crisis are everywhere—Nigerian soldiers serving as peacekeepers, high security checks at airports, bombed out and burned down buildings, mass graves, and poverty that is unspeakable. . . .

1

Everything is broken here—the buildings, the machines, the dogs, the people—but in the midst of it all there is a resiliency, like the ocean beyond my window in this dilapidated hotel. We are at the intersection where worlds are colliding!

On the Sunday before I left Freetown, I preached at the historic Regent Road Baptist Church, the oldest Baptist congregation on the African continent founded in 1792 by returning former slaves who fought in the American War of Independence. My sermon was titled "Building New Roads to the Future." In the sermon I expressed my deep feelings of solidarity with the local people and spoke about the hope that comes from commitment to the gospel of peace. All the while, I was acutely aware of the destruction of rich but frail traditions that had sustained them through slavery and colonialism. As I looked upon the faces of the people in the congregation of the small wooden church, I searched for signs of hope amid the despair that had enveloped their world. And there were signs, especially among the youth who had endured their nation's devastation. Somehow, they believed that in spite of the present, they would survive and again know the joy of family and community.

I closed the sermon with a story of a stranger who rescued starfish from the ocean's shore. As the tiny, delicate starfish, removed from their source of nurture and life, struggled on the shore, the stranger would reach down, lift them up, and return them to the ocean. Soon others joined the stranger, creating a community of searchers who assisted the stranger in reaching down, lifting up, and restoring the beautiful creatures to their home. I left the church that morning believing that these people would find their way to the shores of their beloved nation and return to the source of their hope: the deep-seated traditions and rituals that inspired possibility. "Naïve? Perhaps," I thought to myself. But without such hope, they were destined to despair. I discovered later that the church was burned to the ground by the young rebels.

I knew something about young rebels from a different place and time. The experience of Sierra Leone called me back to an experience I had eight years earlier. Two people from my childhood, Enola and Inky, visited me in a dream. Enola was a young woman brought up on the South Side of Chicago who had a reputation for precipitous violence—like the *Enola Gay*, the aircraft that dropped the atomic bomb on Hiroshima. She discarded her own rage and left an ominous cloud of memories that still hovered over places I had tried to forget. Enola, along with other members of her street gang, the Four Corners Blackstone Rangers, crashed a party at our house thirty years earlier. She assaulted my sister and terrorized our guests. When the gang members left, they threw a huge tire drum through the front window. Despite eleven telephone calls to the police, they arrived about a half hour after the rampage was over. I shall never forget the wearied, defeated look on my father's face as he stood there in his undershirt, explaining to the officers the damage wreaked upon his family, but unable to express the harrowing fear and powerlessness of a displaced black Southerner in a complex, post-industrial urban culture.

Inky—I never knew his real name—was a street ruffian. He, too, had a reputation for violence and hung out on 43rd Street, commonly referred to as "the Bucket of Blood." He was a member of a street gang called the Devil's Disciples, the rival of the Blackstone Rangers. I would often see him on street corners, waiting with his cohorts for fresh prey.

Why I would dream of them in my fortieth year? I don't know. I do know that I was afraid of Inky and Enola and of myself. To grow up psychologically abused by an environment that encourages violence is to live in a perpetual state of fear, always watching and postured for the moment of sudden confrontation with the "other." My biography is the story of escape from the fate of young people like Inky, Enola, and countless others who die before they are born. But one never escapes one's history—the stories and epochal events that shape character, dreams, and aspirations. Mine had been a journey away from the pain of living in a world of fear and dread—of unknowing.

After two years of military service, fourteen years of higher education, and several pastoral and academic positions, I had been moving away from the humiliation of being powerless, unable to deal with the violence of my past environment and the awful battle that still raged within. I had forgotten my name. I was afraid to remember, for in remembering, I had to claim responsibility for the creation of a self that sometimes drifted aimlessly through a sea of names—names manufactured and stolen for the sake of comfort and safe zones. James Baldwin wrote in *The Fire Next Time*: "To accept one's past—one's history—is not the same thing as drowning in it; it is learning how to use it." But there is no escape, no safe place from dangerous memories. They are unsolicited and unwelcome intruders that break into places we have sealed off and secured with layers of fictitious scenarios and masks donned to hide from guilt and shame. Enola and Inky just walked in unannounced, uninvited, and crashed the party.

Enola and Inky visited me. They took me for a walk, a kind of tour through the old 'hood. They were escorts, guides of a sort. We started somewhere around 39th and Ellis. They escorted me past Ben and Ray's grocery store, where my father, like many poor African Americans, had a small credit line to hold him over until he was able to pay. Enola and Inky took me up and down the Bucket of Blood. There, again, I saw the faces of the lost and lame, the forgotten and misbegotten, the broken and the bruised. It is still painful to see those faces—faces revealing horrible secrets, repressed memories, and untold stories about America that Alexis deTocqueville, Gunnar Myrdal, Daniel Patrick Moynihan, and Jacob S. Hacker could only write about but never truly experience. I guess the thing I remember most about my tour was the intense gloom, the hollowness, the sense of abandonment and horror. And in these faces, in the looks of powerlessness, I saw my own face, fearful and unknowing.

Strangely, after this tour through hell, my guides brought me into a mansion, a temple of sorts, and we gazed together out a huge window. There, just beyond the window, a lush green field spread before us, each blade of grass saturated with beams of golden light. It was beauty and light, a feeling of release, a healing on the other side of hell. I stood there entranced, enraptured by a joy I have never known. In that splendorous moment, that one God-drenched second—I gazed into myself. Suddenly, I realized I was alone. Inky and Enola had left, yet they spoke to me in one deep, resonant voice: "We just dropped by to tell you there is hope."

How strange that Inky and Enola would visit me in liminal zones, in those mystical time-slits between sleeping and waking, and conjure up these memories. There I was, a forty-year-old African American male—ambiguously "successful," yet lost in America, lost in history, lost in the hell of a million nightmares of memories.

Since this dream, I have inquired about Inky. What he is doing now, I don't know; but if statistics are any measure of fate for African American men like Inky, it is likely that he is unemployed, on parole, and a member of the permanent underclass, which William Julius Wilson calls "the truly disadvantaged."

Enola—well, her story ended the way she lived: in violence. She was found dead in a car, murdered, twenty years earlier. Some think her killing was drug-related. The word is that she became trapped in the cycle of living death, part of a community of people fated by social and economic conditions to spend their lives as inmates of a cultural asylum manufactured by powerful and indiscriminate systems. Inky and Enola were caught at the intersection where worlds collide!

I have often reflected on this dream and my experiences in Sierra Leone and how they relate to the challenges of emerging leadership in the twenty-first century. Clearly, preaching about hope is not enough; calling upon devastated people to return to traditions that have historically nurtured and sustained them in the midst of political and social upheaval is necessary to reconstruct the civic fabric essential to nation-building, but it is ultimately inadequate. When powerful systems that transact business at the speed of light are in the hands of leaders who profit from misery, the call to community, whether in Sierra Leone or on the South Side of Chicago, appears naïve and hypocritical. Tiny Davids who have nothing in their hands but slingshots and stones are no match for the Goliaths of the world. Yet there must be a place of beginning for those who would seek change and transformation. Such a place must be the province of the individual—not the solitary individual who is disassociated from history, but the individual who is rooted in the ambiguities and contingencies of history and yet dares to believe in and hope for a livable future.

Such an individual does not take stock in the "original position" that seeks community through instrumental reason or moral sentiment alone. Rather, through self-discovery, one seeks community as a constituent dimension of his or her being—and in seeking, one finds others of like mind. The goal of the moral life of these seekers begins and ends in community, and their ethical project seeks the same in every dimension of life—personally, socially, and spiritually. As a rational construction and method, community is both the goal and norm of the ethical life; but the "sense of community" is the inner dimension of feelings, emotions, and yearnings that seeks wholeness in all encounters with tragedy, despair, and destructiveness. For leaders at the intersection, it is the basis for their response and practice when "things fall apart." Imagine a community of seekers who in their search for personal meaning and authenticity find not only themselves but others whom they had not known. The future of our world depends on the connections that these lonely seekers make and the kind of communities of discourse and practice that they create.

A favorite exercise that I use in workshops with leaders across various public venues is to ask them to stand, close their eyes, and imagine that they are at the center of a busy intersection with traffic coming from all directions. I ask them to imagine that there are no stoplights or traffic cops—just oncoming traffic. I also ask them to imagine the sounds at the intersection: running motors, screeching brakes, screams and shouts from people on the sidewalks and in cafes. I ask them to visualize the intersection: people moving back and forth with the pulsating rhythm of urban life, the beggar sitting in the wheelchair outside a building, children holding their parents' hands, and the rushing traffic coming toward them from the front, the rear, the left, and the right. Then I ask, "How do you feel?" The responses normally are: I am afraid, confused, paralyzed. "What will you do?" I will run and dodge the traffic. I will tell the traffic to stop! I will cry for help! I will pray to God! I don't know what to do! "Do you know which way is north? Do you even have time to figure out which way is north?" Most do not know which way is north. Compasses of all sorts, material and moral, come in handy when you are on hiking trips or sailing through life, but they really are useless at the intersection. Finally, I ask, "How will you negotiate this traffic at the intersection?" Very few have credible responses. How to negotiate the traffic at the intersection where worlds collide is the question this book seeks to answer.

Nobody gets out of the intersection alone. There is no such thing as a solitary individual who escapes the intersection and saves the world. Every great leader who has brought about creative change and transformation has done so with a community of fellow travelers who are organized around vision, mission, and specific goals and strategies. Hope without a plan is a dangerous fantasy. Creative change and transformation begin and end with a sense of community. The ethical leader seeks community as both a starting point and the end of her existence. In doing so, she stands in candidacy for a hope that cannot be diminished by external forces of power and dominance. In the midst of worlds colliding, she dares to raise the primary ethical question in public life: What's going on? It is not enough to ponder the ideas of morals and values as isolated, unrelated, individualistic phenomena. It is necessary to analyze and interrogate complex internal and environmental issues, to interpret data that do not fit into convenient categories or principles, and to discern one's fitting decisions and actions. A threefold process ensues from this initial question: discernment, deliberation, and decision, all of which will find greater elaboration in the following chapters.

PRIVATE AND PUBLIC SPHERES OF THE INTERSECTION

First and foremost, the intersection is fiercely private—it is personal and intimate. It is a place of the convergence of dreams, aspirations, ideals, and hopes. It is also the place where dreams, aspirations, ideals, and hopes are often disappointed, defeated, demolished, and dashed against the rocks. This place is not merely psychological or social but profoundly spiritual. In respect to the formation and role of leaders, my concern is with spirituality as a basis for ethical orientation. We ask, "How might we prepare leaders to recognize the need and place of spirituality in the development of habits and practices that nurture morally anchored character, transformative acts of civility, and a sense of community?"

The intersection is also public in the sense that it is the space where citizens meet and engage in meaningful discussion and action about values, and where they hold one another accountable for what they know and value. As Thomas McCollough suggests, "Meaningful discussion about values presupposes a common lifeworld, a shared cultural context within which persons respect one another and care about ideas and values as determinants of their life together."[1] In the public sphere, issues such as class, gender, sexual orientation, race, ethnicity, and religion both form and inform how one understands the private self. Yet the private self must have a public connection. That is, through a web of relationships and networks, individuals are able to actualize their deepest dreams, hopes, ideals, and aspirations. The intersection represents, therefore, both private and public spaces where a new generation of leadership must stand, negotiate, and redirect the traffic of lifeworlds and systems.

"Lifeworlds" refers to the commonplace, everyday traffic of life where people meet and greet one another, where common values and presuppositions about order and the world are held. "Systemworlds" refers to the vast, often impersonal bureaucratic systems dominated by money and power (economics and politics and the various structures of communications and technology), which are frequently at odds with the pedestrian traffic of lifeworlds. Lifeworlds are built on social practices, traditions, and institutions that are often at odds with systemworlds, where technical reason and the relentless quest for power and money assault their very fragile existence. Leadership in the new century will depend largely on how well new generations of ethical leaders negotiate the traffic at these intersections and inspire and guide others to create community.

Standing at the intersection where worlds collide is, at best, hazardous duty. Sierra Leone is only a microcosm of what's going on around the globe. In fact, the increasing incidence of "political violence" directed at and perpetuated by the United States is symptomatic of the social pathology that plagues our private and public worlds—and of the untold histories that converge at the intersection. The image of leaders standing at the intersection reminds me of a poster I once saw that depicted three little kittens cuddled together in a basket of yarn with mischievous gleams in their eyes, ready to brave some immediate adventure. The caption underneath the poster read "You and me against the world. Boy, are we going to get creamed!" When you stand at the centermost place of your convictions and dare to speak and act in public, expect to get creamed! The intersection is dangerous territory.

Ronald Heifitz and Martin Linsky offer sound advice to leaders at the intersection: "You appear dangerous to people when you question their values, beliefs, or habits of a lifetime. You place yourself on the line when you tell people what they need to hear rather than what they want to hear. Although you may see with clarity and passion a promising future of progress and gain, people will see with equal passions the losses you are asking them to sustain."[2] They add that leaders must distinguish between adaptive challenges and technical challenges that arise in advocating for change. Technical challenges ask leaders, as authorities, to apply current knowledge to the problem that needs to be addressed, but adaptive challenges demand that the people who do the work learn new ways of addressing problems. Adaptive challenges are fraught with danger because the leader is asking for changes that result in loss, disloyalty to old beliefs and assumptions, and a sense of incompetence. According to Heifitz and Linsky, danger has many faces—faces of seduction, diversion, marginalization, and attack, which are tactics people use to resist change. When leaders ask people to change, they must expect resistance at the intersection.

DEBATES AT THE INTERSECTION

The intersection is noisy, and as a result, it is often difficult to hear what others are saying. It is also a place dominated by fear, deceit, and threats of violence. I often think that road rage is more symptomatic of the crowded roadways and intersections of our day-to-day lives than simply a psychological phenomenon. This is true also for the extremist points of view represented in culture wars—bombings, assassinations, and subversive tactics that could easily be labeled "terrorist" by most standards.

One of the major examples of incivility is rooted in the dangerous contest between religious and secular discourses. Much of the incivility that characterizes this contest is a consequence of what Michael Walzer calls "maximalist moral language," which is public discourse that is embedded in specific moral contexts and used in confrontational political speech. Walzer also identifies this kind of moral argument as "thick" moral discourse as opposed to "thin." Thin descriptions of moral problems are rather easy points of agreement, as in applying the golden rule: "Do unto others as you would have them do unto you." But thick descriptions demand more than broad areas of agreement, because they involve the critical issues of difference. Contemporary issues of same-sex marriage, abortion, and euthanasia are embedded in long-standing religious convictions, traditions, and interpretations of truth. Conflict surrounding thick moral disagreements results in an inability to hear the other with empathy and respect.

Kwame Anthony Appiah has suggested that the future of cosmopolitanism hinges on how well we distinguish between thin and thick moral arguments in public debates. He identifies three kinds of disagreement about values: failing to share a vocabulary of evaluation, giving different interpretations to the same vocabulary, and giving the same values different weights. The challenge, however, is not always to come to consensus on right and wrong or good and bad, but to seek ways of understanding, because the particularity, or thickness, of some arguments does not allow for ready agreement through moral argumentation. Appiah suggests that, in the final analysis, learning to live with different interpretations of values relies more on practice than on argumentation. Some scholars suggest that it is for this reason that religious citizens, when they engage in public discourse, should refrain from appeals to faith-based or sectarian language that does not have a common vocabulary; the emphasis ought to be on listening to the other, which is a disciplined practice that involves personal virtues—integrity, empathy, and hope—that are related to character and analogous public values—recognition, respect, and reverence—that form the basis of civility.

How then might leaders learn to move beyond thick moral discourse to a more balanced interrogation of the possibilities inherent in the contentious debates at the intersection? I believe that leaders must begin by examining their own assumptions, beliefs, and presuppositions about order and power. Such examinations involve more than critical methodologies concerned with analytic and cognitive processes; they must also include affective undertakings that are rooted in a sense of community that is personal, public, and spiritual. The spiritual dimension is decidedly communal and requires practices that we call "virtuosities" or spiritual excellencies of courage, a sense of justice and compassion. Remembering, retelling, and reliving our own stories are important steps in that process. Leaders at the intersection must also look, listen, and learn from others whose lifestyles and traditions are radically different from their own.

LEADERSHIP AT THE INTERSECTION

Finally, the intersection poses another problem that is even more fundamental to our present state. Not only is society in crisis; leadership itself is in crisis. There is a lot of quarreling at the intersection over which way to go. My childhood pastor used to tell a story about two snakes in a barn that caught fire: one snake had ten heads and the other had one. The pastor would always ask, "Which snake will get out?" He would answer, "The snake with one head will escape while the other burns up arguing over which way to go!" My pastor's story represents the traditional understanding of leadership as one person who serves as the authority for decisions and actions relative to the direction that the group will take. This response, however, is highly problematic, given the multiplicity of complex challenges and issues that confront leaders at the intersection. Leaders of the future will need to reimagine creative ways of constructing responses at intersections where worlds collide. What if we were to explore ways in which all ten snake heads would respond if they were able and willing to collaborate and organize a communal response for the crisis at hand? Surely, ten heads with twenty eyes can see more possibilities than only one head with two eyes.

The critical issue at stake is the need for leadership to envision itself as a community of discourse and practice that is attuned to the kind of networking and decision-making that uses all available resources to respond to the crisis at hand. A community of leaders who are adept at communicating with one another requires more than the traditional approaches that highlight individual leaders as the center of authority. It requires the identification and training of a new generation of leaders who are able to look, listen, and learn together at the intersections. Moreover, it requires certain virtues, values, and virtuosities (or moral excellencies) that encourage collaborative leadership. The skills we are recommending revolve around three pivotal concepts: character, civility, and community, which are the defining concepts of ethical leadership.

Chapter One

HOWARD WASHINGTON THURMAN AND MARTIN LUTHER KING JR.

CRITICAL RESOURCES IN THE DEVELOPMENT OF ETHICAL LEADERSHIP

As we enter a new century beset by ethical issues and challenges, the leadership legacies of Howard Washington Thurman (1899–1981) and Martin Luther King Jr. (1929–1968) provide critical resources for spirituality and social transformation in the development of leaders. At stake in this discussion is not the claim to a metaphysical model or mandate for spirituality. Instead, I am looking at these African American leaders as resources for a developmental model that allows us to examine the ways in which spirituality, ethics, and leadership are linked and to provide a resource for training a new generation of leaders who are spiritually disciplined, morally anchored, and socially engaged.

THE BLACK CHURCH TRADITION

Howard Thurman and Martin Luther King Jr. are products of the "black church tradition," and it is within this long-standing American tradition that we best understand them and the relevance of their legacies for the development of ethical leadership. The "black church tradition" is used advisedly in this context, given its recent *discovery* during the controversy surrounding Dr. Jeremiah Wright. Interestingly, most Americans still associate the black church with the media-stimulated images of the Blues Brothers or with occasional encounters with televangelists while surfing television channels. Remarkably, few remember the role of the black church in the modern civil rights movement. Most forget, in fact, that Martin Luther King Jr. was a pastor before he became a civil rights leader, and few have ever heard of Howard Thurman and many other illustrious leaders of this tradition who have shaped many of the basic institutions and laws of this nation.

The controversy surrounding Pastor Jeremiah Wright has been significant in shaping public perceptions of black churches, and especially black ministers. From the beginning of Senator Barack Obama's campaign, his pastor posed a problem for his nomination. Politically, it was problematic for Obama to embrace Pastor Wright, because he feared that the preacher's incendiary and often colorful statements about race in American society would ignite a firestorm that he could not extinguish. Yet, by his own admission, he was torn; though he loved his pastor and his white grandmother, he could not abide their public commentary on race in America:

> I can no more disown him [Reverend Wright] than I can my white grandmother—a woman who helped raise me, a woman who sacrificed again and again for me, a woman who loves me as much as she loves anything in this world, but a woman who once confessed her fear of black men who passed by her on the street, and who on more than one occasion has uttered racial or ethnic stereotypes that made me cringe.[1]

While both his grandmother and pastor honestly expressed their feelings about race in America, Dr. Wright committed the unpardonable sin—he spoke about it publicly. Lurking always beneath the surface of American culture is the ominous threat that race will become public and that we will have to deal with it.[2] But this has been precisely the public mission of the black church since its inception in American slavery.

First, the designation "black church tradition" encompasses a variety of highly syncretistic religious survivals and retentions from traditional African belief systems and Christian culture, which are more properly referred to under the canopy of the "black church." The black church tradition, at its best, is an argument about the meaning and destiny of American democratic dogma. It finds creative affinity with what the late James M. Washington called "the American dissenting tradition," which included "abolitionists and many other varieties of social reformers. Many Americans do not understand or have forgotten how indebted we are to the stubborn tradition of loyal opposition in American history. The opposition's determination to put righteousness, conscience, and morality before social and political expediency helped to shape some of our most fundamental values and institutions."[3] The moral argument represented by this tradition is a significant contribution to a national community in search of its soul.

The definition of "the Black Christian tradition" offered by Peter Paris in his enlightening book, *The Social Teaching of the Black Churches*, captures the distilled formulation of the many arguments for the syncretistic view and the position represented in this proposal. Paris claims that "the tradition that has always been normative for the black churches and the black community is not the so-called Western tradition per se, although this tradition is an important source for blacks. More accurately, the normative tradition for blacks is the tradition governed by the principle of *nonracism*, which we call the black Christian tradition. The fundamental principle of the black Christian tradition is depicted most adequately in the biblical doctrine of the parenthood of God and the kinship of all peoples." This critical principle of *nonracism*, according to Paris, is fundamental for "justifying and motivating all endeavors by blacks for survival and social transformation." Moreover, the black Christian tradition has functioned both in priestly and prophetic functions—"the former aiding and abetting the race in its capacity to endure racism, the latter utilizing all available means to effect religious and moral reform in the society at large."[4] A biblical anthropology (view of persons) that affirms the equality of all persons under God is the locus of authority and basis for the moral and political significance of black churches. Paris's definition is also helpful, as we will see, in understanding the priestly and prophetic functions that Thurman and King respectively demonstrated in their leadership roles.

Second, the black church tradition is not monolithic; rather, it spans a broad spectrum of denominational, theological, and cultural diversity. The particular strand of the black church tradition referred to here represents a long stream of thought and activism in the African American community in which liberation and integration are inextricably linked. Theologically, Martin Luther King Jr. labeled this quest "the search for the beloved community," and Howard Thurman, "the search for common ground." Lawrence Jones contends that "ever since blacks have been in America, they have been in search of the 'beloved community,'"[5] a community grounded in an unshakable confidence in a theology of history. The approaches of representatives of this particular strand of the black church tradition to the problem of community in American society clearly constitute an analysis of the broader problematic of religion, race, and culture.

The role and place of women in this tradition have remained largely invisible with the exception of recent research and writing, but the advances and progressive democratic politics of this nation owe a great deal to their courage, organizational prowess, and commitment to equality and justice. It is difficult to imagine what America would be without the activism of black church women like Ida B. Wells, Mary Church Terrell, Mary McLeod Bethune, Nannie Helen Burroughs, Fannie Lou Hamer, Pauli Murray, Ella Baker, Marian Wright Edelman, Vasthi McKenzie, and so many more who constitute the best in American democracy.[6] Even in its most anemic and debilitating circumstances, the black church tradition has called America to live up to the better angels of its nature.

Throughout African American history, the black church has provided the pool of leadership that led to the creation of social institutions and organizations that have prophetically challenged the world to move toward a "beloved community." Because of the black church's distinctive socio-cultural location and long history of producing quality leadership, it is a prime candidate for offering direction for the development of leaders for our national and global communities.

At the center of discussion among scholars involved in research and writing on the black church tradition is the development of critical concepts and methods for a social ethic that takes seriously the indigenous sources and experiences of African American people. Most claim that, historically, the black church tradition has been the chief social locus for the ethical foundations of leadership in the African American community. For the most part, African American leadership has been influenced by the distinctive ethos of the black church tradition. The black church, however, is not the only repository of moral and social practices of African American leadership. Black colleges and universities have long-standing traditions of excellence dating back to early postbellum American cultures. Morehouse College was the alma mater of both Thurman and King. Since its humble beginnings during Reconstruction, Morehouse College has been a veritable "candle in the dark" for generations of black men who have sought higher learning and greater visions of service to the black community and the larger society.[7] Morehouse men learned early a sense of personal worth and their responsibility to those less fortunate. Thurman says, "We understood that our job was to learn so that we could go back into our communities and teach others."[8] At Morehouse College, Thurman and King were privileged to study with some of the ablest minds in America and to learn the relationship between education of the head and the heart. King, during his last year, wrote in the Morehouse student journal, *The Maroon Tiger*, that "the function of education . . . is to teach one to think intensively and to think critically. But education which stops with efficiency may prove the greatest menace to society. The most dangerous criminal may be the man gifted with reason, but with no morals."[9]

The contemporary issue at stake in African American moral traditions, as in the larger society, is the role of systems and their impact on the moral development of individuals.[10] Simply stated, individuals are socially constructed, yet by definition are responsible and accountable for moral choices within the context of their social histories and stories. Hence the pertinent questions for the ethical and moral development of leaders in this respect are: What stories are the individual a part of, and how do those stories inform moral practices and habits? What is the role of institutions in this narrative perspective, and how might leaders develop habits and practices that conspire against unjust institutional practices that promote unhealthy and self-destructive existence? The operative assumption here is that African American moral traditions have played a significant role in shaping the moral languages of this nation and, consequently, can serve as a strategic resource in the formation of ethical leadership in the national community.

The point of departure in this inquiry into African American moral traditions is complemented by an interdisciplinary approach, which identifies critical resources and methodologies for the retrieval and appropriation of discourse that shapes character, civility, and community. In this endeavor I rely heavily upon the works Howard Washington Thurman and Martin Luther King Jr. In an earlier book, *They Looked for a City*, I compared the concepts of community in their thoughts and practices with the aim of making a statement about the traditions that had furnished their creative social visions for America and the world. While there was a large body of developing scholarship on King, few scholars had focused on Thurman's contributions as a social critic. Thurman's mystical orientation and emphasis on the primacy of the individual as the basis for social transformation had, for the most part, been relegated to the province of religious life and spiritual moorings. I demonstrated that their respective visions of community were not exclusive but compatible—one emphasizing individual transformation through religious experience as a basis for social change and the other calling attention to the social fabric of American life and the need for the restructuring of American society through nonviolent resistance and a renewed vision of global community. With respect to their concepts of community and their points of entry, I argued that they represented two sides of the venerable tradition of loyal dissent that sought the highest and noblest ideals of American democracy: the black church tradition. Thurman and King, in many ways, represent the best in the American dream. Barack Obama, reflecting on their legacies and his obvious role as beneficiary of their achievements, affirms, "Howard Thurman, I think, represents some of the best in America. I constantly refer back to the work that has been done by Dr. King, Dr. Thurman, and others whose shoulders I really stand on." Their views of inclusive participatory democracy within American society and the method they upheld as the only moral and practical one available to men and women of conscience were, at once, a critique on American society and a distant goal to which the nation is called.[12]

HOWARD THURMAN:
THE OPENER OF THE WAY

Howard Thurman met leaders at the intersections where worlds collided and tutored them through spiritual renewal and social activism. His career as pastor, scholar, teacher, university chaplain, preacher, and administrator extended over fifty-five years and touched the lives of many highly visible leaders within and beyond the modern civil rights movement.[13] Born in Daytona Beach, Florida, at the turn of the twentieth century in the midst of the dehumanizing onslaughts of segregation and Jim Crow, Thurman committed himself to transforming parochial and dogmatic pockets of organized religion into a community transcending barriers of racism, classism, sexism, denominationalism, and religious exclusivism. Although women and men from various racial, socioeconomic, cultural, and religious backgrounds found affinity with this universal spirit, the peculiar genius of Howard Thurman was rooted in his location on "the underside of history," that is, the African American experience of oppression in the United States.[14] The genesis of Thurman's vision of community is properly located within the context of black oppression and was significantly shaped by his encounters with the extremes of race and class domination in America's Deep South at the turn of the twentieth century. His early wrestling with this problematic serves as a "site of dangerous memories"[15] that shapes the central, unifying theme of his life and thought, which he refers to as "the search for common ground." Thurman's self-perception as a solitary brooder, moreover, sheds light on a vital, though neglected, dimension of American discourse on spirituality, ethics, and leadership.[16]

Thurman saw his role in the movement as always calling those individuals involved in the struggle back to that primary experience of encounter with, in his language, the "literal truth" or "the truth of God." Thurman's ministry of teaching and healing extended beyond the walls of the church to personal encounters with individuals who found in his presence a place, a moment to declare, "I choose!" This was part of the ministry performed for so many African American leaders who had to deal with the brutal and harsh realities of living in a society that rendered them nameless, faceless, and sexless. This dimension of Howard Thurman was one of the peculiar graces of the man. Somehow, he was able to dig deep into the inner recesses of the other's being, into places others could not reach. Thurman seemed to be able to find the hidden treasures of the soul and to navigate forsaken wastelands of the heart, the shattered hopes and the flickering visions of yesteryear. He taught those in despair how to dream again, how to begin again, how to resurrect the crucified and forsaken symbols of their lives and make of them redemptive messengers in a world that conspires against faith, hope, and love. In the words of his wife, the late Sue Bailey Thurman, "He helped to move the stumps out of the way for so many people."[17]

The testimonies from many notable leaders within and beyond the African American community are legion.[18] Crusaders like Jesse Jackson proclaim that "Dr. Thurman was a teacher of teachers, a leader of leaders, a preacher of preachers. No small wonder, then, that Martin Luther King Jr., Whitney Young, Samuel Proctor, Vernon Jordan, Otis Moss . . . sat at his feet, for we knew it was a blessing to give this prophet a glass of water or to touch the hem of his garment."[19]

Those closest to Thurman report that, while in his presence, the inimitable Mr. Jackson literally sat at the master's feet.[20] But Jackson is not alone in his adulation. Vincent Harding, a noted historian of the African American struggle, remembers the quiet idiom that marked the gracious manner of Thurman's presence. Harding writes, "I remember our silences. They were filled with wisdom and compassion. Indeed, it may be that he was the wisest and most compassionate man I have ever known." He continues, "Howard Thurman opened doors. . . . Many of us have become more fully human because of his opening love. Many of us have been challenged by his life to do our own moving, deep into the heart of our own 'spiritual idiom,' thereby drawing nearer to the inside [of] all peoples, all cultures, all faiths."[21] Marian Wright Edelman, founder of the Children's Defense Fund, draws on the spiritual wisdom of Thurman for generations of children by counseling them to heed the words of Thurman "to wait and listen for the sound of the genuine," which for her is a lesson in "discipline, solitude and prayer."[22] For the late Arthur Ashe, tennis champion and humanitarian, Thurman represented "the supreme example of the black American's capacity for achieving spiritual growth and maturity despite the incessant blows of racism. Born in the shadow of slavery, black and poor, he developed his understanding of the human and divine to such an extent that he influenced thousands of people."[23]

For the civil rights leader and presidential adviser Vernon Jordan, "Dr. Thurman was one of the greatest and most influential preachers the world has produced. He was a spiritual leader of the nascent civil rights movement, and in later years would give wise counsel to Martin Luther King Jr., Whitney Young, James Farmer (who was his student), Jesse Jackson, and I am very proud to say, me." Jordan first heard Thurman preach in 1953 when he was a freshman at DePauw University. He was so enamored by the gifted preacher's eloquent and soul-stirring explication of the Lord's Prayer that he rushed to shake his hand at the close of the chapel service. "He didn't know me from anybody," writes Jordan, "but that would change." And change it did! Thurman became for Jordan a hero and mentor. Over the years, the young civil rights leader sought his counsel. On one occasion, after he became the head of the National Urban League, Jordan sat with Thurman an entire evening until dawn, discussing life and the lessons that Thurman had learned over the long years of the struggle. Jordan reflects, "Thurman is seen by some as a mystic, but I found him firmly grounded, a repository of wisdom." Indeed, Jordan shares that during his hospitalization after being shot in Fort Wayne, Indiana, Thurman sent him a collection of his taped meditations, which provided for him a point of focus and inner healing.[24]

Perhaps the remarks of Pulitzer Prize–winning author Alice Walker capture best the power of Thurman's presence as a veritable *angelos* incarnate in his written word. She called him "one of the greatest spiritual resources of this nation. . . . The essence of his thought emerges in a message of hope, reconciliation, and love. . . . In those long midnight hours when morning seems weeks away, the words of Howard Thurman have kept watch with me."[25]

How came this intriguing personality to such a prominent place in the lives of many leaders who labored in the civil rights movement of the 1950s and '60s and who continue to struggle for justice in America? What was the secret of his comforting presence and profound insight into the spiritual moorings of leaders engaged in social transformation? I use the designation "Opener of the Way"[26] to express the distinctive characterization of Thurman's contribution to leaders in the forefront of the movement. As a discursive pointer, it also provides a window through which we can examine his understanding of spirituality and how it is wedded to healing and social transformation in Thurman's thought and praxis. By utilizing this language, I also want to highlight Thurman's conscious role as pedagogue in teaching and explicating the spiritual and ethical significance of the political, economic, and social arrangements in which these individuals found themselves.[27]

Mozella Mitchell's depiction of Thurman as "a sophisticated modern-day shaman" and "a technician of the sacred" is helpful.[28] For Mitchell, Thurman stands somewhere between the priest and the shaman while maintaining a distinctive posture as a social prophet. Unlike the prophet who speaks to the community, "Thus says the Lord," the shaman leads the community to God by "giving others access to the spiritual world and effecting a care for their ailing condition." According to Mitchell, "Thurman, in his shamanistic function, does not simply bring the message of truth from God to the religious community, but he leads individuals and the community to have an experience with the divine from which they may gain a sense of wholeness themselves."[29]

Mitchell's description of Thurman places him alongside a company of African American healers and teachers whose roots reach beyond the American clime and find affinity with a long and neglected tradition.[30] While it is helpful to compare Thurman with the shaman of archaic societies, Thurman's linkage with his African past is a more fruitful way to understand his role as Opener of the Way from the underside of history. In this paradigm, one sees exciting parallels with the enslaved preachers of the African Diaspora. Like his precursors, Thurman provided a symbol for leaders of the movement to center upon. James Weldon Johnson and W. E. B. DuBois attributed the centrality of the enslaved African preacher to his or her role as teacher and healer. Johnson wrote that "it was through him [*sic*] that people of diverse languages and customs that were brought here from diverse parts of Africa and thrown into slavery, were given their first sense of unity and solidarity. He was the first shepherd of his bewildered flock."[31] Speaking of the "priest" and "medicine-man," DuBois wrote, "He early appeared on the plantation and found his function as the healer of the sick, the interpreter of the Unknown, the comforter of the sorrowing, the supernatural avenger of wrong, and the one who [c]rudely, but picturesquely expressed the longing, disappointment, and resentment of a stolen and oppressed people."[32]

From early childhood, Thurman felt himself "marked."[33] Most illuminating is this characteristically modest statement about his peculiar gift:

> One day, how early in my life I do not recall, I discovered a little scar tissue in the center of both ear lobes. When I asked about it, I was told that my ears had been pierced when I was a baby. I was told that at the time of my birth my eyes were covered by a film. This meant, according to the custom, that I was gifted with "second sight"—a clairvoyance, the peculiar endowment of one who could tell the future. No parent wanted a child so endowed. It spelled danger and grief. If the ears were pierced, however, the power of the gift would be dissipated. How deeply I was influenced by this "superstition" I do not know. Who is there who can understand such things? One thing I do know, there are times when I am visited by the emergence of a quick memory, the vivid recollection of a face, a person, an event that shoots up from the unconscious on its own errand. Or it may be an insight or an inspiration, an "opening," to use a phrase from the Society of Friends. It is idea and more than idea. We say this thought came into our minds or we had a "hunch" that this was going to happen; our language is full of such references.[34]

Thurman represents an important symbol of America's past—a past torn by what Mircea Eliade called "the massive terror of history" and indicted by the cacophonous tyranny of a fragmented public discourse that has collapsed on itself. Yet it is precisely his wrestling with the interstices of race and culture through the agency of religious experience that bequeaths to us a key to the meaning of what Reinhold Niebuhr called "the irony of American history," and maybe its redemption.[35] Thurman's intellectual and religious project teaches us how to reenter time, lost time, time-swept-under-the-rug and to establish a new rhythmic harmony among disparate and conflicting histories in the search for common ground.[36] His steady insistence on the search for common ground between groups finds creative resonance at this critical impasse of American history.[37] With the increasing ideological tensions in the public square and the concomitant need to carve a fresh and critical approach to the often violent usages of religious discourse as warrants for moral action, Thurman's gentle wisdom and clear analytic provides a resource for a spiritually inspired public ethic that does not pay homage to greedy, grinning gods of modernity.

Thurman has long been heralded as a stellar exemplar of American religious leadership, a theoretician of nonviolent direct action, and a cultivator of spiritual insight into the ethical dimensions of community.[38] More recently, scholars like Gary Dorrien have advanced the argument that Thurman along with Benjamin Elijah Mays, Mordecai Wyatt Johnson, and William Stuart Nelson were "proponents of a black social gospel." However, he accentuates an important difference in respect to their embrace of American theological liberalism. "To them," he writes, "the social gospel movement had barely begun; what was needed was an American Christianity that took seriously its own best preaching and ethics on behalf of equal opportunity, racial integration and peace. They took little interest in theological trends that obscured or relativized these goals. They were preachers, movement leaders and institutional builders, not academic theologians. The most promising religious thinker among them, Thurman, gave up his academic career to launch a model ministry of inclusion. He called American Christianity to its best religious vision and in several ways exemplified it."[39]

Dorrien's observation underscores an important dimension of African American intellectual life since its beginnings: intellectual inquiry and engagement have always sought a public analogue. In this respect, Thurman's imaginative and pragmatic project of community has it origins in the "endless struggle to achieve and reveal and confirm a human identity."[40] His spiritual vision is forged on the *borderlands* between American liberal theology and the powerful black Christian tradition of protest, racial uplift, and social advancement of the race. Leaders in this tradition, such as Thurman, created an "autonomous third zone" where cultures could meet and interact. This feat of "straddling" diverse worlds may be the most distinctive contribution of Thurman to American theological discourse.[41]

Apostles of Sensitiveness

At the intersections of race, class, and religion, Howard Thurman called for leaders who were "apostles of sensitiveness." To be an apostle of sensitiveness is to have a sense of what is vital, a basic underlying awareness of life and its potentialities at every level of experience.[42] The human project for Thurman is the quest for meaning, understanding, and purpose in the midst of tragic existence—and it is this quest, for him, that marked the primal center of *innocence* and *becoming*. "The transition from innocence to knowledge is always perilous and fraught with hazard," writes Thurman.[43] This transition from innocence to knowledge marks the way in which Thurman understood the encounter with the other as simultaneously a quest for self-recognition and understanding and the source of transformative action in the world. For him, spirituality is "the tutor" or "the unseen model" by which one structures the facts of his or her experience. For this reason, Thurman counseled, "The person concerned about social change must not only understand the materials with which he has to do, the things which he is trying to manipulate, to reorder, to refashion but again and again he must expose the roots of his mind to the literal truth that is the tutor of the facts, the orderer and reorderer of the facts of his experience."[44]

This must be done, Thurman contended, so that in the quest for social justice, one's vision of society never conforms to some external pattern, but is "modeled and shaped in accordance to the innermost transformation that is going on in his spirit."[45] He insisted that those engaged in acts of liberation must continually examine the sources of their motivation and the ways in which the social processes that they seek to change are related to their spiritual pilgrimage. Always, the primary questions for leaders involved in social transformation are: "What are you trying to do with your life? What kind of person are you trying to become?"[46] It was Thurman's conviction that the leader in his or her actions "is trying to snare into the body of his facts, his conviction of those facts." He cautioned, however, that faith thus understood always runs the risk of becoming idolatrous as in uncritical patriotic visions of "the American way."[47] Therefore, one must examine the motivational content of action that involves a tutoring of the will by the unseen model, which for him was the truth resident within the individual. Here the questions of *identity*, *purpose*, and *method* are combined in relation to the individual's social context. These three questions frame the inquiry into the development of the leader's character that will be discussed in chapter 3 below.

At the funeral of civil rights leader Whitney Young in 1971, Thurman stated, "The time and place of a person's life on earth is the time and place of the body, but the meaning and significance of that life is as far-reaching and redemptive as the gifts, the dedication, the response to the demand of the times, the total commitment of one's powers can make it."[48] He often asked, "What does it mean to *live* life seriously (not to *take* life seriously), to live freely unencumbered by the necessity of always conforming to external things that limit our potential to be authentically human in the world?" Thurman thought it demanded a journey into the interior, into those places we have sealed off and placed no-trespassing signs around. It meant, for him, an inward journey into dangerous territory, where the real issues of life and death must be confronted, where "the angel with the flaming sword" greets us, where we are not allowed entry unless we yield "the fluid area of our consent."

In his *Meditations of the Heart*, Thurman writes,

> There is in every person an inward sea, and in that sea there is an island and on that island there is an altar and standing guard before that altar is the "angel with the flaming sword." Nothing can get by that angel to be placed upon that altar unless it has the mark of inner authority. Nothing passes "the angel with the flaming sword" to be placed upon your altar unless it be a part of "the fluid area of your consent." This is your link with the Eternal.[49]

This journey into the interior, according to Thurman, is not extraordinary; in many respects, it is far removed from what we normally call "religion." The angel with the flaming sword is encountered in the mundane, earthly experiences of living and being in the world. At any juncture in the road, there may suddenly appear a sign, a flash, a burning bush, which places us in candidacy for this experience. Often in struggle, in crisis, in the heart of suffering and trial, one encounters the angel, the truth about oneself, the mendacious stereotypes about self and others, and the subtle and surreptitious ways in which one has been named. His ministry to Martin Luther King Jr., which is discussed below, is an example of the ways in which Thurman saw his ministry to leaders caught in the thick of the struggle.

MARTIN LUTHER KING JR.: TRANSFORMED NONCONFORMISTS

More than any other American leader in the twentieth century, Martin Luther King Jr. stood at the intersection where worlds collided. In doing so, he challenged the nation to take seriously the role of spirituality and ethics in resolving what the authors of *Habits of the Heart* called the most important unresolved contradiction in our history, the tension between "self-reliant competitive enterprise and a sense of public solidarity espoused by civic republicans."[50] It was King's spiritual genius that provided for him the essential assets and tools to lead a revolution of values that expanded the moral grammar of American history and culture from parochially applied democratic principles to concrete proposals for inclusiveness and action. This amazing feat, performed in a brief period of our history—from 1954 to 1968—was no doubt the nation's finest example of what Martin Buber called "turning." In doing so, King also changed the leadership equation: public leadership no longer belonged to the strict province of position, power, and privilege, but also to the marginalized moral minority—those whom King labeled "transformed nonconformists."[51]

Much of the scholarship on Martin Luther King Jr. has centered on his role as a civil rights leader, his eclectic intellectual formation, and his distinctive place within the black church tradition.[52] Little attention, however, has been given to the relationship among spirituality, ethics, and leadership in his thought and praxis.[53] This, of course, strikes one as surprising since the most casual observer of King's life and work cannot help but be struck by a deep-seated spirituality wedded to a strong sense of Christian character and vocation. It is not surprising, however, that with the noble heritage bequeathed to him by his family, the Ebenezer Baptist Church, Morehouse College, and the larger black Atlanta community, King emerged as a luminous exemplar of the black church tradition of spirituality and social transformation. Equally revealing is his articulation of the thematic that characterizes the wedding of the notions of "spirituality" and "social transformation" in the language of "transformed nonconformity." Embedded in his formulation of transformed nonconformity are significant elements of King's biography and thinking regarding the place of spirituality, ethics, and leadership in his dream of human community.

Transformed Nonconformists

In Martin Luther King's language, ethical leaders are transformed nonconformists who become aware of the transforming power of the encounter with the *other* within themselves and in community with others. King firmly believed that inner transformation was essential to involvement in social transformation. Transformation, however, is not equated with moral perfectionism; rather, it is understood as an inner quality of life that issues forth in deeds of goodwill and love for the neighbor. "In the final analysis," says King, "what God requires is that your heart is right. Salvation isn't reaching the destination of absolute morality, but it's being in the process and on the right road."[54] For him, the transformed nonconformist experiences a new birth and a reorientation of values that enables her to struggle for social transformation. "Only through an inner spiritual transformation do we gain the strength to fight vigorously the evils of the world in an humble and loving spirit," King writes.[55]

King's sense of character and calling was intricately related to his spiritual life and his quest for social justice. The pre-Montgomery King or the faces of "Little Mike," "Tweed" and "the Philosopher King"[56] do not readily lend themselves to the character that is disclosed in the moments of testing that followed his public ministry in Montgomery and thereafter. It is rather in engagement with the struggle for social justice that one begins to see the deep, furrowed glance of the preacher become leader of the people. I am reminded of the poetic meditation of the late Archbishop of Recife, Brazil, Dom Helder Camara:

Lord, guide me
If you try me, send me out into the foggy night,
so that I cannot see my way.
Even if I stumble, this I beg,
that I may look and smile serenely,
bearing witness that you are with me and I walk in peace.

If you try me,
send me out into an atmosphere too thin for me to breathe
and I cannot feel the earth beneath my feet,
let my behavior show men that they cannot part me forcibly from you
in whom we breathe and move and are.
If you let hate hamper and trap me,
twist my heart, disfigure me,
then give my eyes
his love and peace,
my face the expression of your Son.[57]

This understanding of spirituality is not the same as the market-stimulated self-help philosophies on spiritual growth that crowd the shelves in mega bookstores and that promote personal development and solipsistic narcissism as the means to attain spiritual awareness. Rather, King's brand of spirituality stands in direct contradiction to the conforming, anesthetizing cultural deluge that dominates the printed and audio-visual media on leadership.

I cite here an event in his life where one sees clearly the relationship between spirituality and social transformation in King's portraiture of character: the often-cited "kitchen vision." David Garrow maintains that the kitchen vision of January 27, 1956, which took place in the early stages of the Montgomery boycott, was the paradigmatic moment in King's spirituality.[58] The experience captures for us an example of the way in which King understood spirituality to be part of a larger dynamic of ethics and leadership. It is also a revealing portrait of the testing of character that is integral to the spirituality of transformed nonconformity. Caught in the early phases of the Montgomery bus boycott, he received a chilling telephone call threatening his life and the life of his family: The chilling voice on the other end of the phone said, "Nigger, we are tired of you and your mess now. And if you are not out of town in three days, we're going to blow your brains out and blow up your house." King says he "sat there and thought about his little daughter who had just been born" and his "devoted and loyal wife," who was asleep. He thought about how he might be taken from her or she from him. He thought about his father and mother who had always been the steadying influences for him in trying moments, but they were 175 miles away in Atlanta. He said to himself:

> You've got to call on that something in that person your Daddy used to tell you about, that power that can make a way out of no way. . . . And I discovered then that religion had to become real to me, and I had to know God for myself. And I bowed down over that cup of coffee. I never will forget it. . . . I prayed a prayer, and I prayed out loud that night. I said, "Lord, I'm down here trying to do what's right. I think I'm right. I think the cause we represent is right. But, Lord, I must confess that I am weak now. I'm faltering. I'm losing my courage. And I can't let the people see me like this because if they see me weak and losing my courage, they will begin to get weak.

Then it happened:

> And it seemed at that moment that I could hear an inner voice saying to me, "Martin Luther, stand up for righteousness. Stand up for justice. Stand up for truth. And lo I will be with you, even until the end of the world." . . . I heard the voice of Jesus saying still to fight on. He promised never to leave me, never to leave me alone. No, never alone. No, never alone. He promised never to leave me, never to leave me alone.[59]

King's belief in the primacy of inner transformation in the struggle for social justice informed his thinking about the relationship between law and justice. In his many statements about resisting unjust laws, he questioned the underlying assumption that the opinions of the majority should dictate the rightness of moral action. He reasoned that since the rational nature of human beings seeks conformity to law, people are inclined to make conformity the normative equation for truth and justice. Such conformity, according to King, yields to blindness of action and staleness of culture. Blind conformity makes us paranoid and distrustful of opinions that go against the majority; stale conformity quietly supports the status quo through inaction that leads to apathy and neglect of our duties as citizens. "Most people," he writes, "and Christians in particular are thermometers that record and register the temperature of majority opinion, not thermostats that transform and regulate the temperature of society."[60]

He also resisted the temptation to *untransformed nonconformity* and anarchy. Nonconformity is not a good in and of itself; rather, it must be transformed through spiritual regeneration, which is an ongoing, disciplined, and deliberate practice characterized by love for the neighbor. Untransformed nonconformity, for King, leads to unwarranted suspicion and callous intolerance. Important for King, therefore, was the pragmatic thrust of law as an active, dynamic article that is renewed through conflict and struggle, through negation, preservation, and transformation. Democracy at its best, for King, is a squabble, a contentious exchange of ideas, opinions, values, and practice within the context of civil relations. When King speaks of a "revolution of values and priorities" and of overcoming the triplets of oppression (poverty, racism, and war), he speaks within the framework of American democratic society with the willingness to suffer the penalties imposed by law for civil disobedience.[61] King was acutely aware of the dangers that meet transformed nonconformists at the intersection where worlds collide. As a Christian, he believed that as coworkers with God, leaders are called to create a just and loving society through redemptive suffering. In a revealing personal testimony, King writes,

> My personal trials have taught me the value of unmerited suffering. . . . I have lived these past few years with the conviction that unearned suffering is redemptive. There are some who still find the cross a stumbling block, others consider it foolishness, but I am more convinced than ever before that it is the power of God unto social and individual salvation. So like the Apostle Paul I can now humbly say, "I bear in my body the marks of the Lord Jesus."[62]

THURMAN AND KING AT THE INTERSECTION
WHERE WORLDS COLLIDE

Thurman states in his autobiography that on more than one occasion he felt a premonition to minister to those engaged in the thick of the struggle. His relationship with Martin Luther King Jr. is exemplary.[63] After King was stabbed in Harlem on September 20, 1958, Thurman felt the inner necessity to go to him. In reference to this movement of the Spirit upon him, Thurman writes,

> Many times through the years I have had strange visitations in which there emerges at the center of my consciousness a face, a sense of urgency, a vibrant sensation, involving some particular person. On a certain Friday afternoon, Martin emerged in my awareness and would not leave. When I came home I said to Sue [my wife], "Tomorrow morning I am going down to New York to see Martin. I am not sure why, but I must talk with him personally if the doctors permit."[64]

During his visit with the young civil rights leader, Thurman encouraged King to extend his convalescence four weeks beyond those recommended by his doctor in order "to reassess himself in relation to the cause, to rest his body and mind with healing detachment, and to take a long look that only solitary brooding can provide." Thurman suggested, "The movement had become an organism with a life of its own to which he [King] must relate in fresh and extraordinary ways or be swallowed up by it."[65] King's biographers indicate that he did indeed take an extended convalescence culminating in his trip to the land of Gandhi in February 1959. Taylor Branch writes, "Recovering at home, King settled into a period of relative stillness unique to his entire adult life. He delivered no speeches or sermons outside the Dexter pulpit for many weeks. Nor did he travel." Branch also reports that King turned down pressing agendas within the movement during this period.[66] Stephen B. Oates reports that "as he convalesced, King had time to do what he had longed for all these months: he read books and meditated. And he talked a good deal about the trial he was going through. He decided that God was teaching him a lesson here, and that was personal redemption through suffering. It seemed to him that the stabbing had been for a purpose, that it was part of God's plan to prepare him for some larger work in the bastion of segregation that was the American South."[67]

In a series of letters between Thurman and King, it is possible to glean some of the content of the conversation that ensued from the visitation.[68] This correspondence also offers rare insight into the nature of Thurman's role as Opener of the Way in the civil rights movement. The relationship with King is of particular importance because it reveals the level of the struggle in which Thurman was self-consciously engaged as healer and teacher. Earlier that year, on July 7, 1958, King had written Thurman inviting him to come and preach at the church where King pastored, Dexter Avenue Baptist in Montgomery, Alabama. In a letter dated July 18, Thurman replied that if his schedule could accommodate, he would gladly come. The closing sentence, however, is most revealing. He wrote, "In the event that I can come, I hope there will be time enough to have a long, unhurried, probing conversation." This statement suggests that Thurman had desired opportunity to spend time with King before the Harlem incident. One month after the stabbing and subsequent to Thurman's visitation, he wrote King another letter. Two matters of concern were raised by the seasoned sage to the younger visionary. The first was the item mentioned above regarding an additional four weeks of convalescence. The second comment raised his concern for King's safety and the effectiveness of his ministry. In reply to the October correspondence, King, in a letter dated November 8, thanks Thurman for his visit and counsel:

> It was certainly kind of you to come by the Harlem Hospital to see me. The few minutes that we spent together were rich indeed. Your encouraging words came as a great spiritual lift and were of inestimable value in giving me the strength and courage to face the ordeal of that trying period.
>
> I am happy to report that I am feeling very well now and making steady progress toward a complete recovery. I am following your advice on the question "Where do *I* go from here?"[69]

One would not want to make much ado about nothing, but clearly the probing question "Where do *I* go from here?" is a more personal formulation of King's broader social problematic addressed in the last chapter of his 1958 book *Stride toward Freedom* and later expanded into a full-length inquiry in his last book, *Where Do We Go from Here: Chaos or Community?*[70] More important, this question arises from the same schema of the methodology used by Thurman as the initial step of commitment as a spiritual discipline, that is, the questions of identity (Who am I?), purpose (What do I want?) and method (How do I propose to get it?).

Commitment, for Thurman, is more than mere intellectual assent or emotional attachment to an ideal, as in the quest for social justice; rather, it is at the heart of one's personal religious experience, however defined. Commitment involves "singleness of mind." He writes, "This means surrendering the life at the very core of one's self-consciousness to a single end, goal, or purpose. When a man is able to bring to bear upon a single purpose all the powers of his being, his whole life is energized and vitalized."[71]

This is particularly true, Thurman suggests, in the experience of suffering or crisis. In crisis, one is forced to ask the question of purpose, "What is it that I want, really?" He opines:

> When a man faces this question put to him by life, or when he is caught up in the necessity of answering it, or by deliberate intent seeks an answer, he is at once involved in the dynamics of commitment. At such a moment he knows what, in the living of his life, he must be *for* and what he must be *against*.[72]

On November 19, Thurman wrote King:

> It is wonderful to know that you are better and that plans are afoot in your own thinking for structuring your life in a way that will deepen its channel. It would be a very good thing if we could spend several hours of uninterrupted talk about these matters that are of such paramount significance for the fulfillment of the tasks to which our hands are set.

In the last two letters, dated September 11 and September 30, 1959, respectively, the two busy men share their disappointment in not being able to confirm a preaching date for Thurman at Dexter Avenue Baptist Church and missing one another while King was in San Francisco earlier that month. Thurman's closing remarks in the earlier letter reflect his concern for the young civil rights leader: "I think of you in my prayers and quiet time very often with the hope that you will continue to find all the things that are needful for your peace." King, in reply, writes, "I hope we will be able to talk together in the not-too-distant future." Whether this conversation took place is unknown. However, nearly five years later, Thurman was one of the thousands of pilgrims who gathered at the foot of the Lincoln Memorial to hear King share his dream for America. This dream was also Thurman's. In his later years, long after King's tragic death, he reflected on the heroic image of Martin:

> I joined my friend Frank Wilson in the memorable March on Washington and was part of the vast throng who heard and felt the unearthly upheaval of triumphant anguish: "Free at last! Free at last! Thank God A'mighty, I am free at last." Perhaps the ultimate demand laid upon the human spirit is the responsibility to select *where* one bears witness to the Truth of his spirit. The final expression of the committed spirit is to affirm: I choose! and to abide. I felt myself a fellow pilgrim with him and with all the host of those who dreamed his dream and shared his vision.[73]

Thurman's healing ministry to King and others in the movement is suggestive of a much-neglected dimension of American leadership discourse and practice. His approach to social justice issues has been labeled "mystical" and unresponsive to the concrete realities of oppressed peoples. This reading of Thurman is misinformed and unjustified. Any serious, reflective reading of the Thurman corpus reveals a fundamental concern with the plight of the oppressed. Luther Smith suggests that this misreading of Thurman is based primarily on the fact that he does not provide specific proposals for social transformation. Yet Smith contends that while none of Thurman's writings offer a blueprint for social policy, he does offer "a heightened awareness of human suffering that is at stake, he clarifies how fundamental religious principles are involved in issues, he challenges our attitudes and commitments that contribute to social crises, and he inspires us to respond to the issues."[74] Thurman's contribution to spirituality, ethics, and leadership rests on his provision of an intellectual framework for a proper *sense of self* and *urge toward community*, which will find greater elaboration in the following chapters. Otis Moss Jr. captures well the significance of Thurman's contribution to the civil rights movement: "It might be that he did not join the march from Selma to Montgomery, or many of the other marches, but he has participated at the level that shapes the philosophy that creates the march—and without that, people don't know what to do before they march, while they march or after they march."[75]

For Thurman *commitment* is fundamental to character. Commitment involves volition, which may be a radical, self-conscious yielding on the part of the individual or a systematic, disciplined effort over a period of time.[76] The result of the commitment of the individual is a new, integrated basis for moral action; a new value content and center of loyalty inform his actions in the world.[77] The person's loyalty to God, which proceeds from the personal assurance of being loved by God, forms the ground of the moral life. What is discovered in private must be witnessed to in the world. Thurman comments on the nature of the individual's spiritual experience and its relationship to moral action:

> His experience is personal, private but in no sense exclusive. All of the vision of God and holiness which he experiences, he must achieve in the context of the social situation by which day-to-day life is defined. What is disclosed in his religious experience he must define in community. That which God shareth with him, he must inspire his fellows to seek for themselves. He is dedicated therefore to the removing of all barriers which block or frustrate this possibility in the world.[78]

King and Thurman demonstrate that for ethical leaders, each encounter with the *other* carries within itself the danger of disfiguring, of being tested and proven so that that which is hidden (and that which *calls* us) discloses itself in acts of courage, justice, and compassion. Ethical leaders, therefore, are *apostles of sensitiveness*, transfigured and transforming actors who present themselves to the world as symbols and for instances of what is possible and hopeful. In the experience of encounter, one is readied or predisposed to hope, hope being simultaneously the transformation of threat, temptation, danger, and death into a vision of the possible, a sense of values, a sense of the future, that is, having faith to move on in creative activity that aspires to goodness.

The task of the ethical leader is to *inspire* and *guide* others in the process of transformation through courageous acts of defiance and resistance against systems of injustice. At the personal dimension of character (which will be discussed later), this process involves reliving and recovering their cultural futures through life stories, rituals, and creative actions that give meaning to life. The focus is placed on reconciling acts of community, with the spiritual and ethical question being, What can I hope for? Through their personal narratives and their respective analyses of the power of hope, Thurman and King provide key concepts for leaders who must have the courage to hope at the intersections where worlds collide.

Chapter Two

WHAT IS ETHICAL LEADERSHIP?

I describe ethical leadership as the critical appropriation and embodiment of moral traditions that have shaped the character and shared meanings of a people (an ethos). In fact, ethical leadership does not emerge from a historical vacuum but from the lifeworlds of particular traditions and speaks authoritatively and acts responsibly with the aim of serving the collective good. Ethical leaders, therefore, are those whose characters have been shaped by the wisdom, habits, and practices of particular traditions—often more than one—yet they tend to be identified with a specific cultural ethos and narrative. Finally, ethical leadership asks the question of values in reference to ultimate concern.[1] Ethical leadership as described here will receive elaboration in the chapters that follow.

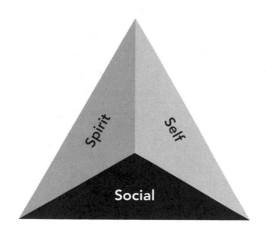

FIGURE 1. THE ETHICAL LEADERSHIP MODEL™

SELF, SOCIAL, AND SPIRITUAL

The above definition of ethical leadership is based on a triangular model that incorporates three dynamically interrelated dimensions of human existence: self, social, and spiritual. In the dimension of the *self* or the personal, the concern is with questions of identity and purpose (Who am I? What do I want? What do I propose to do and become?). The *social* or public dimension involves the relationship with the other (To whom and what am I ultimately accountable?). The *spiritual* addresses the human need for a sense of ultimacy, excellence, and hope in reference to the great mystery of being (Who am I? What do I want? What do I propose to do and become? Who is the other? How am I to respond to the actions of the other on me?). This latter dimension should not be narrowly identified with religion, although religious experience is a vital resource in one's spiritual quest. For this third dimension, I am more interested in answering the questions of identity and purpose in respect to how leaders perceive their own quests of meaning. This is fundamentally a spiritual exercise. Howard Thurman was fond of telling the story of the musk deer of North India:

> In the springtime, the roe is haunted by the odor of musk. He runs wildly over hill and ravine with his nostrils dilating and his little body throbbing with desire, sure that around the next clump of trees or bush he will find the musk, the object of his quest. Then at last he falls, exhausted, with his little head resting on his tiny hoofs, only to discover that the odor of musk is in his own hide.[2]

The dreams, the keys to the meaning of life, the answers to the problems we face are not only outside of us but also within. While the external world of nature and human society is the arena of social contracting, action, and work, the world of values is within.

In his book *Let Your Life Speak: Listening for the Voice of Vocation*, Parker Palmer comments on Václav Havel's 1990 address to a joint session of the U.S. Congress that took place shortly after his election as president of the Czech Republic. Havel thanked the United States for its assistance in helping to reorganize the former Soviet state but added that his people also had something to give to our nation. From their experience of oppression and suffering, they had discovered something that perhaps we had forgotten or had never known: "a special capacity to look, from time to time, somewhat further than those who had not undergone this bitter experience." Havel suggested that his nation had learned that *consciousness precedes being*. For Palmer, this means that "material reality is not the fundamental factor in the movement of human history," but *consciousness, awareness, thought,* and *spirit*. Havel remarked, "The salvation of this human world lies nowhere else than in the human heart, in the human power, to reflect in human modesty and in human responsibility. Without a global revolution in the sphere of human consciousness, nothing will change for the better . . . and the catastrophe toward which this world is headed, whether it be ecological, social, demographic or a general breakdown of civilization, will be unavoidable."[3]

The three dimensions of self, society, and spirit, therefore, cannot be understood as separate but are dynamically interrelated and form the basis for community (*integration, wholeness,* and *harmony*) within persons, society, and the universe. The movements of these three dimensions are not linear but circular and cyclical, as in a spiral or "a liberated circle." The geometrical form of the spiral is an unfinished circle, spiraling inward and outward in infinite patterns of opening and closing, moving deeper into the recesses of consciousness and outward in the world of people and things. The song "Spiraling into the Center"[4] captures the movement of life, individually and collectively, represented in the spiral of infinite progress and regress, extending and returning to the Center of All Things:

> Spiraling into the Center
> The Center of our Wheel
> Spiraling into the Center
> The Center of our Wheel
> I am the Weaver
> I am the Woven One
> I am the Dreamer
> I am the Dream . . .

The Dance of Bees

The late physicist David Bohm, in *Wholeness and the Implicate Order*, argued that traditional Western ways of knowing inhibit this dynamic aspect of reality—the constant flow of the inner and outer in respect to the infinite character of living things of which human beings are only one aspect. According to Bohm, the relationship between reality and knowledge is a dynamic process analogous to "the dance of bees." As bees locate honey-bearing flowers, they communicate to the others through a pattern of activity that resembles a dance. The activity, says Bohm, does not origi-nate in the "minds" of the bees as "a form of knowledge in relative corre-spondence to the flowers"; rather, it appears to be a process that is at one with the bees and the activity of collecting honey. He writes, "This activity is not separate from the rest of what is involved in collecting the honey. It flows and merges into the next step in an unbroken process. So one may propose for consideration the notion that thought is a sort of 'dance of the mind' which functions indicatively, and which, when properly carried out, flows and merges into an harmonious and orderly sort of overall process in life as a whole."[5]

To understand the vibrant character of a dynamic and living universe is to enter into a different relationship with self, the other, and the mystery in which one is participating. It is also to realize a way of *knowing* that is not limited to mere analytic processes but involves what we sometimes call "intuition." For our purposes, I am identifying this sense of knowing with the dimension of *spirit*. But spirit, as we shall see, is not detached from nature, history, or the world, but is *embodied*. I am arguing that the funda-mental issue besetting civil society is the absence of the third dimension of spirit in most constructions of social reality. Consequently, in such limited constructions, the self is treated as an isolated, discrete sphere of meaning without any necessary connection to the other and the larger mystery of the cosmos. Joseph Jaworski, who was deeply influenced by Bohm's phi-losophy, suggests in his book *Synchronicity: The Inner Path to Leadership* that *relatedness* is the organizing principle of the universe and thus is the missing link in the way we think about leadership.[6] Ethical leadership, as it is presented here, addresses this two-dimensional pursuit of meaning by calling attention to *relatedness;* and also addresses the place of the third dimension and the relationship of *spirituality*, *ethics*, and *leadership*.

SPIRITUALITY, ETHICS, AND LEADERSHIP

Discussions of spirituality cover a broad and increasingly complex spec-trum of beliefs, practices, and approaches within and beyond traditional religious circles. For our purposes, spirituality refers to a way or ways of seeking or being in relationship with the other, who is believed to be wor-thy of reverence and highest devotion. With this definition I am concerned with the *other* as inclusive of both individuality and community. The other is not impersonal but intimately related to who I am and who I become.

According to Emmanuel Levinas, the other has a *face*—and the face of the other is the foundation of ethics and the origin of civil society.[7] Beyond our private quests for meaning and authenticity, we are connected to others. Indeed, in order to be fully human and ethical, we must "face the other."

I encounter the face of the other in everyday life but also in its strangeness and transcendence, in its force of obligation and interdependence. James Hillman writes:

> The Other's face calls upon my character. Rather than thinking my character shows in my face and that my face is my character exteriorized . . . character requires the face of the Other. Its piercing provocation pulls from us every possible ethical potential. In bad conscience we turn away from the face in the wheelchair, the face of the beggar; we hood the face of the executed, and we ignore the faces of the socially ostracized and hierarchically inferior so that they become "invisible" even as we walk down the same street.[8]

The human face is also the face that is hidden and present for me in all its power and meaning. Indeed, in its deepest expression it is *spiritual*—in the heat of passion and desire, lovers *face* one another; in courtrooms, victims *face* their assailants; in reconciliation, the penitent child *faces* a forgiving parent; and in reverence and conviction, the devout *faces* the God she serves. But in the final analysis, spirituality requires that we face ourselves—our stories and memories. The face invites me to revel in memory—my own memories and in collective memory as diverse and old as the world. If such a face were to visit me, I would understand that I am not alone, unrelated neither to history nor to memory.[9]

In C. S. Lewis's classic retelling of the story of Cupid and Psyche, *Till We Have Faces*, the dying Queen Orual remembers her sad story and comes to the great realization that Psyche, the sister she envied because of her beauty and the god's love for her, was never the problem that she *faced*. Nor was it the faceless stone gods in the temple who needed faces. Rather, she first had to see her face, which she despised, before she could see the gods'. In the end, she discovered that her face and the face of Psyche were one and the same, mirroring the mystery of all that was and is to come. How can the gods speak to us face-to-face till we have faces? And how shall we face ourselves until we have faced the *other*?[10]

Spirituality involves facing the other as we face ourselves. This experience of facing the other reveals the deep longing and yearning to be in unity with ourselves. The following meditation from my journals speaks to this dimension of *facing the self*:

> *I am climbing the mountain with him who has invited me to come.* He is climbing as though there were nothing to it. He must know the mountain well; he seems to like the climbing itself. My joints ache and I have the wrong attitude for climbing. I am fussy and absorbed in myself—my struggles, my pain, my loneliness, my likes and disappointments. I have not noticed that he is really tired too—but for him the journey is non-negotiable.
>
> I fear that tomorrow I will awaken from this sleep and will curse myself for being so easily deluded, smooth-talked into making this climb, knowing my temperament and deep feelings about such things. "I am a mother hen!" "There I go again. Stop it! Just climb!"
>
> "I believe I shall see the goodness of the Lord in the land of the living." "The Lord is my shepherd, I shall not want." "I would have fainted if it had not been for the Lord."
>
> "Now faith, hope, love abide—but the greatest of these is love." "I believe in the universal church, the resurrection of the body. . . . I believe in God the Father Almighty, creator of heaven and the earth. . . . I believe all mountains are illusions and only faith says that we have arrived."
>
> "I believe that the Transfiguration is completed not when we arrive at the top of the mountain, but when we come down."
>
> "Maybe today, I will see the goodness of the Lord in the land of the living . . . maybe . . . if I continue to climb."
>
> *I am climbing the mountain today. I am alone with the Alone. Who then is this fellow-traveler? His face is very familiar. I must become better acquainted with him if I am to continue this journey. Friend, tell me, who are you? And what is your name?*

Spirituality is also a discipline that places emphasis on *practice*—spirituality is something that we *do*. Prior to any act of cognition, spirituality has to do with the practical, day-to-day encounter with the other, the other being both friend and stranger, comrade and opponent, individual and collective, divine and demonic. In its active, dynamic expression, spirituality is *life-generating* and *disfiguring*. Using these indicators, spirituality can be viewed from three perspectives: (1) formal notions of spirituality that are related to established religions; (2) informal notions of spirituality that are "self-actualized" or self-defined by individuals or small groups that may or may not be associated with an established religious institution; and (3) philosophical or ethical notions of spirituality related to values and perceived goods, for example, truth, beauty, justice, and so on. I also use these three categories as heuristic devices that provide lenses through which to look at the vast landscape of a developing literature that incorporates ideas, beliefs, and practices from an array of traditions and perspectives—health, science, technology, politics, business, and education.[11]

In my discussion on the Ethical Leadership Model,™ spirituality plays a key role in the development of ethical leaders. Moreover, spirituality demands that leaders cultivate and nourish a sense of self that recognizes the interrelatedness of life or a sense of community. A "sense of community" refers to the larger extended ecological sphere made tangible by nature, defined as the universe and the cosmos, but in its final essence, it is *spirit*. This idea of *spirit* finds resonance with Peter Paris's definition of spirituality in the African context: spirituality is never individualistic but is part of a larger sphere of unity that is diverse in its dynamics and character. "The spirituality of a people," he writes, "refers to the animating and integrative power that constitutes the principal frame of meaning for individual and collective experiences."[12] For Robert M. Franklin, spirituality refers to "a person's sense of identity in relation to other people and that which is conceived as ultimate concern. Rooted in spiritual identity are a person's fundamental values, moral commitments, and ability to engage in ethical reasoning. Spiritual health is reflected in a person's ability to trust and care for others."[13] In summary, spirituality demands that we *face* the other, personally and collectively—and in facing the other we are transfigured and transformed and called to the larger quest of building community in the world.

Spirituality is the core of the inner and social lives of ethical leaders. It informs the relationship between the private and public spheres of leadership at the intersections where worlds collide. How then do leaders utilize spirituality as a resource in making fitting ethical decisions in the various contexts and situations that lead to transformation of powerful, intransigent systems?

The relationship among spirituality, ethics, and leadership is important because leaders in many public venues are increasingly turning to approaches that emphasize some form of spirituality as an authoritative source in making decisions that impact the lifestyles, attitudes, and behaviors of many people, especially in the areas of education, government, health, science, and business. Often these appeals to spirituality fail to address the larger ethical questions of justice, equity, and truth-telling that are raised in public life.

They also speak to the role that spirituality and ethics will increasingly play in the development of leadership for the future. A significant challenge for the next generation of leadership is the increasing promotion and advancement of science, technology, and business to serve the interests of human development and the environment. The changes produced by this triumvirate have already resulted in a significant upheaval in society, the meaning of life, intelligence, and work. For example, there is a growing movement within nonprofit and for-profit sectors to incorporate ethical principles and practices pertaining to issues of transparency, diversity, transcultural dynamics, sustainability, the environment, and human development. Increasingly, large corporations, think tanks, and political leaders are relying on spirituality as a form of human resource development to address these larger structural issues. Thurman's and King's approaches to these ethical questions will receive attention throughout the following discussions on justice, fairness, and integrity in the Ethical Leadership Model.

Finally, in order for a just civil society to exist, persons in responsible leadership roles must make decisions based on ethical guides.[14] For historically marginalized peoples, the relationship of spirituality, ethics, and leadership is most urgent. With the long-range economic, political, and social costs of war, a troubled market economy, and rapid advances (crusades) in technology, science, and globalization, we now have the makings of a social anarchy that threatens the very foundations of our social purpose. The impending catastrophic fallout of the present situation will have far-reaching negative consequences for the least of these, those whom the late Samuel DeWitt Proctor called "the lost, the left-out and left behind."[15] At a deeper level, however, there *is* a spiritual malaise, a nihilistic threat promoted by the predominance of a utilitarian individualism that appeals endlessly to therapeutic remedies that begin and end with self. Who will lead in the twenty-first century? Better yet, how shall they lead? *Who will go for us, and whom shall we send?* For answers to these questions, it is instructive to inquire regarding fundamental assumptions of ethical theory and how these inhere in our construction of spirituality and leadership.

WAYS OF DOING ETHICS

There are different ways of *doing* ethics. Note that the emphasis is on *doing*, not simply *thinking* about ethics. Ethics, like spirituality, is essentially a practice—it is something that we do and hence our basic moral beliefs are shaped by habits and practices that are formed in specific communities. Although the words "morality" and "ethics" are often used interchangeably, for our purposes, it is important to make a distinction between them. Morality refers to commonly accepted rules of conduct; patterns of behavior approved by a social group, and values and standards shared by the group; and beliefs about what is good and right held by a community with a shared history. Morality has its primary location in *lifeworlds*. Ethics, in its normative sense, is the critical analysis of morality. It is reflection on morality with the purpose of analysis, criticism, interpretation, and justification of the rules, roles, and relations in a society. Ethics is concerned with the meaning of moral terms, the conditions in which moral decision-making takes place, and the justification of principles brought to bear in resolving conflicts of value and of moral rules in public space. The practice of ethics is not unlike the practice of a doctor, lawyer, or technician. Although one "knows" the rules and procedures, excellence in one's field of endeavor involves practice.[16]

This understanding of ethics and morality is important because one of the most difficult questions for leaders is how one goes about making an ethical decision, whether personal or public, at the intersection of lifeworlds and systemworlds. Most of our moral perspectives arise from particular lifeworlds, which have their own histories and communities of memory that determine what is *right* and *good*. By virtue of their particular contexts and horizons of meaning, our moral perspectives are often in conflict with other perspectives, values, and conceptions of the *good* and the *right* that compete in public life.

There are basically three prevailing assumptions and perspectives that have driven the debate on ethics and leadership in the modern world: rationalism, empiricism, and communitarianism. For each of these, there are corresponding perspectives of human nature and consequently of moral agency, which I will refer to respectively as (1) *the rationalist*, (2) *the realist and the retooler*, and (3) *the relationalist*. I will propose a non-exclusive fourth way of looking at spirituality, ethics, and leadership that provides a conceptual framework for making moral decisions as *the way of the storyteller*, which involves the interrelated processes of remembering, retelling, and reliving our stories; looking, listening, and learning from our stories and the stories of others; and discerning, deliberating, and deciding on appropriate strategies and actions at the intersections where worlds collide.

The Way of the Rationalist: Rules-Based Ethics

The rational model of ethics, technically known as *deotontological* ethics, depends largely on the role of reason in creating and sustaining human society in it various dimensions. At the heart of the rationalist view is the belief that reason is the supreme source for ordering and giving coherence to the moral life. It focuses on the question "What is my duty?" In this perspective, one cannot ultimately trust the insights of experience or the wisdom of traditions to inform decisions related to moral and ethical issues. The rational functions of the self are viewed as the most reliable in ascertaining appropriate conduct in given situations with others. This view also relies heavily on a picture of the moral agent as a discrete, individuated being who, though situated among others both in history and in nature, seeks abstraction from particularity in order to seize upon the universal. For the rationalist, the individual is primary and must seek conformity through reason by subordinating personal idiosyncrasies *to* it, and constructing social and corporate relationship *from* it.

In regard to the ethical life, the rationalist is concerned with principles, rules, and laws that maintain order within the self and in relationships with others and the larger society. The basic issue here is the assumption that the determination of *rights* precedes determination of the *good*. In other words, different individuals and groups entertain different and even conflicting conceptions of what is good. Any hope of reconciling these ideas must proceed from some initial and mutual respect for one another's autonomy. It is not that the rationalist believes the self is completely autonomous or is fully self-regulating but rather that the self cannot enter into orderly relations with others apart from some basic acknowledgment of and respect for their will, even where it is ill—or at least where one thinks it so.

The obvious strength of this way of doing ethics is that, at its best, it seeks rules-based egalitarianism and is concerned with order. It helps us to know when we are out of line with what Michel Foucault called "the order of things." To transgress the rules that we have mutually agreed upon, as the basis for moral obligation to the other, is to violate something intrinsic to human nature; it is to go against reason and human freedom. The popular movie serial The Matrix captures this view. The Architect, a Platonic form, is the primary lawgiver and custodian of the truth. If Neo (the new man) is to function without danger in this world constructed by reason, he must submit to its rules or face the fate of all those who have preceded him. Reason holds it together. When rules are broken, there are penalties. Moral life, therefore, is governed by conformity and obedience to law that is universal in its intent. Reason is suspicious of and therefore monitors carefully the dynamic other side of the equation, which is experiential and creative. For the question of ethical leadership, as we shall see, this observation is critical for reframing and addressing complex leadership issues and experiential learning.

Much of the recent controversy surrounding ethical compliance falls into this scenario of the rules-based ethical perspective. Questions repeatedly raised in these discussions are, finally, Who makes the rules? Who determines what is just? and When rules are broken, are penalties enough to sustain a just and equitable society? But these are always the wrong questions, according to the rationalist, unless we are undertaking some sort of sociological and cultural investigation. They are the wrong questions, in a moral sense, according to theorists like the late John Rawls, because the prior concern must always be less Who makes the rules? but What are the rules? In other words, in what frame of mind ought those who are charged with framing or interpreting them to proceed? It can never be possible, for the future, to say with certainty who will end up as leaders. But it should at least be possible to say by what principles they should be led and in what frame of mind. Recent responses to ethical improprieties in government, military, business, and religious institutions are examples of the limitations of the rationalist approach.[17]

The Way of the Realist (Reality-Based Ethics) and Retooler (Ends-Based Ethics)

A second model of ethical discourse, which we divide in two parts as the realist and the retooler, has its basis in empiricism. As ethical theories, the realist and retooler are more formally associated with *teleological* ethics. This ethical perspective begins with goals with the end in mind or with the vision that informs the leader's behavior. It is rooted in Aristotelian philosophy and has as its focus the idea of human beings, respectively, as "practical realists" who are concerned with the end product or outcome in mind, or as "tool makers" who are constantly constructing from experience the necessary skills, competencies, and tools essential for adaptation and fulfillment of the vision. Values derived from this perspective are based on experiential models that are developmental, pragmatic, and, often, utilitarian. The emphasis is on the appropriate calculi and tools for shaping and remaking meaning and ensuring the efficient delivery of intended outcomes. There tend to be two major schools of thought that hold this view: utilitarianism and pragmatism, or what we shall call *realists* and *retoolers*.

Realist Leaders

On the utilitarian side of this equation, the way of the *realist* is committed to efficiency and measurable outcomes. It is consequentialist in that it asks the ethical question in respect to its short-term and long-term goals in relation to other alternatives. Both Jeremy Bentham and John Stuart Mill, its modern progenitors, formulated this philosophical perspective as a way of enhancing the social good and providing a means of ensuring equal justice. The classical formulation of utilitarianism is found in the maxim "One should always choose the option that allows the greatest good for the greatest number."[18]

All utilitarians, however, do not focus on good as happiness alone but identify good from a plethora of human activity, including fraternity, knowledge, human development, and so on. There are "act utilitarians," who focus on specific, individual actions as sources for moral deliberation, and "rule utilitarians," who are concerned primarily with measuring the consequences of general principles or rules from specific actions. In all cases, the obvious strength of utilitarianism lies in its direct empirical/moral commitment to the diminution of pain wherever and to whomever it occurs. Leaders who use utilitarian-based ethics as a guide for improving the quality of an organization tend to ask questions like "Have we considered all alternative actions and selected the one that produces the greatest good? How can we best serve the ends of the collective rather than the individual? What specific actions or general rules will either maximize or minimize the good?"[19]

The realist approach bears affinity with the rationalist approach as it relates to technical reasoning, which is concerned with quantitative measurements or the utilization of some form of calculus as the means for determining successful outcomes. There are severe limitations in a shallow utilitarian approach for leaders involved in ethical decision-making. One is the temptation of failing to see people as individuals inhering with equal dignity and worth. Whenever individuals are treated as a means to an end, this fundamental principle is violated. Another question for the utilitarian approach is that it can involve perilous consequences for the minority. When the guiding assumption is that the majority is numerical, whether that majority is human beings or interests, the minority is ill served. It is in this sense that shallow utilitarianism fails to acknowledge that ends and means should cohere in order to respect human life and dignity. For instance, military strategists often use a utilitarian calculus in scenario games to determine collateral damage in war.[20] If one has to choose options based upon how many civilians will die in an attack over against how many lives will be spared, utilitarianism can be seen as disrespecting the human rights of those who are killed. The same argument applies to business leaders who are called to lay off hundreds of employees based upon maintaining shareholders' interests and company earnings without exploring other options like reorganization and providing proportionate pay cuts across the organization.[21]

In the absence of adequate principles of justice, procedures and rules proliferate ad nauseum. Organizational and governmental policies that adhere to rules-based ethics, as we have indicated, are constantly engaged in the production of rules and penalties that are ultimately ineffective in staving off a tide of corruption and impropriety. Though necessary, principles and rules derived from a social contract by which all parties theoretically consent to abide are ultimately insufficient. According to some moral theorists, this approach only responds to one side of the question of justice; leaders should also embody and employ a *moral sense of justice* in the construction of community. I will return to this important distinction in my discussion of justice in chapter 5, "Community at the Intersection."[22]

Neither rationalist nor realist perspectives on leadership adequately address the deeper questions of human desire and need to be connected with others in acts of empathy, respect, and justice. In determining the distribution of goods among competing interests, the ethical leader is faced with the need to balance rationalist and realist claims with her sense of justice as fairness that seeks connectivity and community. This balancing act, however, can be fraught with perilous consequences. In the absence of consideration of essential relationships or connections that bind one to the other, the primary motivating force of leaders is utilitarian individualism.[23] For ethical leaders, this observation is most important. In organizational and civic life, if the individual leader or team becomes the primary moral resource and behavioral model, then building community becomes highly problematic. On a larger scale, leadership that is driven by utilitarian individualism exacerbates the central problematic of lifeworlds and system-worlds: the building of a moral ethos that informs behaviors and practices that promote community. Most leaders and managers would agree, however, that an inordinate embrace of a communitarian ethic or what is viewed as the soft side of management creates problems of governance and efficiency without which a viable and strong organization can exist. This challenge is not limited to business leaders but affects leaders across public venues, especially nonprofit and community-based organizations.

The challenge of balancing rationalist and realist approaches to leadership also has a cultural analogue in respect to multiculturalism and difference. The authors of *Habits of the Heart* argued that the national community has lost its moral languages of expressive individualism (represented by Walt Whitman), biblical piety (represented by John Winthrop), and civic republicanism (represented by Thomas Jefferson), while retaining only one dominant mode of moral discourse, utilitarian individualism. This latter language is expressed socially in the representative characters of the entrepreneur, manager, and therapist. According to these thinkers, these models of self-understanding cannot serve as moral resources for re-thinking the meaning and destiny of the democratic experiment. Their recommendation is that we return to the lost languages of the republic (expressive individualism, civic republicanism, and biblical piety) as a basis for reconstructing a new moral ecology that would be a successor of the moral authority and energy demonstrated in the modern civil rights movement.[24]

Retoolers

Retoolers are pragmatic leaders who see the call to reconstructing a new moral ecology as precisely the issue at stake, but with important differences to the rationalist and realist approaches. In the more general pragmatist sense of the retooler, promoted essentially by William James, John Dewey, and more popular pragmatists like Richard Rorty, the questions for ethics deal more with the contingency of history and the limited autonomy of ethical claims and decisions. In other words, the retooler does not extol the virtues of absolute truth, laws, and rules but asks the more immediate questions: What are the essential assets and tools at our disposal to deliver the intended outcome? What are the limits of our moral language when we speak of the good life and work toward fulfillment of our vision? Truth for the pragmatist retooler is not a prescribed formula given once and for all, nor is it a finished product; rather, it is part of an ongoing human project of reconstruction, which involves identifying the appropriate methods and strategies for understanding and enhancing the perceived goods of our collective lives. Human beings are builders, technicians who are constantly retooling and adapting to changes in the environment that signal more productive outcomes. Leaders who are retoolers work with the materials at hand and refashion them into usable tools in order to meet mutual goals.[25]

Many adaptive leadership theorists use the pragmatist approach as a way of innovating and changing organizations. Warren Bennis and Robert Thomas define adaptive capacity as applied creativity, "the ability to look at a problem or crisis and see an array of unconventional solutions."[26] Ronald Heifetz's excellent work *Leadership Without Easy Answers* is an example of this approach.[27] Retoolers challenge traditions, beliefs, and assumptions about the good and inquire, Does it work? Does it have any practical value for the goals that we seek to achieve? The pragmatist leader sees reconstruction as part of a dynamic, ongoing project that strives toward an end that is authentically human in its production.

The approach of the retooler is helpful for our purposes in that it provides leaders with a methodology for remembering, retelling, and reliving their personal life stories in the context of larger cultural narratives. The remembering, retelling, and reliving of personal stories helps leaders, in the words of American philosopher John Dewey, to "form, reveal and test" themselves, which is part of the ongoing work of developing character.[28] Its emphasis on the value of communities of discourse and practice highlights the pertinent issues at stake for the leader in gaining a sense of wholeness in continuity with her past without romanticizing the inherited practices that are antithetical to her quest for character, civility, and community. As we shall see, the leader is called upon to retell or reframe his or her story by self-revising and reframing memories in respect to integrity, empathy, and hope (character); recognition, respect, and reverence (civility); and courage, justice, and compassion (community). In the critical processes of reframing, the leader is called upon to exclude, include, and reconfigure fragments of self in historical context in a creative and imaginative process of *moral bricolage*.[29]

The Way of the Relationist: Relations-Based Ethics

A third view that has been part and parcel of Western culture is relational ethics, which posits that all life and experience are interrelated—to understand oneself is to understand how we are fundamentally connected. The questions of knowing (epistemology) and valuing (axiology) are interrelated. What one knows cannot be divorced from beliefs, values, and visions of the good. The quest for the good life is in all places and at all times centered in a community of practice. This is the way of the relationist. The list of leaders in this tradition is long and hallowed with examples from early Christians who practiced *koinonia* to experiments in communal living led by the likes of Leo Tolstoy, Gandhi, Martin Buber, and many others. Martin Luther King Jr. called this practice the quest for "the beloved community." Howard Thurman called it "the search for common ground." The basic thesis of the relationist leader is that human beings are related in mutuality and interdependency, as is all existence. We are a part of a larger I-Thou relation, which means that we are always addressing and responding to the other in a relational web of existence. In this model, the moral self is essentially relational and moral actions are based more on covenant than on contract as depicted in rationalist and utilitarian constructions. The appeal is to conscience or some form of mutually agreed-upon norms that derive from relationships that promote community. The major value constructs tend to be love, peace, friendship, empathy, hope, and reconciliation, which appeal to the formation of community.

The claim of relationist leaders to create community is both their liability and their hope. While relational models presuppose a certain nature or quality in human beings that predisposes them to communal existence, the requirements of rational bureaucratic models that dominate society often conflict with their projects. Reinhold Niebuhr referred to this conflict as "moral man in immoral society." On the other hand, their dream of a friendly world under friendly skies is at once a critique of existing social arrangements and a call to reimagine possibilities at the intersection. The salient question for the relationist is, How might leaders in the new century who seek community survive and transform the intersections of rational/utilitarian systemworlds and lifeworlds, while adhering to traditional understandings of community and the values that uphold them?[30]

The Ethical Leadership Model, described here, takes as its point of departure the relationist understanding of ethics. The use of thinkers like Thurman and King as representative characters of a particular tradition of justice and compassion, which we call the black church tradition, provides leaders with a framework that explores the relationship between spirituality, ethics, and leadership. This framework, however, is not exhaustive; it seeks, rather, to uphold the values of constant criticism, reevaluation, and modeling. Since relational models always run the risk of extolling utopian visions that transcend self, history, and culture, it is important that they be linked to particular traditions of discourse and practice in which the leader finds herself. The poet Robinson Jeffers says, "Nobody that I know of ever poured grain from an empty sack."[31] The relationist, therefore, is in constant pursuit of habits and practices that aspire to the construction of just and loving communities that are rooted in particular strands of traditions. In this respect, it finds creative affinity with the way of the storyteller, the primary ethical theory that our model espouses.

The Way of the Storyteller: Narrative-Based Ethics

The approach that this model advocates is based on narrative or story. Narrative or "virtue ethics" takes seriously experience and tradition as primary resources for ethical life and practice. It does not eschew the approaches of the rationalist and empiricist, but unlike rules-based, ends-based, or relations-based ethics, this perspective is narrative-based; that is, human life and history are seen as a network of interlocking stories that aspire to truth. The essential dynamic of "connectedness" or "relatedness" as espoused by the relationist is significant, but more is at stake for the storyteller than simply being related. The storyteller emphasizes the place of traditions that authenticate and ground relatedness in the context of larger historical narratives or stories. The substantive discourse of traditions yields long-standing virtues, values, and social practices embedded in institutions that have historically provided an understanding of the good life in respect to the individual and the collectivity.

Alasdair MacIntyre, for instance, traces the contemporary ethical crisis of Western civilization to "the failure of the Enlightenment project," which effectively cut off the power of traditions through the introduction of instrumental reason and moral visions unconnected to the historical narratives and communities that provided coherence and instruction for the moral life. The present impasse that is dominated by the moral views of rationalists, realists, and retoolers, MacIntyre suggests, is due to the extraction of a situated self from the historical-social context (social telos) for which ethics (moral rules and language) and the classical/medieval conceptions of human nature existed. The result is the modern era's "emotivist self," an empty, vacuous concept of human nature that has no coherent basis for justifying moral claims and, hence, moral agreement. The moral claims of the rationalist and utilitarian ("rights" and "utility"), MacIntyre argues, are incommensurable, precisely because there is no overarching social canopy to give them meaning and coherence.[32]

Harvard philosopher Michael Sandel agrees, with important exceptions, that in order for communities to exist, there must be an adequate political theory that sees the self as connected to traditions of justice that are rooted in a larger vision of what constitutes "the good." This sense of a just and beloved community is the basis for self-understanding and knowing one's ends and purposes within the larger society. In other words, to conceive of society as the product of a social contract in which parties agree to live by certain rules and principles but without a sense of connectedness to common visions of morality is to exist as an outsider in a story that is about you. He writes:

> To ask whether a particular society is a community is not simply to ask whether a large number of its members happen to have among their various desires the desire to associate with others or to promote communitarian aims—although this may be one feature of a community—but whether the society is itself of a certain kind, ordered in a certain way, such that the community describes its structure. For a society to be a community in this strong sense, community must be constitutive of the shared self-understandings of the participants and embodied in their institutional arrangements, not simply an attribute of certain of the participants' plans for life.[33]

The way of the storyteller seeks to identify these shared understandings that provide for connectedness in institutional life by excavating from communities of memory the stories and myths that underpin the enduring virtues and values that have historically shaped certain moral beliefs and actions. A critical issue in this perspective is that the error of Western liberalism lies not in rights and utilitarian ideology per se but in the failure of memory or what Jan Assmann calls "mnemohistory," which investigates the history of cultural memory. Assmann reasons that since we are what we remember, then "the truth of memory lies in the identity that it shapes." In other words, memory has a face, a name and a story; and the truth of memory "is subject to time so that it changes with every new identity and every new present." Therefore, identity and consciousness lie in the story, "not as it happened but as it lives on and unfolds in collective memory."

At the collective level, these stories are called myths. They are the stories by which a group, a society, or a culture lives. Myths are narrative constructions with their own inherent logic and history that "organize action, experience and representation" for groups and individuals.[34] Claude Levi-Strauss stated that "the kind of logic used in mythical thought is as rigorous as that of modern science, and the difference lies not in the quality of the intellectual process, but in the nature of things to which it is applied."[35]

Likewise, Paul Ricoeur suggested that separation of myth from history does not imply a rejection of myth's power to speak to our contemporary concerns. Rather, he sees the modern person as being in a unique situation, since she, unlike traditional peoples, can recognize myth as myth.[35] Myth functions at two levels: one, it answers questions regarding origins and death; and two, it explains and justifies existing social systems and gives an account for values, customs, and rites.[37] In the latter function of myth, especially for our argument, it plays a profound role in shaping ethos and ethnic identities (ethnogenesis). As bearers of collective memory, myths shape the character of individuals and the community of discourse and practice of which they are a part.

A number of folklorists and anthropologists have considered the folk-tale as a special form of the myth, that is, as a traditional and dramatic oral narrative. Some argue that, like myth, the basic characteristic of folk-tales consists in their concreteness and ability "to render intellectually and socially tolerable what would otherwise be experienced as incoherence."[38] Black folktales, spirituals, sermons, *witnessing* and *testifying* in respect to their concreteness and didactic nature, reflect this character of myth.[39]

The point to be made here is that through the remembering, retelling, and reliving of their stories and by the telling of tales and singing of songs, enslaved Africans fashioned an ethos, a community rooted in dialogue with the past (memory) whose future (vision), though untested and unrealized, afforded them a basis for hope in the present.[40] Alex Haley's epic, *Roots: The Saga of an American Family*, which remembers and retells the story of his great-great-great-great-grandfather, Kunta Kinte, is along this line of thinking. Upon his arrival in his ancestral village in The Gambia, West Africa, Haley was met by a senior *griot* (a traditional oral historian) who sat for nearly two hours and remembered his family's story identifying the capture of Kunta Kinte in 1767 by slave-raiders near the Gambia River. Haley writes:

> [the Gambian elders who accompanied him to the ceremony with the griot] reminded me that every living person ancestrally goes back to some time and some place where no writing existed; and then human memories and mouths and ears were the only ways those human beings could store and relay information. They said that we who live in the Western culture are so conditioned to the "crutch of print" that few among us comprehend what a trained memory is capable of.[41]

My fondest memories of my father were those cold, wintry evenings when my brother, my sister, and I would gather around his feet and listen to him tell stories. Daddy was not an educated man, at least by accepted standards, but he had an amazing gift for storytelling. He was a repository of folktales and jokes. I guess the peculiar grace of Daddy's storytelling was how he was able to draw our young imaginations into a world that transcended the ordinary and mundane. There were moments when we were literally translated into the drama of folk heroes like Stagolee, High John the Conqueror, and Brer Rabbit as they outsmarted their more powerful adversaries. There were other times when our hair would stand on our heads as he talked about the ghosts that inhabited the country churchyard where he grew up. He would make the Bible come alive. My father was a master storyteller. I know, for instance, that Goliath can be defeated because I saw him fall at my father's feet.

Little did I know then, in fact, only in recent years have I begun to understand how my world was shaped by those stories. The stories that I heard from Daddy were more than just tales about distant, fantastic characters who were unrelated to history. They were veritable tutors that helped to shape my view of the world and my place in it. History is a network of interlocking stories; it is a type of ongoing drama of the struggle between good and evil, power and powerlessness, tragedy and comedy, courage and cowardice, and love and hate. Human beings are essentially storytelling animals; that is, we become through our histories tellers of stories that aspire to truth. We are not the authors of the stories, but in a strange and interesting way we are the bearers of our stories. We are "storied creatures."

> I can only answer the question, 'What am I to do?" if I can answer the prior question "Of what story or stories do I find myself a part?" We enter human society, that is, with one or more imputed characters—roles into which we have been drafted—and we must learn what they are in order to be able to understand how others respond to us and how our responses to them are apt to be construed. It is through hearing stories—about wicked stepmothers, lost children, good but misguided kings, wolves that suckle twin boys, eldest sons who receive no inheritance but make their own way into the world and youngest sons who waste their inheritance on riotous living and go into exile to live with swine—that children learn or mislearn both what a child and what a parent is, what the cast of characters may be in the drama into which they have been born, and what the ways of the world are. Deprive children of stories and you leave them unscripted,

anxious stutterers in their actions as in their words. Hence, there is no way to give us an understanding of any society, including our own, except through the stock of stories that constitutes its initial dramatic resources.[42]

What is the black church tradition if not the ongoing story of men and women too proud to yield to and too wise to curse the darkness of the experiences of marginalization and oppression in pursuit of the highest and noblest American dream of democracy, justice, and equality?

Tradition and the Way of the Storyteller: The Hand of the Gardener

As defined earlier, ethical leaders are leaders whose characters have been shaped by the wisdom, habits, and practices of particular traditions, often more than one, yet they tend to be identified with a particular ethos and cultural narrative. Moreover, ethical leaders ask the question of values in reference to ultimate concern that is emphatically spiritual.[43] Tradition refers to the customs and meanings around which a community unites as well as the transmission of these customs and ways of thinking to the next generation. The return to tradition, of course, as a repository of meaning and direction for present and future leadership has its inherent dangers. Any causal observation of the national and global conflicts surrounding religion, race, and ethnicity should sound a warning to unreflective attachment to tradition. What I have in mind is more closely akin to what the great sociologist Edward Shils had in mind when he referred to tradition. He suggests, "Traditions are beliefs, standards and rules, of varying but never exhaustive explicitness, which have been received from the preceding generation through a process of continuous transmission from generation to generation. They recommend themselves by their appropriateness to the present situation confronted by their recipients and especially by their provenience to the past." He adds that the authority of tradition is not registered for its own sake or "because it's always been this way." "Tradition is not the dead hand of the past, rather *the hand of the gardener*, which nourishes and elicits tendencies of judgement which would otherwise not be strong enough to emerge on their own."[44]

In respect to the development of ethical leadership, tradition as "the hand of the gardener" provides a methodological approach that is pragmatic in respect to the retrieval of the substantive discourse of tradition and its reconfiguration and appropriation for the perceived needs of the present. Here Jeffrey Stout's recommendation of a process of *moral bricolage* informs our basic methodological approach. Key to this approach is the perspective that reflection on and retrieval of tradition constitute a return to a community of memory, defined in part by its past and its memory of its past.[45] Implicit in the accentuation of memory is that emerging and existing leaders must remember their stories and the ways in which these stories are formed and informed by countless other stories that mark their place in existence and define in large part the context of their understanding of values and leadership. To become aware of the power of tradition to restore the ethical center through a process of narration that is open to the present and the future frees leaders to explore new options and strategies while still being anchored to values that guide, inform, and project. Returning to tradition, however, is not a static but dynamic process of analysis, interpretation, and response.[46]

An important feature of the return to tradition as a source of memory is to identify habits and practices that inform one's ethical center. William James referred to this idea of habit and practice as "plasticity." "Plasticity, in the wide sense of the word, means that possession of a structure weak enough to yield to an influence, but strong enough not to yield all at once."[47] Plasticity is analogous to resilience, the inner strength and fortitude of character that allows the individual to withstand the external forces that threaten his or her existence without yielding that inner core which is sustained by life-affirming virtues, values, and virtuosities (spiritual excellencies).[48] Diane Dreher suggests that leaders who have this inner flexibility are like the bamboo: "Able to bend, blend with circumstances, adjust to change and overcome adversity, they can meet any challenge with courage and compassion."[49] Plasticity, however, does not function without a community of discourse and practice, which is involved in a time/space continuum of memory (remembering the story), vision (retelling and reframing the story), and mission (reliving the story).

The assumption here is that leaders are a part of living traditions that are also parts of ongoing narratives that are at once personal and communal. The identification of particular traditions and institutions that are bearers of memory and perpetuators of habits and practices provides leaders with opportunities to look at the role that certain values have played in the formation of leaders in communities; and how leaders within those traditions have dealt with complex issues and challenges over time.[50]

The significance of this approach of returning to memory and retrieving substantive discourse is that it also creates space for the reframing of beliefs and assumptions, as well as learning from these experiences so that there is a continuous creative cycle of remembering, reframing, and learning. In this process, values that have been the long stay of a said tradition find resonance in new contexts of meaning and are enabled because of their "plasticity" to inform and guide the leader in discerning, deliberating, and deciding on the appropriate course of action. A sterling example of this process is seen in the leadership styles of African American leaders, especially black church women. Marla F. Frederick's excellent ethnographic study of black women's spirituality in Halifax County, North Carolina, depicts the role of faith in the everyday struggles of black life. She writes, "Spirituality provides a space for creative agency, which gives voice to the multifaceted ways in which women interpret, inform and reshape their social conditions."[51] In a creative interplay between structure and agency, these women transform "not only institutions, but also themselves."[52] Such leadership has a certain improvisational artistry, which yields without breaking and holds its central values without losing its integrity as it challenges recalcitrant structures of injustice and evil. Martin Luther King Jr.'s dialectical appropriation of knowledge and faith is another example of what is at stake in this perspective of ethical leadership. This approach enabled King to develop a methodology for dealing with conflict and struggle in both his personal and public life. More revealing, however, is the fact that dialectical thinking has long been a hallmark of the black church tradition.[53] I will refer to this methodology as "balancing."

DRINKING FROM OUR OWN WELLS

In 1984 a Peruvian theologian, Gustavo Gutierrez, wrote a powerful treatise titled *We Drink from Our Own Wells: The Spiritual Journey of a People*.[54] Following the lead of the twelfth-century mystic Bernard of Clairvaux, who commented that the place where our own spiritual nourishment comes is the place where we think, pray, and work, Gutierrez was concerned that spirituality be located within lifeworlds, the concrete lived situations of a people.[55] In the case of the people of Peru, their wells were located in the struggle for liberation and their reinterpretation of traditions of Catholicism and native Indian cultures. In respect to the argument for ethical leadership, I am also positing that the eventful language of spirituality, ethics, and leadership is best appropriated from where leaders find their own spiritual moorings. It would be hard to imagine Albert Luthuli, Mahatma Gandhi, or Mother Teresa without considering how their morally anchored character, their transforming acts of civility, and their deep, throbbing sense of community were related to the traditions of which they were a part. These are leaders who drank from their own wells and appropriated their substantive discourse into strategies and actions for personal and political transformation.

Returning to our traditions as guides for the appropriation of values and practices that can give new meaning and hope to the American democratic experiment is not just a response to the moral dramas that play out in the public lives of contemporary leaders. Rather, the issue at stake is how we might learn from traditions that have provided hope and a sense of community in the past in order to refashion and inspire a vision for the future. This is not the strict province of any tradition and certainly not just religious traditions, but drinking from our own wells provides an opportunity to reconnect with a community of memory, which has the power to retool our moral vision and perspectives. Jacob Needleman's work *The American Soul: Rediscovering the Wisdom of the Founders* is an example of what is at stake in this kind of endeavor. He suggests:

> Great ideas, ideas that meaningfully reflect something of the world's ancient tradition of wisdom, have the power to bind people together and to bring unity under a goal and vision that are stronger and deeper than all personal, short-term gain. This is the mark of great ideas: they *unify the disparate parts of the human being*; they speak of a social order that is possible *on the basis of an ordering within the individual self* [emphasis added]. The idea of America once had something of this power of unification.[56]

Leaders who stand at the intersection, where they are caught between the often conflicting moral languages that form and shape moral vision and action, need to think about strategies that both heal and prevent the rupturing of their ethical centers. It is important, therefore, that leaders pay close attention to personal narratives that inform thoughts, feelings, and behaviors at the intersection. Leaders who are unable or ill prepared to reenter their own personal constructions of morality have difficulty appreciating and participating in the lifeworlds of others. But *morals* are part of larger stories, historically grounded narratives that are rooted in traditions that shape ethical vision and practice. The way of the storyteller is the principal method that we are recommending in the following discussion of character, civility, and community. Throughout the remaining chapters, utilizing the examples and insights of Thurman and King as exemplars of black church tradition, I will also look closely at ways in which spirituality and ethics inspire and inform ethical decisions at the intersection where worlds collide.

Chapter Three

CHARACTER AT THE INTERSECTION

THE QUEST FOR CHARACTER

The quest for character is a significant element in the ongoing debate on race, religion, and politics in American society. Generally, when we speak of character, we refer to it as something that a person possesses or as an attribute, as in, "Sally is a person of good moral character." Or we say that "Madge has excellent character," as though we were speaking of her good dental work. In both respects, character is something that we have, not an experience that we undergo or seek. In the following, I am interested in character as an adventure of sorts, a quest for unity of self and consciousness—more like a prize or a goal that is sought. As we shall see later, it is a narrative quest for unity in the context of a larger social-historical narrative.

This interpretation of character is important for at least two reasons. First, character as a possession or something that a person *has* is extraneous to self rather than being integral to who a person is and is becoming. Character as a quest for unity of consciousness addresses a profound sense of dynamism within the self: the need for identity and purpose. Second, character as an attribute describes what a person does to adjust or polish up what is already there, as if it were an object or thing and all that is needed is that we work on it. Metaphorically, if character is an object or an attribute, it means that it is fixed and can be adjusted, as most of our models of self-development propagate. These perspectives on character figure prominently in religious and political ideologies that collide at the intersection in American life.

Recent discussions on the place of character generally have to do with the decline of and call for renewal in American society, as if America were a huge machine that simply needs fixing or adjustment. Consequently, the emphasis on character education as a means of fixing the complex challenges the nation faces has been at the center of social reform promulgated by political and religious activism. The upsurge in religious activism in the quest for character education reflects the larger issue of ideology and values inherited from a mechanistic model that places emphasis on fixing and adjusting things.[1]

Robert Fogel, author of *The Fourth Great Awakening*, suggests that at the heart of the problem for the new century are three predominating factors: a new technological revolution, a cultural crisis precipitated by technologically induced change in the structure of the economy, and two powerful social and political movements confronting each other across an ideological and ethical chasm. The vast chasm of ideology and ethics is fueled by religiously inspired debates mainly on character and the moral failure of leadership.[2] These debates represent some dangerous signs in our culture; in our political, civic, and religious institutions; and in our own lives.

Public conversations about values and character are increasingly the products of high-tech marketing and political expediency rather than debates on principle and substance. With respect to the ways of doing ethics that we have discussed, these debates portray utilitarian and pragmatist perspectives that shape public perception and behavior about war, poverty, and a host of other issues that collide at the intersections of our private and public lives. Among these are the rise of a new kind of Christian nationalism that propagates "family values" that are narrowly defined and dangerously exclusive,[3] the scapegoating of foreign nationals, and the neglect of our need to seek answers to questions about global peace and national security that are not camouflaged in misinformation.[4]

Leaders of the new century must interrogate spurious assumptions about values, power, and policy that rest on the question of character defined as something that we can fix or adjust. Character, rather, as a narrative quest asks different questions about our present impasse by remembering the past without resorting to romanticization and trivialization of national memory. Romantic remembering that reaches back to a nostalgic past that never really existed will not address the shifting grounds of American social and political reality. John Wayne is dead, and Rocky Balboa is symptomatic of our deepest fears and creative imaginations. Leaders who remember must also retell and relive their own stories within the context of larger social-historical narratives. To understand one's character is to take seriously one's role in shaping the future of our nation and our world. But one cannot begin this quest for change and transformation without coming to grips with the questions of identity, meaning, and purpose, which are dynamically and integrally related to the larger story of America. I am not suggesting here that we do not work hard at analyzing this relationship among values, power, and policy or that we are not persistent in our discussions and dissemination of facts and statistics. Ours is a subtler and more sinister adversary—we have lost a sense of vision, imagination, and possibility inspired by memories of traditions that have been forgotten through nonspecificity and erasure.[5]

The quest for character, however, in both its political and religious affiliations, is linked to the larger quest for community in American society. The arguments from the right and the left reveal a formidable concern that is at the center of the debate on character: the question of race and the subtle configurations of power that have played out disastrously in political elections and religious debates. Even more glaring is the absence of the place and promise of African American moral traditions from most discussions on the development of character. African American moral life and practices have been rendered nonspecific and, in certain cases, erased with respect to their efficacy in preparing leaders of character for the new century. But one can understand neither the genius nor the tragedy of American moral life without taking into account the place and role of African American moral traditions. To trace the moral practices of all Americans, we must acknowledge the common tragedy of race in this culture. As Toni Morrison writes:

> Race has become metaphorical—a way of referring to and disguising forces, events, classes, and expressions of social decay and economic division far more threatening to the body politic than biological 'race' ever was. Expensively kept, economically unsound, a spurious and useless political asset in election campaigns, racism is as healthy today as it was during the Enlightenment. It seems that it has a utility far beyond economy, beyond the sequestering of classes from one another, and has assumed a metaphorical life so completely embedded in daily discourse that it is perhaps more necessary and more on display than ever before.[6]

Barack Obama's speech "A More Perfect Union" is a powerful example. Prompted by his pastor's sermons that received exaggerated media coverage, the speech is a revealing commentary on the subtle and damning configurations of race, religion, and politics in American life and culture. As the first serious African American contender for the presidency of the United States, his candidacy represented the difficulty that "we the people" have in speaking the truth about race and character. It is instructive to note that religion provided the context and the energy for placing the issue of race in the center of the debate on his character, defined as loyalty to American values. In his call for unity and a return to the bedrock American values of freedom and equality that made his candidacy possible, he was also reminding the nation of the terrible secret that everyone knows: in America we live and breathe race, but we are not allowed to speak about it openly and honestly without penalty.

Telling the truth about race in America may be the hardest lesson to learn about what constitutes ethical leadership and character in the national debate. Jim Wallis, in his book *God's Politics*, states that telling the truth about race means acknowledging that racism is "America's original sin."[7] The ideals of freedom and equality upon which America's quest for character rests must also include an intelligent and honest debate on race and the ways in which it continues to define the political and religious life of citizens. Langston Hughes expressed it well when he wrote:

> I am the American heartbreak—
> Rock on which Freedom
> Stumps its toe—
> The great mistake
> That Jamestown
> Made long ago.[8]

The "American heartbreak" continues and informs leadership practices at the highest levels of government. The conundrum of moral languages that we speak in American society has created a veritable Tower of Babel that evades the historical entrapment of race and disallows the possibility and dream of America. We no longer speak *to* one another, but speak *past* each other. This is the point that Barack Obama so eloquently made when he spoke to the problem of race in America and its lingering legacy of anger and distrust in both black and white communities. The resolution, he suggested, involves addressing issues that "reflect the complexities of race in this country that we've never really *worked through*—a part of our union that we have yet to perfect. And if we walk away now, if we simply retreat into our respective corners, we will never be able to come together and solve challenges like health care, or education, or the need to find good jobs for every American."

Working through our history will require listening to the other with empathy and respect with all the attendant challenges and risks. But this national conversation cannot start from scratch; we cannot hide our heads in the sand like the proverbial ostrich and pretend that the past does not inform the present, or as Obama aptly stated, "Understanding this reality requires a reminder of how we arrived at this point," and then quoting William Faulkner: "'The past isn't dead and buried. In fact, it isn't even past.'" This is a conversation that evokes dangerous memories with redemptive possibilities. It begins, however, by acknowledging the inequities and injustices that persist in American life within the context of a larger vision inspired by courage, justice, and compassion.

The error of many public leaders is that they have failed to acknowledge the presence of masses of disinherited and dispossessed groups within the power configurations of this culture. Consequently, those public leaders have allowed ideology to predominate their understandings of national community, and their resultant analyses and recommendations are bereft. *Working through race* is a risky proposition, given the spiritual and moral eclipse that has simultaneously occurred in the communities of the marginalized and poor in our nation, but it is a risk worth taking as we enter the twenty-first century tip-tilted toward a racial and ethnic cataclysm unparalleled in our history.

African American leadership is not immune from the charges of the failure of ethical leadership. Titles like *Losing the Race: Self-Sabotage in Black America*; *Transcending the Talented Tenth: Black Leaders and American Intellectuals*; *The Head Negro in Charge Syndrome: The Dead End of Black Politics*; *We Have No Leaders: African Americans in the Post Civil Rights Era*; *Capitalist Nigger: The Road to Success*; and, more recently, *Enough: The Phony Leaders, Dead-End Movements, and Culture of Failure That Are Undermining Black America—and What We Can Do about It*; and *Come on People: On the Path from Victims to Victors*[9] are reflective of the self-critique that abounds with respect to post–civil rights African American leadership. The state of many black church leaders is even more damning.[10] Clearly, any reasonable assessment of the political, intellectual, and religious leadership of African Americans indicates that they are no better off than others. To use the metaphor of the miner's canary, in a book by Lani Guinier, the state of black leadership is symptomatic of a larger and more fundamental issue in American society. In the past, miners would take a canary with them into the deep regions of the mine in order to test the toxicity of the environment. If the canary died, it was a signal that the mine was too dangerous for the miners to perform their work. In a similar respect, the plight of African American leadership is a sign and a warning of the toxic environment of the larger question of leadership in American society.[11]

Character and Ethical Leadership

Following the triadic model outlined in chapter 2, my work addresses the psychological, social, and spiritual dimensions of ethical leadership in respect to character, civility, and a sense of community. Within each dimension of character, civility, and community, there are attendant *virtues* (good habits), *values* (good habits that drive social practices in public space), and *virtuosities* (the excellencies of a virtuous life that drive behavior at personal and public levels). Ethical leaders come into being through the development of character, civility, and a sense of community. This triune of virtues, values, and virtuosities is the bedrock for genuine human development, productivity, and peaceful coexistence.

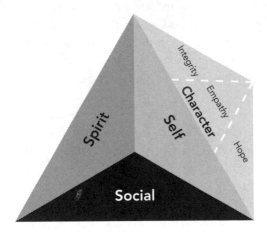

FIGURE 2. THE ETHICAL LEADERSHIP MODEL™

THE DEFINING VIRTUES OF CHARACTER

Character as Narrative Quest

The notion of character, as the personal dimension of leadership, refers to the narrative script that defines the individual, the stories that name the individual's experience, the "inner experience" or core philosophies espoused by the individual.[12] Leadership theorist Manfred F. R. Kets de Vries has suggested that there is an "inner theater" that represents those core themes that affect an individual's personality and leadership style. He writes, "For each of us, our unique mixture of motivational needs determines our character and creates the triangle of our mental life—a tightly interlocked triangle consisting of cognition, affect, and behavior. No one of these dimensions of the triangle can be seen as separate from the other."[13] The cultivation of the private life or one's "inner theater" is the basis for spirituality and ethical awareness. Leaders involved in acts of social transformation must begin by *remembering, retelling,* and *reliving* their own stories. Again and again, leaders must ask themselves what and whom they are seeking to change. This is the first step in the realization of calling and character.

Character, in this sense, refers to "the morally-anchored self in the context of sociohistorical narrative."[14] For our purposes, this means that leaders must examine their life experiences in relation to larger historical and cultural narratives. Reclaiming the ethical center requires that the unfinished business of one's life story (the pains, the hurts, the unresolved contradictions) be addressed. It also means reattachment to historically grounded virtues, values, and virtuosities that have protected the community through ritualistic healing, bringing about integrity and self-esteem, trust and empathy, courage and hope as personal and political practices. One should not (or, better, cannot) begin the work of creating a just and healthy civil society until one has explored the deepest regions of self-knowledge and the motivational content of agency that mark the core of individuality, personal morals, and practices. While there are formidable social, political, and economic issues that must be confronted, I am convinced that a critical dimension of the battle must be waged from within.

Howard Gardner's definition of a leader is helpful in this regard in that he emphasizes the tripartite construction of cognition, affection, and behavior. "A leader is an individual (or, rarely, a set of individuals) who significantly affects the thoughts, feelings, and/or behaviors of a significant number of individuals."[15] I would add to Gardner's definition by emphasizing the *body* as a critical source and ground for the ethical life. One can hardly imagine living ethically, or unethically for that matter, without a body. Moreover, the body constitutes a critical frame of reference for the aesthetic life, apart from which ethics as a narrative quest is impossible. Ethics as a discipline not only seeks answers to questions of right and wrong but seeks responses to beauty, balance, and symmetry that are equally significant for the moral development and deportment of leaders. In a discussion on what he calls *somaesthetics*, Richard Shusterman makes the lively argument that the body is the occasion for ethical life and practices. Therefore, it is incumbent upon leaders to care for and develop their sensory capacities in the pursuit of ethical living. "Every man," says Thoreau, "is the builder of a temple, called his body, to the god he worships, after a style purely his own, nor can he get off by hammering marble instead. We are all sculptors and painters, and our material is our own flesh and blood and bones. Any nobleness begins to refine a man's features, any meanness or sensuality to imbrute them."[16]

Woefully absent in leadership literature are discussions on the place and the role of the body in framing moral and ethical dilemmas faced by leaders in multifarious circumstances that bring shame and resentment. This is because we have borrowed our theories primarily from the rationalist perspective that places high premium on reason, which is used synonymously as mind. Human beings, some leaders included, are more than mind. Leaders are embodied beings and spirits as well. Toward the end of his last year at Rochester Theological Seminary, Thurman met with George Cross, his major professor, to discuss his future plans. At this meeting, Cross unveiled his own plans for Thurman's future, which later proved a source of encouragement and bewilderment for Thurman. Cross said to his brilliant young student:

> You are a very sensitive Negro man, and doubtless feel under great obligation to put all the weight of your mind and spirit at the disposal of the struggle of your people for full citizenship. But let me remind you that all social questions are transitory in nature and it would be a terrible waste for you to limit your creative energy to the solution of the race problem, however insistent its nature. Give yourself to the timeless issues of the human spirit. . . . Perhaps I have no right to say this to you because as a white man, I can never know what it is to be in your situation.[17]

Thurman says that he "pondered the meaning of his words, and wondered what kind of response I could make to this man who did not know that a man and his black skin must face the 'timeless issues of the human spirit' together."[18] Thurman's recommendation to King, which is noted earlier, "to reassess himself in relation to the cause, to *rest his body* and mind with healing detachment, and to take a long look that only solitary brooding can provide" is along these lines.[19]

The construction of human agency is tripartite or three-dimensional, comprising body, mind, and spirit. Mind as *noetic* primarily refers to the rational dimension of self, but the cultivation of mind as rational center is not a sufficient condition for the formation of leaders. The bodily senses (*somatic*) as well as the spiritual (*pneumatic*) are essential to the *thinking-feeling continuum* and behaviors of leaders. These three dimensions are dynamically interrelated and cannot be separated in practice, but are simply portrayed above in Figure 2 for the sake of analytical discussion. We shall see later how they interact in the ethical decision-making of leaders.

Attendant to character, there are three *virtues* that ethical leaders must allow to become part and parcel of their focus and personal deportment. They are, respectively, *integrity*, *empathy*, and *hope*. I am defining *virtue* in the sense of Aristotle as good habits. More precisely, virtue refers to William James's idea of character as existing in an "organized set of habits of reaction"[20] For James, the building of character is essentially a matter of habit formation, which requires practice. James cites four maxims for the formation of habits. First is that "in the acquisition of a new habit, or the leaving off of an old one, we must take care to launch ourselves with as strong and decided an initiative as possible." Second, "Never suffer an exception to occur till the new habit is securely rooted in your life." Third, "Seize the very first possible opportunity to act on every resolution you make, and on every emotional prompting you may experience in the direction of the habits you aspire to gain." And fourth, "Keep the faculty of effort alive in you by a little gratuitous exercise every day" (italics removed).[21]

Integrity

Integrity is essentially a product of *habit*. For Thurman, integrity refers to a sense of wholeness, a sense of community within self—in sum, what he calls *a healthy sense of self*. The threefold process (identity, purpose, and method) begins with the development of a healthy sense of self, which is the basis upon which one comes to understand one's own unique potential and self-worth. Without a sense of self, one drifts aimlessly through life without a true understanding of one's place in existence. This is an especially significant issue for leaders of marginalized groups who have been misnamed by a culture in often subtle and surreptitious ways.[22] For Thurman, a healthy sense of self is garnered out of a dynamic tension between the individual's *self-fact* and *self-image*. A leader's self-fact is his or her inherent worth and dignity; it is the central fact that he or she is part of the very movement of life itself and therefore deserves *recognition* and *respect*. A person's self-image is formed by relationships with significant others and society, which to a large extent determines one's destiny. However, the individual's case must ultimately rest with his or her self-fact of intrinsic worth. He writes, "The responsibility for living with meaning and dignity can never be taken away from the individual."[23] This is a significant point for the leader's response to dehumanizing actions and other forces that work against human potential and community.

Integrity informs the leader's actions and practices. Diane Dreher has suggested that the Chinese symbol for character, *Te*, though variously interpreted as "virtue," "goodness," "power," and "morality," literally means "integrity or character: living straight from the heart."[24] Integrity as the primary virtue in our model draws upon this sense of character. It is the practice of speaking and living *straight from the heart* without neglecting the rational processes of the mind. Integrity incorporates both head and heart. Stephen Carter's definition of integrity places emphasis on the wedding of cognitive and affective dimensions of integrity as a practice. He suggests that there are three steps to integrity: (1) *discerning* what is right and wrong; (2) *acting* on what you have discerned, even at personal cost; and (3) *saying openly* that you are acting on your understanding of right and wrong.[25] These three steps are important because they underlie what is at stake for leaders in public space. We are aware of leaders who believe strongly in honesty and truth-telling, yet they fail miserably at carrying out what they believe to be true. Nonetheless, the failure to exercise integrity within organizations and systems can be monumentally destructive and costly. What if someone at Enron had followed the simple steps outlined by Carter regarding the ballooning value of stocks and had critically pursued this three-step process of discerning, acting, and saying openly what came straight from the heart? Or if someone within the FBI had really paid attention to the memo written by the whistle-blower agent in Minneapolis? Would September 11 have been a day of terror and tragedy or a grand moment in the annals of national security? Integrity is not simply a matter of personal choice, but has huge implications for how we live together and function in community.

I heard Warren Buffett speak about integrity as it relates to shared vision and values.[26] When asked whom he would like on his team, Buffett responded that the values that he looks for are *intelligence, energy*, and *integrity*. The most important of these three, he added, is integrity. He reasoned that individuals with whom he works might possess great skill and intelligence, energy, and stamina, but if they do not share his value of integrity, it will prove ruinous for the business. Integrity, for Buffett, refers to honesty. I would like to add that integrity begins first and foremost with identity. The idea of integrity has its roots in "integer," the mathematical equivalent of a prime number. "Wholeness" is the underlying value that integrity seeks to portray. Integrity has much to do with personal identity, purpose, and the means by which one responds to his or her environment and to others. If a leader cannot carry a sense of wholeness, a healthy sense of self into all of her practices, then she is doomed to external temptations of rewards and penalties.

Integrity has also to do with freedom and self-regulation. What I stand for in any given situation is determined by the measure of my inherent dignity and self-worth. Integrity is demonstrated through the choices that I make regarding what is of value to me. I can no more make a wise, ethical decision without a sense of wholeness and self-worth than I can fly a kite without a string attached. Integrity is the thread in my hand that guides the kite along the currents of air that toss and turn it in various directions. But if the string is held firmly, the kite may dance in the air and ride the currents, yet it is always grounded and guided by the hand that controls its flight. Many of the recent revelations of unwise, unethical leadership practices are examples of misguided, unclear, and ungrounded values that find their basis in the lack of integrity. Decisions that lack integrity are decisions that are inevitably driven by winds of change in the performance of the market, driven by changes in the makeup of the organization and political changes and pressures that determine direction and course of action. A strong core of integrity is essential for ethical decision-making.

At a deeper level, however, the leader must examine the motivational content of his or her behaviors as they relate to integrity. While integrity has to do with wholeness, harmony, and integration at the personal level, it is also the product of critical self-examination. Here, the personal dimensions of leadership come to the fore as they relate to issues of transparency, trustworthiness, and fair play. Our emphasis on this dimension of character, which begins with integrity as the foundational virtue—*community within the self*—seeks to draw attention to the leader's need to make a distinction between cognitive and affective dimensions of self, although they are intricately related. Because of the ways in which we have been formed by habit, training, and tradition, it is often easy to forget that I am also a "feeling" as well as a "thinking" being. Integrity, as I am using the term, does not make an either/or distinction between the two but rather seeks *the relation* between both in a *feeling-thinking continuum,* so that at all times the leader seeks to be in balance with these dimensions that inform behavior. As it relates to integrity, the feeling-thinking continuum must grant that the affective dimension drives unconscious behaviors and practices that can be positive or negative, genuine or disingenuous. Careful attention to this deep motivational dimension of the self is an important element of the leader's practice. One does not behave genuinely or disingenuously as a result of some predetermined disposition; rather, we learn early the practice of truth-telling or of deceit. Habits of integrity form over time and crystallize into reflective behaviors. How might leaders begin to recognize these motivational forces that shape responses to ethical situations?

First, it is important to understand that leaders must *consciously* seek a sense of wholeness in thoughts, feelings, and behaviors. Self-awareness begins with the desire to know oneself; it involves a quest for self-discovery. For instance, when one asks the question of identity, Who am I? she must also ask, Who is asking the question? Is it I? And if it is "I," then who is the "I" who asks the question? Watch the answers, because they tend to come from many regions within the self, and it is no accident that they are multiple because we have so many "selves" that speak for us. Hence, one of the initial understandings that comes from self-examination is that there are always multiple voices that answer questions regarding identity—and also regarding ethical challenges with which we are confronted in leadership roles. Leaders who are unaccustomed to discerning which voices are authentic and who lack the courage to act make unhealthy decisions that hurt themselves and others.

What of these multiple voices that respond to our deep moral convictions and often compete at the private intersections of our inner lives? Should we seek to mute some voices that speak to the situation to which we are responding? I think not. In fact, I believe that under no circumstances should we seek to silence voices that belong to our inner lives. Instead, we should seek a way or method to bring them to some unanimous forum where they can all cast their votes. When we mute internal voices with which we disagree, we do damage to the self by forcing our deepest feelings and motivations into retreat, but they do not go away. Rather, they wait for a more propitious moment when life's challenges awaken them. The secret to an authentic life that informs leadership practices and skill development at this level is discipline—a discipline of calling to attention the plurality of our inner lives and the seemingly innate response that seeks unity of the self in all that we say or do.[27] Thurman writes:

There must be a core of wholeness at the core of man
That must abound in all he does;
That marks with reverence his ev'ry step;
That has its sway when all else fails;
That wearies out the evil things;
That warms the depths of frozen fears,
Making friend of foe,
Making love of hate,
And lasts beyond the living and the dead,
Beyond the goals of peace, the ends of war!
This man seeks through all his years:
To be complete and of one piece, within, without.[28]

The cognitive task of the leader is to engage the self critically—by probing, examining, and asking the hard questions of identity, purposes, dreams, and aspirations—but only with the aid of the affective can there be an authentic response.

Second, the leader who seeks integrity is really seeking balance and harmony between two poles, the affective and the cognitive. As it pertains to the spiritual life, she is seeking balance between two extremes that are a part of every quest for wholeness, integration, and harmony: *innocence* and *brokenness*. Thurman's treatment of innocence and goodness is helpful here. Thurman begins his examination of the ideal of community in collective memory by analyzing creation myths. His purpose is to explore what the memory of the human race has to say about the nature of community and its ageless concern for "lost harmony." His central question is, "What is there that seems to be implicit or inherent in racial (human) memory that is on the side of community?" He examines the creation myths of the Judeo-Christian tradition and the Hopi Indians. Thurman maintains that a consistent theme in both accounts is "creation with the harmony of innocence; the loss of innocence with the disintegration of harmony."[29] This theme has significant implications for Thurman's understanding of innocence and goodness, and of community as an ideal or goal that must be achieved.[30] In each account, the original experience of community by humans is both *potential* and *actualized potential* within the framework of innocence. In the state of innocence, that which works against community is dormant or unactualized, but once actualized by the agency of free will, disharmony results and innocence is lost.[31] The loss of innocence or *brokenness* marks the loss of community within persons, in interpersonal relationships, in divine-human relationships, and in nature. Thurman argues that once innocence is lost, it can never be restored. After the fall from innocence, the project of "goodness" or "community" becomes the goal toward which human endeavor must be directed. Unlike innocence, "community" or "goodness" must be achieved through free, responsible actions. Goodness as *achieved community* is predicated on the radical freedom of the individual to make a conscious, deliberate choice to strive for wholeness, harmony, and integration within the self and in relations with others and the world.

The idea of the loss of innocence or *brokenness* is a key concept in Thurman's view of the self and his ethical theory. Innocence is given without knowledge; goodness, however, is achieved through knowledge and responsibility. He writes:

> When the quality of goodness has been reestablished, a great change has taken place. Eyes are opened, knowledge is defined, and what results is the triumph of the quality of innocence over the quality of discord; a new synthesis is achieved that has in it the element of triumph. That is, a child is innocent, but a man who has learned how to winnow beauty out of ugliness, purity out of stain, tranquility out of tempest, joy out of sorrow, life out of death—only such a man may be said to be good. But he is no longer innocent.[32]

Consequently, there is at work in the quest for integrity as wholeness (goodness, achieved community) the dialectical tension between innocence and brokenness. Hence, the initial step in the quest for integrity is the acknowledgment by the leader of his or her brokenness. As this perspective applies to leadership practices, I am referring to the presumption of the leader that she is really faultless, never was implicated in any scandal or impropriety that would bring shame or reflect badly on the organization or group. If this were true—and maybe in some remote village in the Himalayas it is—still it would not abstain the leader from fault. It would only suggest that she has never been tried and tested. Leaders make mistakes and sometimes willingly engage in practices that they know to be out of line. Leaders who practice integrity do not hide their faults and failures—they offer no presumption of innocence. They know, rather, that all are susceptible to improper behavior and that all can be tempted. These are the leaders who are able to empathize with the other because they have shared his or her challenges. Therefore, they consciously seek points of connection through creative and imaginative techniques that invite the other to be authentic.

After twenty years of reading and grading exams, I can readily recognize plagiarism. Some years ago, I was teaching a class at a prestigious university in New England. It was an undergraduate class, but I made special arrangements for several graduate students who wanted to register for the class as well. I noticed early that the undergraduate students, like young racehorses, dashed out of the stalls and left two of the graduate students far behind. I sought ways to recognize and compensate for the obvious disparities in background and education for these students but without great success. I could really feel their struggle, because I had shared their lot on a number of occasions and had found creative strategies to saddle up and at least run in the pack with the others. I was not surprised, therefore, that when I read their final papers, there was evidence of plagiarism. I called them in, one by one, and reviewed with them the error of their ways—and I shared that though I had never actually plagiarized, I had done some other pretty underhanded things, like borrowing books that I never returned to the lenders or neglecting to pay my bills in a prompt manner. But plagiarism, I counseled, is a very naughty habit to get into because it steals from you the genius and potential that are yours if you dare to do the hard but rewarding work of studying. I did not nail these students, as I could have, but I demanded that they redo their entire papers and submit a revised annotated bibliography. They were of course repentant, but most important they understood me (better, they *felt* me). Years later, I met one of the students, who was leading a major conference at a college where I was invited to speak. We never once mentioned that affair, but we both knew and valued the experience. Did my attempt to empathize with him make a difference? I know it saved him from the shame and humiliation of being caught and suspended or even expelled. I hope that, at least, he learned to practice the virtues of integrity and empathy in his leadership role in higher education.

Empathy

Related to integrity is *empathy*, the psychosocial dimension of character. Empathy has to do with sympathetic imagination or, as some have come to call it, *emotional intelligence* and *resonance*. The authors of *Primal Leadership* list four dimensions of emotional intelligence that are exhibited by leaders. They locate empathy under the category of social competence, the capabilities that determine how leaders manage relationships. Empathy, for them, is *sensing the other's emotions, understanding their perspective, and taking an active interest in their concerns*.[33] For our purposes, empathy is the capacity of the ethical leader to put him- or herself in the other's place. It is correlated with respect of the other and thrives best where there are shared visions and goals. Empathy is really about feelings, intelligent feelings that have been cultivated through practice. At the personal level of character, it occupies the social dimension and is the first step toward respect, which will be discussed under civility.

Empathy, first and foremost, is a good habit. Leaders must intentionally practice empathy for others as a way of creating a contagious atmosphere or culture (*a moral ethos*) within organizational life. This can only be done through the use of disciplined imagination. Imagination is a constituent part of the individual's nature as a spiritual being. Imagination can be used as a veritable messenger of spirit, when the individual through self-transcendence puts himself in another's place. Imagination, in this sense, is the pathway to empathy. Through the use of imagination, the individual is enabled to transcend himself and reach the other at the core of his being, at the seat of "common consciousness." In doing so, the other is addressed at a place beyond all blame and fault. This, according to Thurman, is the experience of compassion. When an individual is addressed at the centermost place of personality, she experiences a sense of wholeness and harmony. This is the "common ground" of our relations with others. For Thurman, imagination is "the peculiar quality of mind that enables a man [*sic*] to stand in his own place, defined by the uniqueness of his life's story, and project himself into another person's life or situation. He makes soundings there, looking out upon life through the other's eyes, even as he remains himself. It is to inform one's self of the view from 'the other side.'"[34]

Empathy, like integrity, is a vital dimension of the leader's private life—and is related, as well, to unconscious drives and motivations of which we are not often aware. For instance, have you ever met someone with whom you simply connected? We often say it was déjà vu or that the individual reminded us of someone else. The deep features of recognition tend to exist at the level of memory or recollection of past experiences of color, sound, voice, an experience or situation that still resides in the deep self, which is provoked by their presence. Who knows? But what is important to note is that empathy tends to operate in this way—but *consciously*. Learning to use the imagination is not at all a flight of fantasy or a figment of anything, except that we do have radar capacity—the ability to sense the other, his needs, desires, and thoughts—if we dare cultivate it through habit and practice.

How does this work? Long ago, when we did not have the tools and technologies that make life so easy, we used to pay close attention to the face and the body of the other. We had natural instincts for listening and sensing movements, signs, gesticulations, and feelings of others, much like your pets who really know you and your mood hands down! Empathy begins with openness to the other—it assumes vulnerability and risk in the *face* of the other because as you see her face, she can also see yours. But this facing of the other can also be a grand opportunity for the realization of courage, a sense of justice and compassion, because at a deeper spiritual level, we are really recognizing ourselves in the other.

The human organism, according to Thurman, reveals an evolutionary process characterized by *directiveness* and purpose. He suggests that the emergence of mind in the human organism may be a product of the species' response to the history of the organism itself. The human mind does directly and deliberately what nature has done through ages of trial and error. He suggests that the "mind *as* mind" evolved from the body as part of the unfolding process of this potential resident in life; and that the mind as such is the basis for the evolution of *spirit*. The imagination as *mind-evolved-spirit* continued the same inherent quest for community that is resident in nature and the body.[35] When an individual consciously seeks community, therefore, he will discover that "what he is seeking deliberately is but the logic of meaning that has gone into his creation."[36] Philosopher Emmanuel Levinas suggests that "the face of man is the medium through which the invisible in him becomes visible and enters into commerce with us."[37]

Incorporation and Indifference

Empathy has two extreme sides of which leaders must be aware and which they must seek to balance. Leaders who are not balanced in respect to empathy tend to *incorporate* or to be *indifferent* to others' stories. Incorporation is derived from the Latin *incorporare*, meaning "to form into a body." In Freudian terminology, the concept refers to identification, as in a primitive wish to unite with or cannibalistically destroy an object. Leaders who *incorporate* will listen to the other as a way of consuming the other's story; and because of their unresolved sense of self and uninhibited need for potency, they tend to "disregard their subordinate's legitimate needs and take advantage of their loyalty. . . . This kind of leader can be exploitative, callous, and over competitive and frequently resorts to excessive use of deprecation."[38] This is a statement about power that clearly arises from a deep need for control and narcissistic impulses.

A severe expression of the impulse in leaders to incorporate is what Erich Fromm called *necrophilia* or the *love of death*. According to Fromm, necrophiles "are fascinated by all that is not alive, all that is dead; corpses, decay, feces, dirt . . . and they come to life precisely when they can talk about death." They tend to dwell in the past, not in the future, and are enamored by force and violence, which supplant sexuality and spiritual relations with visions of power and conquest. For Fromm, leaders like Hitler and Stalin were examples of this orientation. Contemporary leaders who fit this description I will leave the reader to identify, but the essential problem of the necrophilic leader is his or her inability to embrace life as an organic, creative, dynamic process; rather, he or she is "driven by the desire to transform the organic into the inorganic and to approach life mechanically, as if all persons were things." Leaders who have necrophilic orientations tend to see ethics only as rules-based and adhere relentlessly to codes of justice that are absolute and binding, which in turn make them feel secure and powerful. They are like the woman who asked King Solomon to cut the disputed child in half. They "would rather have a properly divided child than lose a living one."[39]

Indifference is another extreme that makes empathizing with the other impossible. Leaders, especially "organizational men," tend to lack the ability to listen to the other. Manfred de Vries calls these *alexithymic leaders*.[40] These are leaders who are emotionally illiterate and cannot feel or sense the other's needs or desires. They have "no words for emotions" and appear as "dead souls." They are characterized by an inability to recognize intrapsychic conflicts and are involved in "doing" rather than "being" and "experiencing." Some are very adept at appearing to listen and connect, but in fact they are simply working from external stimuli in the environment that they have learned to manipulate from habit. Like the *necrophilic* leaders, *alexithymic* leaders find comfortable nesting places in large bureaucratic systems where they are allowed to function by conforming to rules and procedures that camouflage their deep emotional emptiness. These are leaders whose basic ethical orientation tends to be rules-based and therefore unsympathetic to contingencies that arise in the context of groups and interpersonal networks.

Resonant Leaders and the Sound of the Genuine

Leaders who incorporate and are indifferent to the stories of others create dissonance in organizations and teams because of their own unresolved emotional needs and stories. The kinds of leaders who are able to empathize with others at the intersections where worlds collide are what the authors of *Primal Leadership* refer to as "resonant leaders." These are leaders who are able to listen to others empathetically and to create synchrony in groups and teams. Resonant leaders are able to read a group's feelings and to move them toward their goals by speaking and acting authentically from their own values and *resonating* with the emotions of others. Most important, resonant leaders leave people feeling understood and cared for.[41]

The mark of the resonant leader is his or her authenticity or genuineness. Authors Rob Goffee and Gareth Jones outline competencies of authentic leaders as the capacity to display a consistency between words and deeds, coherence in role performances, and comfort with oneself.[42] These three competencies are interrelated. The consistency of word and deed emanates from a sense of self that is not betrayed by the various roles or performances that are essential to the leader's responsibility in communicating and interacting with different audiences. Nor does the leader, in shifting between audiences and tasks, place himself or herself in a disingenuous position that contradicts core values and beliefs, because the true core is the authentic character that is molded by integrity or what Howard Thurman calls "the sound of the genuine."

Thurman believed that "there is something within every person that waits and listens for the sound of the genuine within herself. . . . There is something in everybody that waits and listens for the sound of the genuine in other people."[43] *The sound of the genuine* in Thurman's language addresses the need to begin with a fresh approach to the place of spirituality in leadership discourse and practice. The sound of the genuine is the spiritual and moral source of the interrelated concepts of character, civility, and community and is the basis for the creative encounter with one's own self and with the other.[44]

Empathy begins not with *speaking* but with *listening*; and it is in this creative encounter of waiting and listening for the other that a new and fresh moral purpose is inspired so that one is enabled to empathize with the other. This dynamic relational matrix, or "inter-isness,"[45] for Thurman, is in direct contradistinction to systems that place leaders as the primary authority and speaker. Rather, the emphasis is on the listener, the one who hears the other's story with empathy and respect. The traditional construct of leader as authority and speaker militates against wholeness—integrity in the self and the other.[46] But the emphasis on waiting and listening to the other dramatically shifts roles and functions and creates the synchronous relations that Goleman and others refer to as "primal leadership."[47]

Moreover, *the sound of the genuine* suggests that it is a moral obligation to hear the other's story. In other words, the freedom and responsibility to hear the other involve more than auditory stimulation. It must be activated by the moral imagination, that fluid area of consent that is at once one's spiritual and moral duty and one's duty to self. This perspective has positive implications that reach far beyond teams and organizations to society and the larger questions of civil society and culture. The substantive benefit to society is the articulation and creation of a new and fresh form of civil discourse that reaches out to the neighbor with empathy and respect. In theological terms, it is to hear and see the voice and presence of God in the other person; the other being more than the individual representation of conscious being, but rather the representation of the complex and jagged contours of culture itself mirrored through the eyes and resounding in the voice of the other.

Finally, for Thurman, *to wait and listen for the sound of the genuine in the self and in the other* is to enter into another sphere of discourse that is primordially spiritual and imaginative.[48] Here, the reference is not to the spirituality of religion per se, but to the spirituality of the *event*. Indeed, spirituality is eventful, a *word-event* incarnated in a language that is familiar in the common place and common sense of things, yet *strange* in its ability to move the hearer beyond fixated moral discourse. The sound of the genuine is first-order language. Unlike story discourse embedded in second-order language, which is thick and descriptive, first-order language is imaginative and eventful.[49] In first-order language, the emancipatory and enlightening character of narrative is disclosed, unrestricted by the abstraction of signification in the story discourse of public narratives; it translates the hearer into the sphere of *possibility*, connecting the past with the future.

Gerhard Ebeling comments on the liberating power of word at this level: "It is the power of word to make present what is not at hand. The fact that word brings us what is past and future . . . is only an illustration of the way in which man [*sic*] is dependent upon confrontation by a word that comes his way, and liberates him, both from the frightening restrictions that bind him to what is present and from the anxiety of his own heart, and that thus frees him for the things which are outside his power to command but are offered him to believe. *[Human beings] need language more for hearing than speaking, for believing than acting.*"[50]

Leaders who *incorporate* and are *indifferent* to the emotional needs and desires of others cannot create communities of empathy and respect; rather, they breed suspicion, contempt, and mistrust. Empathy that proceeds from the sound of the genuine helps to create and maintain environments of trust and mutual respect. Empathy is at home with integrity much in the same way that parents make up a household. The children of their union are strong, healthy, and wise. It is absolutely impossible to grow a healthy organization or business without integrity and empathy. Where leadership lacks integrity and empathy within the organizational culture, the products, the outcomes, and the offspring are born impaired and susceptible to destructive and degenerative failures throughout the system. Think about it. How many stories have you heard of individuals who have worked for systemically toxic organizations where goodwill, good intentions, and good thoughts were not valued but wasted in the squabbles about power and who goes first? Businesses, unlike any other social organizations, are highly susceptible to these faults and failures because they are driven always to perform in highly competitive, often dysfunctional systems that demand that we mask incompetencies and inadequacies. It is for this reason, among others, that communities of trust and mutual respect are important. Such communities thrive on *integrity*, *empathy*, and *hope*. These are the communities and organizations that learn to hold hands at the intersection where worlds collide and imagine new and different ways of fulfilling shared visions.

Hope

Hope is a strange word for thinking about organizational life and culture, but, given the often chaotic twists of the market and the overwhelming need to adjust to the patterns that are at work in society as a whole, I believe that hope will emerge as the primary motivation for keeping our visions and work in perspective. But far more is at stake in learning the virtue of hope for our society and the larger global community. I am defining hope as genuine anticipation of the future. Genuine anticipation of the future is rooted in what James Gustafson describes as confidence in the future that is carried by human freedom: "Hope is carried by the confidence that life is more reliable than unreliable, that the future is open, that new possibilities of life exist, that the present patterns of life are not fated by the blind god Necessity, but are susceptible to change, to a recombination of aspects and elements of the world. Hope is carried by freedom."[51]

There are two extremes to the virtue of hope: *despair* and *a sense of fatedness*; and they act as spiritual vortices that drain the moral and ethical resources leaders need for overcoming the challenges that meet us at the intersection where worlds collide.

Despair and Hope

I attended a conference in honor of Warren Bennis, the great leadership theorist and mentor to thousands of us who are deeply indebted to his legacy. During one of the panels, the discussion turned toward the contemporary perception of U.S. citizens outside of the country and the need for hopeful leadership that could inspire and guide our nation through the challenges and issues that are taking a toll on the souls of leaders. One well-known corporate CEO spoke of his growing despair that American leaders were seen in less than positive ways by most of the people he met around the globe. Others on the panel and in the audience echoed his sentiments. I responded by suggesting that the problem of hope lies not just in how we see America, but in how we dare to envision leadership of the future. I referred to a question from a student at a lecture I delivered at Penn State some years ago on the legacy of Martin Luther King Jr. The student asked whether I believed that we would ever see another leader like Martin Luther King Jr. I responded that the jury is out on whether we will see another King or even if such a leader at this point in our history is desirable and appropriate, but I was sure that if *she* does appear, she probably will not be "made in America." My point was that leaders like King do not emerge from historical vacuums but are the products of traditions that shape character and attendant virtues like hope. Traditions of struggle for justice and peace form certain kinds of people who are deeply intertwined with the narratives of hope and possibility. I further suggested that if such leaders who inspired hope were to emerge, they probably would not come from the builders of the American Tower of Babel whose children have eaten sour grapes and whose teeth are set on edge, but from the stones that the builders rejected. Leaders in traditions where hope is not a matter of sentimental longing for a better world or at worst the personal hope for a better position within an organization or political party are in scarce supply in America. At the end of my response, I invited the audience to sing with me an old song that I first heard in the church. Its point is simple, but its passion is riveting:

> There is hope for this world
> There is hope for this world
> It's all going to be all right
> There is hope for this world!

Hope as "the genuine anticipation of the future" is not the same as the superficial optimism that is so in vogue in romantic understandings of the world and of human nature. In fact, it has become increasingly difficult to speak about hope in the midst of all the violence, abandonment, fears, and pains that beset our society. The error that plagues the modernist project is the elusive ideal of progress that issues forth in superficial optimism. The late Christopher Lasch, in *The True and Only Heaven*, suggested that this "optimism" feeds on a nostalgia in which memory of collective innocence supersedes and erases the boundaries of history. Hope, on the other hand, according to Lasch, is the product of garnered faith in the potential goodness of life. This hope is not sentimental; it does not feed on fictitious innocence but acknowledges the limitations of history. Lasch writes:

> Hope implies a deep-seated trust in life that appears absurd to those who lack it. It rests on confidence not so much in the future as in the past. It derives from early memories—no doubt distorted, overlaid with later memories, and thus not wholly reliable as a guide to any factual reconstruction of past events—in which the experience of order and contentment was so intense that subsequent disillusionments cannot dislodge it. Such experience leaves as a residue the unshakable conviction, not that the past was better than the present, but that trust is never completely misplaced, even though it is never completely justified either and therefore destined inevitably to disappointments.[52]

Hope, like love and faith, is one of those rather amorphous virtues that is seldom spoken of, with the rare exception of leaders like Barack Obama, but in reality is the driving force of all human relations. Without hope, individuals and groups plunge into despair. When despair informs practice, desperate people do desperate things! Businesses, organizations, and nations that are bereft of hope are doomed to fail because people need to know that the future is not predetermined; that they can make a difference that will affect outcomes. Hope has a tenacity of vision. It refuses to yield when confronted with despair because it dares to see beyond the present and to work toward the envisioned future with all its challenges and ambiguities. The greatest of leaders are those who inspire hope for change and transformation and then guide others in the implementation of the vision.

Fatedness and Hope

Sydney Hook's classic *The Hero in History* distinguishes between *the event-ful leader* and *the event-making leader*. The former is caught in the flow of historical circumstances and does not make a unique contribution to the group or the world; but the event-making leader inspires hope and brings about change and transformation.[53] Bernard Bass makes reference to this distinction in respect to Abraham Lincoln and his predecessor, James Buchanan. Bass writes, "Buchanan was content to stand by and allow the Union to disintegrate slowly; but Lincoln was determined to hold the Union together and to reverse what seemed at the time to be the inexorable course of history."[54] What made Lincoln an event-making leader was not his superior intelligence, uncanny timing, and political skill but his moral vision of hope, which he maintained until his death.

Hook identifies the issue at stake when eventful leaders are paralyzed by a sense of *fatedness* as the belief that the inexorable logic of history cannot be changed and that human agency is at the mercy of circumstance. A sense of fatedness drives and perpetuates the cycle of despair and apathy that destroys the inner will and creative possibilities of leaders at the intersection. A classic example of this type of leader is found in every extreme rationalist and utilitarian position that believes that the universe is fixed, that certain customs, laws, and values are mandated by some grand metaphysical design that relegates some to lives of misery and poverty and others to lives of prosperity and affluence. Systemworlds that regulate and prescribe these values are at odds with human freedom and responsibility. Event-making leaders who dare to hope and inspire others at the intersection of systemworlds and lifeworlds reject fatedness as morally unsound and rationally unjustifiable.

Transformed Nonconformists and the Call to Hope

More than any other American leader in the twentieth century, Martin Luther King Jr. fits the description of the event-making leader. King dared to hope by challenging the nation to see the inherent contradictions in segregated statues that were based upon values and practices that were rooted in fatedness. When King spoke of a "revolution of values and priorities" and of overcoming the triplets of oppression (poverty, racism, and war), he spoke within the framework of American democratic society with the willingness to suffer the penalties imposed by law for his civil disobedience.[55] King was acutely aware of the dangers that meet transformed nonconformists at the intersection where worlds collide.

King's critique of segregated practices that relegated black citizens to lives of inferiority and hopelessness rested upon a profound sense of freedom and responsibility that were centered in his spiritual moorings and commitment. In reflection on the "New Negro" involved in the Montgomery campaign, King wrote:

> Once plagued with a tragic sense of inferiority resulting from the crippling effects of slavery and segregation, the Negro has now been driven to re-evaluate himself. He has come to feel that he is somebody. His religion reveals to him that God loves all His children and that the important thing about a man is not "his specificity but his fundamentum"—not the texture of his hair or the color of his skin but his eternal worth to God.[56]

He also maintained that because persons are created in the image of God, they are free. He understood freedom to be the very essence of human personality. Freedom, however, is always within destiny; that is, it is not limitless nor is it the mere function of the will. Rather, freedom, properly understood, includes the whole person. "The very phrase, 'freedom of the will,' abstracts freedom from the person to make it an object; and an object by definition is not free," King writes. "But freedom cannot thus be abstracted from the person, who is always subject as well as object and who himself still does the abstracting. So I am speaking of the freedom of man, the whole man, and not the freedom of a function called the will."[57]

King defines freedom in three ways: (1) freedom is the capacity to deliberate or weigh alternatives; (2) freedom expresses itself in decision; and (3) freedom is always wedded to responsibility.[58] "The immorality of segregation," King argued, "is that it is a selfishly contrived system which cuts off one's capacity to deliberate, decide and respond."[59] The denial of freedom relegates the person to a level of a thing by treating her as a means and not an end. King's understanding of freedom is essential for understanding moral agency and hope. Moral choice cannot be postulated without the capacity of deliberation, decision, and responsibility.

Considerable work has already been done on King's leadership, but only recently have scholars paid close attention to how his vision of hope informed his overall leadership in the modern civil rights movement.[60] Although beleaguered with controversy and sabotage, the final years of King's life (1964–1968) are the most crucial in understanding the maturation of his personal and intellectual growth as a leader. It is in this period that one sees most clearly King's tenacity of vision in his wrestling with nonviolence as a means of achieving human community, his increased realization of the international implications of his vision of community, his understanding of the nature and role of conflict, and the place of hope in the realization of human community.[61]

The basis for the profound hope in King is found in the experience of transformed nonconformity. In his "Christmas Sermon on Peace" (1967), King spoke of the disparity between his dream of 1963 and his personal nightmare that evolved over the following four years: "Yes, I am personally the victim of deferred dreams, of blasted hopes, but in spite of that I close today saying I still have a dream, because, you know, you can't give up on life. If you lose hope, somehow you lose that vitality that keeps life moving, you lose the courage to be, that quality to go on in spite of all. And so today I still have a dream."[62]

No place in King is this hope more vividly portrayed than in his bold excoriation of the Vietnam War and in his trials within the African American community around the political philosophy of Black Nationalism, articulated by Malcolm X. James Cone suggests that King's perspective on "racism, black empowerment, and war led to a shift in emphasis and meaning regarding the themes of love, justice, and hope," which were operative concepts in his articulation of the beloved community.[63] The theme of hope, according to Cone, became "the shining center of Martin's thinking, revealing new interpretations of love and justice."[64] Hope, for King, was not incidental to his vision but was his most important legacy to leaders of the future.

As we witness the shifting grounds of world change, emerging leaders must ask new questions about the nature and scope of our long, arduous journey on these shores. They must ask what this new season of worldwide struggle means for us, for this nation, and for the world. Who will lead? Dare we hope, or must we conclude that we are at "the end of history"? King did not think we were at the end of history. King believed that what we are witnessing is a worldwide revolution that challenges the very foundations of Euro-Western hegemony. In his last public statements, King said that he was pleased to live during this chaotic and precarious age because beyond the despair and fatedness that abounded, he believed that this was a great moment for the united struggles of people throughout the world. King said:

I know, somehow, that only when it is dark enough, can you see the stars. And I see God working in this period of the twentieth century in a way that men, in some strange way, are responding—something is happening in our world. The masses of the people are rising up. And wherever they are assembled today, whether they are in Johannesburg, South Africa; Nairobi, Kenya; Accra, Ghana; New York City; Atlanta, Georgia; Jackson, Mississippi; or Memphis, Tennessee, the cry is always the same—"We want to be free."[65]

Leaders must not succumb to the fears of Chicken Little, who declares that the sky is falling! The sky is not falling—rather, it simply needs a lift and we are the ones who hold the future. Envisioning new futures at the intersection will become more the province of leaders who are not only able to imagine new futures but also willing and able to share their visions with others. The ability to envision new futures begins with seeing the potential in all the various challenges and problems of the present. It will also involve freedom and imagination that take us beyond our private worlds and into the arena of public life as bold and creative seekers of change. The successful, healthy, life-inspiring leaders of the future will be those who are able to form communities of integrity, empathy, and hope at the intersection where worlds collide.

In one of my favorite meditations of Howard Thurman, titled "The Growing Edge," he speaks to the spiritual foundations of this hope:

Look well to the growing edge. All around us worlds are dying and new worlds are being born; all around us life is dying and new life is being born. The fruit ripens on the tree, the roots are silently at work in the darkness of the earth against a time when there shall be new leaves, fresh blossoms, green fruit. Such is the growing edge! It is the extra breath from the exhausted lung, the one more thing to try when all else has failed, the upward reach of life when weariness closes in upon all endeavor. This is the basis for hope in moments of despair, the incentive to carry on when times are out of joint and men have lost their reason, the source of confidence when worlds crash and dreams whiten into ash. The birth of the child—life's most dramatic answer to death—this is the growing edge incarnate. *Look well to the growing edge!*[66]

Chapter Four

CIVILITY AT THE INTERSECTION

THE QUEST FOR CIVILITY

The quest for civility is a popular subject in various media and discussions about the decline and renewal of community in American society. Civility, as an intellectual discourse, has received increased attention since the publication of Stephen Carter's popular treatise by the same name.[1] The publication of Carter's work coincided with the publication of *A Call to Civil Society: Why Democracy Needs Moral Truths*[2] by the Council on Civil Society, chaired by Jean Bethke Elshtain of the University of Chicago, which was also home to yet another distinguished scholar concerned with civility as an intellectual and practical discipline, the late Edward Shils.[3] The matter of civility, however, has been the subject of serious intellectual debate preceding the rise of the nation-state.[4] In American civic life, our earliest leaders found social and political merit in practicing civility. Fourteen-year-old George Washington is reported to have copied from a seventeenth-century English translation of a sixteenth-century French book of manners for what later became his *Rules of Civility and Decent Behavior in Company and in Conversation*.[5] Civility, as a quest for social dignity and political reward, promised its most loyal practitioners a place within democratic polity, but for those who failed to abide by the rules or who by virtue of race, ethnicity, gender, class, or sexual lifestyles were deemed unfit for civil society, the etiquette, manners, and ways of civility have been punitive and damning.[6]

Civility is used in a variety of contexts, often masking complex historical, sociological, and methodological issues. In common usage, civility refers to a set of manners, certain etiquettes and social graces that are rooted in specific class orientations and moral sensibilities.[7] Civility, however, does not refer simply to etiquette, manners, and social graces but is inclusive of social capital and the inherent benefits accrued by these networks of reciprocity. Civility also has to do with the individual's social dignity within that system. It represents the public space of the leader where she negotiates the intersection between lifeworlds and systemworlds. Without a strong civil society, the experiment in democracy becomes an anesthetizing drama of conformity to the power of the state, procedural rules, and rights that masquerade as moral values.

Much of the current debate surrounding rights and utility has its genesis in the acquiescence of citizens who have failed to fully participate in the discourse and practices that sustain civil society. This debate has underestimated the power of market-stimulated moralities and their impact on civic life manifest in the prevailing financial crises on Wall Street and Main Street. A closer look at this connection forecast an ominous future for American democracy, especially for the poor and those who have been marginalized at the boundaries of a social contract that in its inception was exclusive and xenophobic.

In our model, the term "civility" is used as a framework for understanding the role of social capital within the context of leaders' public life and practices.[8] Robert D. Putnam's *Bowling Alone* is one example of the ongoing public debate on the significance of civil discourse and social networking that is part of a larger conversation about the need to recapture, appropriate, and sustain the habits and practices essential for the survival of an American ethos of generalized reciprocity and mutual obligation. I do not limit civility, however, to social capital, but refer more broadly to the concept as the social-historical script or covenant that the individual citizen negotiates within the context of the larger society. Civility is the psychosocial ecology of the individual; a certain understanding or self-referential index of the individual's place within a social system as it relates to individual character.

Civility, in this respect, is indigenous to healthy civic life. Civic life, however, covers broad territory. Included in civic life are questions of what constitutes civility, civic capacity, and civil society. For instance, Robert Wuthnow suggests that civil society is "the arena in which individual freedoms, even those that are self-interested, are kept in tension with collective values and community participation."[9] Michael Walzer defines civil society as "that 'space of uncoerced human association' and 'the set of relational networks' and institutions that fill it, all trying to harmonize the conflicting demands of individual and group interests and the social good.

Families, schools, churches, synagogues, mosques, voluntary societies, non-governmental organizations, and communications media all belong to civil society."[10] The critical point of leverage in both definitions is the role of values (freedom, self-interest, collective good, and community). Included in the idea of civic life is this larger understanding of the role of values that make civil society possible. Undergirding these values, or better, the practice that infuses and sustains values within a democratic social and political culture, is civility. Civility, in this context, treats social capital and civic capacity as synonymous in that they both refer to "connections among individuals—social networks and the norms of reciprocity and trustworthiness that arise from them." Moreover, social capital is related to civic virtue in that the latter is "most powerful when it is embedded in a dense network of reciprocal social relations." Robert Putnam opines, "A society of many virtuous, but isolated individuals is not necessarily rich in social capital."[11]

This description of social capital and its role in creating and sustaining community is important for ethical leaders in two ways. First, social capital provides networks for community engagement that can be inclusive and socially beneficial for the leader and organizational life; and second, social capital derives its life and power from the norms of reciprocity that it engenders and sustains. Ethical leadership, whether in politics, business, science, education, religion, or the arts, is essential for the maintenance of social capital. Moreover, civic life, social capital, in sum, civility, is the fuel of a strong democratic culture that ensures opportunity and stability for organizations. Civility, therefore, protects and encourages the key values of liberty, equality, and friendship without which democracy is impossible.[12]

DYSFUNCTIONAL AND TRANSFORMATIVE CIVILITY

Civility, however, can be highly dysfunctional, especially for leaders who are called upon to confront powerful systems of injustice that demand speaking truth to power. Our world is filled with examples of leaders who fail to address destructive practices within their own organizations and larger publics for the sake of good civil relations. Such dysfunctional expressions of civility not only are counterproductive but actually contribute to and perpetuate ongoing dramas that mask disingenuous, underhanded, and grossly evil social practices. The revelations with regard to our government's failure to find weapons of mass destruction in Iraq and other failures of authenticity and transparency from public leaders are excellent examples of what is at stake when leaders allow dysfunctional civility to substitute for truth-telling in public life.

Civility can also become a transformative practice that exposes unjust practices and calls upon the highest within the leader's character. The leadership of Martin Luther King Jr. in the modern civil rights movement represents an outstanding example of this legacy of civility. Perhaps better than any other leader of the twentieth century, King was able to forge civility into a subversive weapon in the struggle for equality and justice in American society. By subversive civility, what I have in mind is akin to Jeffery Goldfarb's observation that intellectuals "contribute to a democratic life when they civilize political contestation and when they subvert complacent consensus; when they provide enemies with the discursive possibility to become opponents and when they facilitate public deliberations about problems buried by the norms of civility."[13] King's distinctive contribution in this regard is the way in which he dialectically explored the options afforded by democratic life and forced existing tensions through nonviolent direct action. Stephen Carter makes a similar observation. According to Carter, King and other leaders in the Southern Leadership Conference were able to "spark a dialogue" through nonviolent acts of civility. The ethical leader as *transformed nonconformist* is primarily concerned with the disruption of "negative peace" as a way of bringing to surface hidden tensions that create the conditions for creative understanding and new discursive possibilities.

Critical to this understanding of subversive civility is the practice of what King called "excessive altruism."[14] Excessive altruism is concretely expressed in acts of empathy or sympathetic concern for the other. It is to be distinguished from acts of pity that are general in application; rather, empathy is concerned with particularity. "Sympathy," wrote King, "is fellow feeling for the person in need—his pain, agony, and burdens." Sympathetic concern does not do something *for* others; rather, it does something *with* others. It is only in this respect that the dignity and self-worth of others are preserved. Excessive altruism, therefore, goes beyond the rationalist perspective discussed earlier, which relies on deontological decrees, universality as a criterion for duty, and the sometimes uncritical compliance to law; it goes the "second mile." Therefore, excessive altruism cannot be enforced by external rules but is motivated by unenforceable, self-imposed sanctions. King made a distinction between enforceable and nonenforceable obligations. Enforceable obligations refer to moral demands (rules, laws, statutes) that are externally imposed, while unenforceable obligations refer to inner sanctions, which are self-imposed. Unenforceable laws "concern inner attitudes, genuine person-to-person relations, expressions of compassion which law books cannot regulate and jails cannot rectify."[15] Enforceable obligations are human laws that ensure justice; unenforceable obligations belong to a higher law, rooted in the moral order of the cosmos, and they produce love.[16] Although behavior can be regulated by external decrees, King's view of civility as "excessive altruism" cannot be legislated. This was the logic of his argument against the limits of desegregation as an enforceable demand and integration as an unenforceable demand. "Desegregation will break down the legal barriers and bring men together physically, but something must touch the hearts and souls of men so that they come together spiritually because it is natural and right."[17]

Finally, King's brand of transformative civility was rooted in a profound sense of spirituality and a "searching ethical awareness." Howard Thurman made this observation in his elegiac remarks on the assassination of Martin Luther King Jr. He said:

> Always he spoke from within the context of his religious experience, giving voice to the ethical insight which sprang out of his profound brooding over the meaning of his Judeo-Christian heritage. And this was indeed his great contribution to our times. He was able to put at the center of his own personal religious experience a searching ethical awareness. Thus organized religion as we know it in our society found itself with its back against the wall. To condemn him, to reject him was to reject the ethical insight of the faith it proclaimed. And this was new. Racial prejudice, segregation, discrimination were not regarded by him as merely un-American, undemocratic, but as a mortal sin against God. For those who were religious it awakens guilt; for those who [were] merely superstitious it inspires fear. And it was this fear that pulled the trigger of the assassin's gun that took his life.[18]

Religion, for King, played a prominent role in sustaining the "negative peace" of the culture of conformity. In his "Letter from a Birmingham Jail," King challenged the white religious leadership to imitate the example of the early Christian church by becoming "disturbers of the peace" and "outside agitators." Black religious leadership was not exempt from King's scathing critique. Throughout his public career, King was a critic of the two extremes of emotionalism and classism that he felt plagued black church leadership. Some of King's severest critics were fellow black clergy and elites who saw him as a "disturber of the peace," especially in his decision to speak out against the Vietnam War.[19]

Leaders of the new century can take an important cue from King and other leaders of the modern civil rights movement. The call for a new kind of subversive, transforming civility is echoed from many corridors as war escalates and violent acts of injustice are perpetrated through laws that silently exclude and relegate entire peoples to the margins. How might leaders who stand at the intersection where worlds collide maintain a disciplined yet disruptive movement of presence without succumbing to the temptation to become physically violent and self-destructive in the process? The lessons of transformative civility represented by King and the civil rights movement may well be the salvation of American democracy if we have the courage to experiment with new forms of nonviolent dissent and resistance.

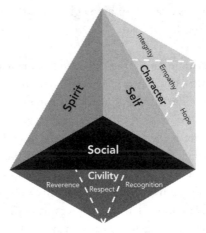

FIGURE 3. THE ETHICAL LEADERSHIP MODEL™

THE DEFINING VALUES OF CIVILITY

Following our model, there are three interrelated dimensions of civility: *recognition* (personal), *respect* (public), and *reverence* (spirit). In each dimension of civility, as we shall see, there is also the circular movement from personal to public to spirit.

Recognition

Recognition in ethical leadership practices begins with consciousness, a focused awareness that is extended to the self, to others, and to ultimate frames of reference. First, recognition as an activity of consciousness has neither moral nor ethical significance. It insists, rather, on the development of a sense of transcendence in which one is able to self-observe as one observes others. This mode of consciousness is sometimes called *reflexive consciousness* or *self-observation*. Self-observation allows the leader to become aware or to *recognize* herself and to better understand the unconscious motivations that drive thoughts, feelings, and behavior. For leaders involved in public life and practices, this focused awareness of the self is of paramount importance. The significance of self-observation for civility lies first in our personal quests for self-dignity and respect. It also serves as a major fount for the quest of remembering one's own story and how that story is intertwined with the stories of others. No greater work can be done by the leader in repairing the ethical center than becoming aware of one's own inherent worth and dignity, especially when confronted with judgment, blame, and mistrust. In civil relations, the aim is to create networks of reciprocity and social capital that are based on trust. Beyond social contracting in the formal sense, civility rests on covenantal relations that require integrity, empathy, and hope, which engender and sustain friendship. Friendship extends beyond utility and duty and rests ultimately upon common purpose and vision.[20]

Recognition also has to do with consciousness of one's self or *being-for-self*. As indicated earlier, consciousness precedes being, or in the language of Jean Paul Sartre, *existence* precedes *essence*. By this he meant that "man [woman] first of all exists, encounters himself, surges up in the world—and defines himself afterwards."[21] It is in this encounter with self that one discovers one's freedom and responsibility to oneself and to others. But recognition also involves *being-for-others*—the encounter with the other that has implications for how one sees oneself. In fact, most of self-perception is dependent on how one perceives the other's perception of him or her. Recognition, then, is about "looking" at oneself and the other; and through the very act of "looking," one makes value judgments about oneself and the other. This looking can have dramatically negative consequences, as in feelings of shame and guilt that are *mirrored* through the eyes of the other. In this sense, Sartre is correct when he says, "Hell is other people," because being-for-others means that one is defined by the other's look and becomes an object for the other. On the other hand, the look of the other, if given with empathy and compassion, can be powerfully affirming and liberating. Much rests upon the look of the other and the power of recognition. Most important, one comes to a sense of identity and character through one's encounter with the other. Leaders who are unaware of the dynamic of being-for-self and being-for-others are often stuck in performances that mask the deep-seated issues of power, guilt, and shame that stunt potential for change and transformation. There are two extremes of this dynamic to which ethical leaders must give attention as it relates to their personal deportment as leaders and the development of civility: *mirroring* and *masking*.

Mirroring

Mirroring, as a psychological term, refers to self-reflection on and *transference* of one's deepest past emotional experiences onto others in situations that are provoked by memory. The leader's self-perception is, in large part, a function of mirroring. The mirrors through which leaders peer and self-reflect determine patterns of behavior that are deeply rooted in images of what they project upon others; the mirrors through which others (in this case, followers) project upon the leaders also inform the leaders' attitudes, decisions and actions. Manfred F. R. Kets de Vries suggests that leaders are mirrors of their inner selves and the images of others that have been variously integrated in their personalities.[22] Recognition as mirroring gives the leader a fragile sense of self that can evolve into a recurring need for justification and approval from others. In Sartre's play *No Exit*, Estelle says, "When I used to talk with people, I always made sure there was one [a mirror] nearby in which I could look at myself. I talked, I saw myself talking, I saw myself as others saw me—that kept me awake."[23] But the inner life of the leader needs more than affirmation of the other; ultimately the leader must find balance in the creative tension of a realistic assessment of self-fact and the self-images that are mediated by the other. For leaders in public space, a healthy sense of self, which is the product of this creative tension, is a critical resource for civility.

Early childhood and later experiences of rejection and humiliation can play out in narcissistic quests for power and control. David Gergen's treatment of Richard Nixon is a revealing portrait of the ways in which these experiences play out in mirroring. Gergen suggests that Nixon was a brilliant strategist who thrived on his knowledge and historical grasp of leadership and power, especially the leadership of General Charles de Gaulle. Like de Gaulle, Nixon was a man of "inner steel" with an indomitable will to succeed in the midst of overwhelming opposition. Gergen cites examples of his resilience in the aftermath of early public rejections in his races for the U.S. Senate in 1950, President Eisenhower's attempt to knock him off the ticket in 1956, and his failed twin election bids in the 1960s. But the "demons within" that eventually led to his fall, Gergen suggests, may be found in his early childhood experience of losing two brothers and facing periodic rejection; the bad luck of family circumstances—after his father sold the family store, oil was discovered on the property—and his awkward romance with his wife-to-be, Pat. It is reported that as a young man he was the chauffeur for Pat as she rode in the backseat with her dates. Gergen suggests that Nixon's romance with Charles de Gaulle and other "strong men," like Benjamin Disraeli and Winston Churchill, provided him with "role models for action" and helped him to maintain the balance between the mysterious mystique of the leader as a protective strategy and as a means for maintaining authority. His famous years "in the wilderness" after the narrow defeat by Kennedy in 1960 was also modeled after leaders such as de Gaulle, Churchill, and Alcide De Gasperi, who used their defeats as fulcrums for self-reflection, writing, and preparation for their return to public life. Nixon's mirroring of these experiences of rejection and the *model of return* provided by de Gaulle and other "strong men" combined to create a character that drew a stringent line between private moral life and public actions that eventually proved ruinous to his career and harmful to the nation. Gergen adds that these models that were mirrored by Nixon, though powerful and helpful in many respects, ultimately failed him because he confused leadership with power as domination and allowed "the demons within" to dictate the decisions that finally led to his downfall. [24]

Leaders must be particularly aware of the power of mirroring both in its negative and positive dimensions. Mirroring can serve as a powerful resource in developing the kind of civic character that promotes values of equality and freedom in democratic life, but it can also become a crippling demonic parasite that feeds on the leader's inner resources and renders her ineffective, frustrated, and prone to unrealistic and dangerous quests for power and control. The model of "the strong man" or "the great leader syndrome," where individual leaders jealously guard the boundaries of private and public life, is ill equipped to correct the negative impact of mirroring.

Ethical leaders who practice integrity, empathy, and hope at the intersection are constantly engaged in practices of self-observation and self-critique that ask the questions of identity (Who am I?), purpose (What do I really desire to achieve?), and method (What is the most ethical and reasonable course of action to achieve these goals?). Moreover, the creation of an ethical community of discourse and practice, a moral ethos within a group or organization, provides the kind of healthy insight and critique that corrects the unhealthy tendencies of mirroring. Manfred de Vries's observation is helpful:

> We should not ignore the fact that playing the mirroring game can have its positive side, as mirroring can, for a while, provide a much-needed adhesion, keeping a company together in times of upheaval and change. Its momentum can create a common vision and committed action, often with good results. Nevertheless, a healthy dose of insight and self-criticism, and the ability to tolerate frank feedback from others, is needed to check the distortion in the mirroring process. Many leaders do not have that capacity, and the seductive pull from mirroring subordinates has led many of them astray.[25]

Masking

The search for power and social recognition often compels leaders to remake themselves or excessively adapt the ideas to which others give value or relevance, thus dismissing their life's purpose and sense of self. As these practices escalate, they can leave leaders feeling isolated or fearful of showing their true selves, so fearful that they actually lose touch with their core values. These self-imposed deceptive practices can bind leaders to controlling dramas where they literally act out the expectations of others to their own detriment and the success of their group, organization, and nation.

The late Dorothee Soelle, a political theologian and human rights activist, relates a story of a young student who approached her at the close of a lecture and handed her a letter. The student's letter demonstrates the confusion people can face when they wear masks that have become controlling and from which they cannot escape. This is particularly relevant to emerging leaders who are often moving into positions of greater power and responsibility:

> Please hear what I am not saying. Don't be deceived by me. Don't let the face I make deceive you. I wear a thousand masks and I am afraid to lay them aside. Not one of these masks is the real I. Pretending is an art that has become second nature to me. Do not be deceived by it; for God's sake don't be fooled.
>
> I give the impression that I am an affable fellow who has not a single inner or outer care in the world. I give the impression that confidence

is my name and "being cool" my game, that I am a quiet stream, so in command of things that I need no one.

But don't believe me—please don't believe me. Outwardly I may appear quite confident and serene, but that is a mask I wear. There is nothing behind that mask. Beneath I am what I really am—confused, afraid, alone. But I conceal all that. I wouldn't want anyone to notice it. If someone shows the slightest awareness of my weakness, it throws me into panic, and I dread exposing myself to others. That is precisely the reason I desperately devise masks behind which I can hide. A clever slovenly façade helps me to pretend and to withstand the look of a knowing eye, which would see through me. And yet such a look would be my salvation. I know it. If such a look were only one of acceptance or of love! That is the only thing which can give me the security I cannot give myself: the assurance that I really am of value and worth.

But I do not say that to myself. I don't dare. I am afraid to say it. I am afraid that you will think ill of me, laugh at me. I am afraid that your laughter would kill me. I am afraid that deep down inside of me I amount to nothing and that you reject me for this.

So I play my little game, my desperate little game. On the outside I show a façade of confidence; beneath I am a trembling child. I am rambling on! I'll tell you everything—which is really nothing—and nothing which really cries out within me. So do not be deceived by the things I say out of habit.

Please listen carefully. Try to hear not what I say but what I really want to say, what I need to hear in order to survive, yet cannot.

I loathe this game of concealment. I detest this superficial game I play. It isn't honest. I wish I could be genuine and spontaneous, just be myself. But you must help me. You must extend your hand, even though it may seem to be the last thing I really want. You alone can take this empty glaze of death from my eyes. You alone can call me into life. Every time you are gentle and friendly to me, every time you encourage me, when you try to understand me because you really care about me, my heart takes on wings. Small and fragile wings to be sure. But wings!

Your intuition, your empathy and the strength of your understanding breathe new life into me. I want you to know.

I want you to know how important you are for me—if you will make me the human being that I really am. How I hope you want to do it! Only you can tear away my mask. Only you can rescue me from my dread and insecurity—and my loneliness. Please do not pass me by. It will not be easy for you. My longstanding sense of worthlessness erects high, thick walls. The closer you get to me the more blindly I strike back. I resist with tooth and nail the very thing for which I cry out. But I am told that love is stronger than any thick wall, and I am counting on that.

Please! Try to tear down this wall with hands that are strong and firm, yet gentle, for a child is so sensitive!

Who am I? I am someone you know very well.[26]

Masking and mirroring are related, but each has its distinctive power to shape character and the performance of leaders in public space. Masking is a game, a very dangerous game especially for leaders in civic life. Masks hide a multitude of feelings, as the student's letter attests, but they also provoke a multitude of harmful practices that can be disastrous for leaders. We all wear masks—from early childhood games in front of the mirror, where we glance at ourselves in roles ranging from ballerinas, clowns, warriors, princesses, or beautiful movie stars to knaves, murderers, and devils. The images of the mirror tell tales of greatness and triumph and of inestimable sorrow. Rainer Maria Rilke writes about his early childhood games of impersonation and the dangers of masking:

It was then that I first learned to know the influence that can emanate directly from a particular costume itself. Hardly had I donned one of these suits when I had to admit that it got me in its power; that it prescribed my movements, my facial expression, yes, even my ideas. My hand, over which the lace cuff fell and fell again, was anything but my usual hand; it moved like a person acting; I might even say that it was watching itself, exaggerated though that sounds. These disguises never, indeed, went so far as to make me feel a stranger to myself; on the contrary, the more varied my transformations, the more convinced did I become myself. I grew bolder and bolder; I flung myself higher and higher; for my dexterity in recapture was beyond all doubt. I did not notice the temptation in this rapidly growing security. To my undoing, the last closet, which I had heretofore thought I could not open, yielded one day to surrender to me, not specific costumes, but all kinds of random paraphernalia for masquerades, the fantastic peradventures of which drove the blood to my cheeks. It is impossible to recount all I found there. In addition to a pautta that I remember, there were dominos in various colors, there were women's dresses that tinkled brightly with the coins with which they were sewn; there were pierrot-costumes that looked silly to me, and braided

Turkish trousers, all folds, and Persian fezzes from which little camphor sacks slipped out, and coronets with stupid, expressionless stones. All these I rather despised; they were of such a shabby unreality and hung there so peeled-off and miserable and collapsed so will-lessly when one dragged them out into the light. But what transported me into a sort of intoxication were the capacious mantles, the wraps, the shawls, the veils, all those yielding, wide, unused fabrics, that were so soft and caressing, or so slithery that one could scarcely take hold of them, or so light that they flew by one like a wind, or simply heavy with all their own weight. In them I first discerned really three and infinitely mobile possibilities: being a slave-girl about to be sold, or being Jeanne d'Arc or an old king or wizard; all this lay to hand, especially as there were also masks, large, threatening or astonished faces with real beards and full or high drawn eyebrows. I had never seen masks before, but I understood at once that masks ought to be. I had to laugh when it occurred to me that we had a dog who looked as if he wore one. I recalled his affectionate eyes that always seemed to be looking as from behind into his hirsute visage. I was still laughing as I dressed up, and in the process I completely forgot what I intended to represent. No matter; it was novel and exciting not to decide till afterward before the mirror. The face I fastened on had a singularly hollow smell; it lay tight over my own face, but I was able to see though it comfortably, and not till the mask sat firm did I select all sorts of materials, which I wound about my head like a turban, in such a way that the edge of the mask, which reached downward into an immense yellow cloak, was almost entirely hidden also on top and at the sides. At length, when I could do no more, I considered myself sufficiently disguised. I seized in addition a large staff, which I made walk along beside me at arm's length, and in this fashion, not without difficulty, but, as it seemed to me, full of dignity, I trailed into the guest-room toward the mirror.

It was really grandiose, beyond all expectation. And the mirror gave it back instantly, it was too convincing. It would not have been at all necessary to move much; this apparition was perfect, even though it did nothing. But I wanted to discover what I actually was, so I turned a little and finally raised both arms: large, almost conjuring gestures were, I saw immediately, the only fitting ones. But just at this solemn moment I heard quite near me, muffled by my disguise, a very complicated noise; much frightened, I lost sight of the presence in the mirror and was badly upset to perceive that I had overturned a small round table with heaven

knows what, probably very fragile objects. I bent down as well as I could
and found my worst fears confirmed: it looked as though everything were
in pieces. The two useless green-violet porcelain parrots were of course
shattered, each in a different malign fashion. A box, from which rolled
bonbons that looked like insects in silken cocoons, had cast its cover
away; only half of it was to be seen, and the other had totally disappeared.
But most annoying of all was a scent-bottle that had been shattered into
a thousand tiny fragments, from which the remainder of some sort of old
essence had spurted that now formed a spot of very repulsive profile on
the clear parquet. I wiped it up quickly with something or other that was
hanging down about me, but it only become blacker and more unpleas-
ant. I was indeed desperate. I picked myself up and tried to find something with which to repair the damage. But nothing was to be found.
Besides I was so hampered in my vision and every movement, that wrath
rose in me against my absurd situation, which I no longer understood.
I pulled at all my garments, but they clung only the tighter. The cords
of the mantle strangled me, and the stuff on my head pressed as though
more and more were being added to it. Furthermore the atmosphere had
become dim as though misty with the oldish fume of the spilled liquid.

Hot and angry, I rushed to the mirror and with difficulty watched
through the mask the working of my hands. But for this the mirror had
just been waiting. Its moment of retaliation had come. While I strove in
boundlessly increasing anguish to squeeze somehow out of my disguise,
it forced me, by what means I do not know, to lift my eyes and imposed
on me an image, no, a reality, a strange, unbelievable and monstrous
reality, with which, against my will, I had become permeated: for now
the mirror was the stranger, and I was the mirror. I stared at this great
terrifying unknown before me, and it seemed to me appalling to be alone
with him. But at the very moment I thought this, the worst befell: I lost
all sense, I simply ceased to exist. For one second I had an indescribable,
painful and futile longing for myself, then there was only he: there was
nothing but he.

I ran away, but now it was he that ran. He knocked against everything, he did not know the house, he had no idea where to go; he man-
aged to get down a stairway, and in his course stumbled over someone
who shouted in struggling free. A door opened, several persons came
out: Oh, oh, what a relief it was to know them! There were Sieversen, the
good Sieversen, and the housemaid and the butler: now for a decision.
But they did not spring forward to the rescue; their cruelty knew no

bounds. They stood there and laughed; my God, they could stand there and laugh. I wept, but the mask did not let the tears escape; they ran down inside over my cheeks and dried at once and ran again and dried. And at last I knelt before them, as no human being ever knelt; I knelt and lifted up my hands, and implored them: "Take me out, if you still can, and keep me," but they did not hear; I had no longer any voice. [27]

Leaders wear many faces—private faces reserved for family, friends, and associates, where trust and acceptance are taken for granted, and public faces that conform to expectations often associated with strength, power, and position. Perhaps one of the greatest assets of leaders in public space is to appear as a master of civility in respect to etiquette and manners, and to conduct oneself with appropriate decorum and taste befitting public respectability. But underneath these masks are untold stories of moral failure, insecurity, and fears that often betray the leader's deepest yearnings and idealism. How do leaders negotiate the intersection between private worlds of meaning and feeling and the public demand for civility without falling prey to the controlling drama outlined by Rilke above—of being held captive to the mask and the controlling drama of recognition as power? Or better put, how do leaders avoid self-deceptive practices born of the need for recognition from the other, however conceived, and speak the truth as they understand it to themselves and to others?

Recognition in Black Leadership Practices

Some of my earlier work in studying civility among black churches helped to further develop the role that recognition plays in the practices of leaders and the challenges of *mirroring* and *masking*.[28] Recognition, in black life, has a long and painful history and does not require extensive commentary here. For Orlando Patterson, the drive for recognition from the master was the basis for the social dignity and honor sought by enslaved Africans— and consequently was the means by which their masters manipulated them. Civility, as a response to the insatiable need for social dignity and respectability, became a chief aim among many black religious leaders, as it did among their secular counterparts. Drawing on Hegel's dialectic of recognition between the Lord and Bondsmen, Patterson writes, "Confronted with the master's outrageous effort to deny him all dignity, the slave even more than the master came to know and desire passionately this very attribute. For dignity, like love, is one of the human qualities that are most intensely felt and understood when they are absent—or unrequited."[29]

A major challenge for black leadership, as with most historically marginalized leaders, is masking and mirroring. Paul Laurence Dunbar's classic
recitation "We Wear the Mask" is revealing in its accent on the pain and
anguish of wearing the mask, but equally revelatory in respect to the complex
act of balancing self-fact and self-image and all the energy one must deploy in
negotiating mask-wearing in the face of resistance, spitefulness, and danger.

> We wear the mask that grins and lies;
> It hides our cheeks and shades our eyes,
> This debt we pay to human guile;
> With torn and bleeding hearts we smile,
> And mouth with myriad subtleties.
>
> Why should the world be over-wise
> In counting all our tears and sighs?
> Nay, let them only see us, while
> We wear the mask.
>
> We smile, but, O great Christ, our cries
> To thee from tortured souls arise.
> We sing, but oh the clay is vile
> Beneath our feet, and long the mile;
> But let the world dream otherwise,
> We wear the mask![30]

For Dunbar, the mask is prophylactic—it conceals and protects one
from pain and sorrow—and yet it is an expression of the will-to-power, the
human need to maintain a sense of dignity and self-respect. Black leaders, for
the most part, have learned the value of masking as a means of balancing self-
fact and self-image often with great public reward. But the inherent danger
of masking in the long run has been costly and counterproductive to leaders
and followers alike. It creates what scholars have called *dilemma* or *doubleness*.
Dilemma has a long, protracted history in black leadership practices, but its
roots lie in the doubleness of American history. A brief excursus provides
insight not only into leadership practices but into its genesis in American
character and the quest for civility.

Since Gunnar Myrdal's classic study *An American Dilemma*,[31] the
term "dilemma" has come to represent broad and conflicting ideologies
in respect to African American life and culture.[32] Myrdal's formulation

of the American dilemma, however, betrayed a deeper and more fundamental problem seldom echoed in quiet, genteel places where the *problem
of whiteness* was suppressed and ignored. W. E. B. DuBois, in artful prose,
forthrightly captured the nature of the dilemma in black life:

> After the Egyptian and Indian, the Greek and Roman, the Teuton and
> Mongolian, the Negro is a sort of seventh son, born with a veil, and
> gifted with second-sight in this American world—a world which yields
> him no true self-consciousness, but only lets him see himself through
> the revelation of the other world. It is a peculiar sensation, this double-
> consciousness, this sense of always looking at one's self through the eyes
> of others, of measuring one's soul by the tape of the world that looks on
> in amused contempt and pity. One ever feels his twoness—an American,
> a Negro; two souls, two thoughts, two unreconciled strivings; two war-
> ring ideals in one dark body, whose dogged strength alone keeps it from
> being torn asunder.
>
> The history of the American Negro is the history of this strife—this
> longing to attain self-conscious manhood, to merge his double self into a
> better and truer self. . . . He simply wishes to make it possible for a man
> to be both a Negro and an American, without being cursed and spit upon
> by his fellows, without having the doors of Opportunity closed roughly in
> his face.[33]

DuBois's depiction of doubleness is a meditation on the psychosocial
condition of the African American at the turn of the twentieth century,
but it is even more. At the core of the problematic is the plea for recognition. *Recognition, respectability,* and *loyalty* were also cornerstones of
racial uplift ideology that dominated the landscape of post-Reconstruction
activities among black leadership. These civic goods were sought through
education, suffrage, political leadership, and jury service based on natural
rights arguments. Most prominent among these strategies, however, was
education.[34]

Before Booker T. Washington and W. E. B. DuBois became the popular representatives of industrial versus classical education among freed
people, the ideological die was cast by the growing white resistance to a
literate black leadership through the work of General Samuel Chapman
Armstrong, the founder and principal of the Hampton Normal and Agricultural Institute. Armstrong believed that political participation by literate black leadership spelled the death of the South as an economic force,

and that with the failure of the South, the economic stability of the nation. His solution was to ensure that freed men and women would maintain a labor force for the agricultural wealth of the South. His strategy was to train a generation of laborers who would teach other blacks the values of hard work, thrift, and subservience. His pedagogy reinforced belief in black subordination to the planter class ideology of minstrelsy and infantilism; that is, an educated black leadership was detrimental to the political economy of the South. He found his perfect pupil in one Booker T. Washington. Washington's genius, it seems, was in his ability to *mask* his own deep personal feelings of justice and equality over against the more pragmatic hope of black political empowerment.[35]

The *dilemma* is hardly resolved; it still exists at the heart of African American life and practices and has far-reaching implications for the ways in which African American leaders understand and participate in civic life. In recent years, a number of scholars working in critical race theory and in historical, literary, cultural, multicultural, and philosophical studies have addressed the problematic in other terms.[36] Broadly speaking, education among freed slaves was used as a means of racial uplift, but it had the paradoxical advantage of inculcating certain habits and practices that encouraged bourgeois manners and morals.[37] The civilizing influences of education, despite great ideological divides as to which type was most effective for uplift, had much the same impact on recognition, respect, and loyalty to democratic values. Black intellectuals and race leaders, such as Ida B. Wells, Anna Julia Cooper, W. E. B. DuBois, Booker T. Washington, T. Thomas Fortune, and Mary Church Terrell, all embraced the polite and gentle pursuits of bourgeois morals embodied in *thrift, industry, self-control, piety, temperance,* and *the work ethic*—all necessary, they believed, for successful citizenship and economic independence. Kevin Gaines adds, "Education of the freedpeople was often tied to moral evolution and industrial training rather than citizenship and political independence."[38] Gaines's observation is important in that it demonstrates the ways in which discursive formations provide the means for the articulation of moral languages that over time become distinct from habits and practices that were originally related to, or assumed to be related to, the historical project of their discursive features—in this case, to the ideology of racial uplift. Black elite ideology of racial uplift was accompanied by a specific moral vocabulary, born of the rigors of slavery and Jim Crow. But in its most basic formulation, it was a language that sought *recognition, respectability,* and *loyalty* to an ideal embodied in democratic life and practices. Furthermore, the moral vocabulary of black elites evolved over time to embrace a bourgeois worldview that promoted self-reliance and social egalitarianism.

This worldview proved to have complex and aggravating features that impacted ways in which black people, especially black leaders, understand civility.

It should come as no small surprise, then, that many prominent black leaders have perfected the art of masking to their own detriment and, for others, their own personal and professional fulfillment. Ellis Cose, in *The Rage of a Privileged Class: Why Are Middle-Class Blacks Angry? Why Should America Care?* has illustrated the negative impact that masking has had on "successful" blacks and the underlying historical connections that play out in highly dysfunctional relations with their white counterparts.[39] Price Cobbs and Judith Turnock, on the other hand, offer advice to blacks who are newcomers in corporate environments:

> Blacks in corporate America always have a second job, one that is intensely personal and never completed. You must add depth and breadth to understanding and insight about your personal experiences, so that you can position yourself in the new environment. You must develop a finely-tuned sense of how to handle racial slights . . . you must develop strategies to manage your own conscious and unconscious discomfort as well as the discomfort of your colleagues, and you must deal with stereotypical responses they may have of you. All of this is critical to your success.[40]

How does one manage "conscious and unconscious discomfort" as well as the discomfort of others without falling prey to the foibles of masking? What insights might be gained from looking closely at ways in which one balances the need for recognition in black life and practices? I believe more is involved than simply outlining techniques and strategies for "managing" the feelings of black leaders. The lessons from *dilemma* and *masking* in black leadership practices have strong implications for *all* leaders who are unaware of the power and danger of recognition, especially for emerging leaders who will negotiate the questions of civility at the intersection. The work of developing morally anchored character is essential for addressing the ways in which leaders will create networks of reciprocity and social capital that have their basis in genuine human concern for what Howard Thurman called *a friendly world underneath friendly skies.*

Recognition and Integrity

Recognition, as the personal dimension of civility, is related to character and the virtue of integrity. Integrity, as I have demonstrated, refers to a sense of wholeness and authenticity and is the cornerstone of a healthy sense of self. Therefore, it is imperative that leaders deepen their own sense of self by cultivating integrity, empathy, and hope. These are spiritual practices that demand "truth-telling." Truth-telling refers to honesty and sincerity in relation to self, others, and one's ultimate spiritual reference.[41] Truth-telling underscores the fundamental dignity and worth of human beings. It highlights the equality of all people, regardless of color, class, status, or social advantage. This is an important observation embodying radical implications for leaders' understandings of themselves and their relationships to others. Deception is never a viable moral alternative for ethical leaders, because it destroys the value structure of the one who deceives and lies. "The penalty of deception," Thurman suggests, "is to become a deception, with all sense of moral discrimination vitiated."[42] But if the leader adheres to the truth, she equalizes the relationship between herself and the one who has the advantage, because deception perpetuates the relationship of the powerful and the powerless.[43] Truth-telling understood thusly liberates the individual from any form of external bondage or need for masking. For within the person who internalizes the truth, there is an inner authority that allows her to say no even at the threat of rejection, violence, and death. This is the essence of the freedom of the individual and her birthright.[44]

Moreover, the ethical leader is also responsible for guarding against self-deception. This was a major concern for Thurman, and the theme arises throughout his writings. Always, the individual is called upon to test her perspective against the facts of her own experience and the experiences of others.[45] As one dares to ask the primary questions of *identity*, *purpose*, and *method* and is willing to be tutored by the "sound of the genuine" that is within, a refreshing occurs; a new sense of self and presence emerges, which enables one to reenter the struggle with new courage and determination. For Thurman, this quest for personal space involves defiant activity, for it presupposes that one's quest for civility cannot ultimately be divorced from one's wrestling with the internal issues of power and dominance. He writes, "It is a strange freedom to be adrift in the world of men without a sense of anchor anywhere. . . . It is a strange freedom to go nameless up and down the streets of other minds where no salutation greets and no sign is given to mark the place one calls one's own."[46]

Lessons learned from the practices of masking and the need for truth-telling among leaders of African American life can be invaluable for all leaders in the quest for civility at this critical passage in our history. Telling the truth to oneself and to others involves what philosopher Cornel West calls a "politics of conversion." The call for a politics of conversion presupposes the nexus of memory and hope. It demands that leaders remember their stories as the stimulus for truth-telling. Masking and self-deceit have long, complex personal histories, and unless leaders can remember, retell, and relive their stories, there is little basis for hope. Leaders who do not remember cannot hope, nor can they offer hope to others. But they cannot begin this spiritual process until there is a willingness to return to their roots. "These days," poet Charles Olson writes, "whatever you have to say, leave the roots on, let them dangle, and the dirt, just to make clear where they come from."[47] This return to the roots, to a sane place, requires a radical deconstruction of self in the midst of a multiplicity of forces that stands guard over one's entry into a new future of hope and possibility. In other words, the *politics of conversion* presupposes *personal conversion*. The transformed nonconformity King talked about involves a type of existential death—a blessed irrationality born of the refusal to submit to market mentalities and cultural cages that inhibit the birthing of new names and redemptive possibilities. The first step for leaders in this process of conversion is to come to grips with the power and danger of recognition as a personal virtue and public value.

Overcoming Thymotic Leadership

There are two negative types of leadership that thrive on the inordinate need for recognition: *thymotic* and *self-deprecating* leadership. Building on Plato's treatment of *thymos* (recognition, honor) in *The Republic*, David Brooks suggests that "All Politics Is Thymotic." Francis Fukuyama calls it *megalothymia*, the inordinate need for recognition and respect, the need to stand out as a symbol of prowess and power, to demand by height what one lacks in depth, to wrest from the other what one thinks is absent in oneself, and to find security in the obsequiousness of the other.[48] Martin Luther King Jr.'s famous sermon on recognition, titled "The Drum Major Instinct," reminds us that "we all want to be important, to surpass others, to achieve distinction, to lead the parade . . . this quest for recognition, this desire for attention, this desire for distinction is the basic impulse, the basic drive of human life, this drum major instinct."[49] The "drum major instinct" can have powerfully negative or positive consequences for leaders and those they serve.

Thymotic leaders fail to balance the drum major instinct. History is replete with leaders who possess drive, ambition, and promise but in the end fail miserably and hurt many because of the insatiable quest for recognition. Daniel Goleman and colleagues call this leadership type "the demagogue." Unlike resonant leaders who possess a refined sense of emotional intelligence, demagogues thrive on fear and anger, threats of "others" and "them" and what others may take from "us." Goleman writes, "Demagoguery casts its spell via destructive emotions, a range that squelches hope and optimism, as well as true innovation and creative imagination (as opposed to cruel cunning)."[50]

Ethical leadership posits demagoguery's opposite, inviting positive and creative exchanges through imaginative leaps of possibility anchored by the virtues of integrity, empathy, and hope. Thus, the development of *morally anchored* character becomes all the more important. The attending virtues of integrity, empathy, and hope are indispensable for ethically grounded leadership. Leaders in public life who have not cultivated a morally anchored character can do great damage to an organization, community, or society. Witness the recent revelations of impropriety, greed, deceit, and violence that mock our nation and world because of the unanchored "drum major instinct."

Thymotic leadership borders on madness. Olive Schreiner (1855–1920), the South African writer and a favorite resource for Thurman, says that once she dreamed that God took her soul to hell. Upon arrival she was astounded by its beauty and exclaimed, "I like this place." And God said, "Really!" As she proceeded further she noticed beautiful women everywhere wearing long flowing robes over their graceful bodies and tasting fruit from the trees. She noticed, however, that they never ate the fruit, but only touched it softly with their mouths and left it hanging on the tree. She asked God why they were only touching the fruit with their mouths but not eating it. God replied that they were really poisoning the fruit. She asked God, "Why are they doing that?" God said, "That another may not eat." She said, "But if they poison all then none dare eat; what do they gain?" God said, "Nothing." She asked, "Are they not afraid they themselves may bite where another has bitten?" God said, "They are afraid. In hell, all [people] are afraid."

She went a little further and noticed a group of men busily at work. She said, "I should like to go and work with them. Hell must be a very fruitful place, the grass is so green." God said, "Nothing grows in the garden they are making." She examined the workers more carefully and noticed they were working among the bushes digging holes, but set nothing in them; and when they were a way off they would hide in the bushes watching. She noticed that as each walked he set his foot down carefully, looking where he stepped. She asked God, "What are they doing?" God said, "Making pitfalls into which their fellows will fall." "Why are they doing this? How will he rise?" God answered, "He will not rise." And she saw their eyes gleam from behind the bushes. "Are these men sane?" she asked. God answered, *They are not sane; there is no sane person in hell.*[51]

Self-Deprecating Leadership

The other extreme of recognition is the leader who is *self-deprecating.* Self-deprecating leaders loathe public space and the recognition that accompanies it. They tend to acquiesce to power and are indecisive in respect to critical moments that demand responsibility and action. Sometimes being overly affiliative—always open to the emotions of others on one's team or in one's organization and offering praise when the moment requires critical feedback and accountability—self-deprecating leaders can actually derail an organization.[52] Just as thymotic leaders thrive on attention and recognition and often bite off more than they can chew, leaders who are self-deprecating tend to shy away from responsibility and any recognition that will draw attention to themselves. This does not mean, however, that they do not desire honor and recognition; in fact, they actually seek it through pleasing everybody.

Jerry B. Harvey calls this leadership challenge "the Abilene Paradox." Stated simply, when leaders and groups take actions in contradiction to what they really want to do in order to please one another, they defeat the purposes of what they are trying to achieve. Harvey suggests that managing conflict among groups may not be the greatest leadership challenge; rather, the inability to manage *agreement* may be the major source of organizational dysfunction. This cycle of dysfunctional civility in the organization begins with individual and private agreement about what is wrong and what steps should be made to correct the problem or situation, but members of the group fail to honestly communicate their desires and beliefs to one another. With inaccurate information and counterproductive actions, frustration peaks and antagonistic subgroups emerge and the result is dysfunction—not because of conflict, but because of the failure to manage agreement.[53] Leaders who are able to communicate their deepest convictions because they want to avoid conflict destroy morale and create climates of dishonesty and mistrust among teams. Even more tragically, they fail to recognize their own inherent worth and dignity by trying to please everybody and failing to speak their truth.

Neither extreme of *thymotic* or *self-deprecating* leadership will enable leaders to recognize the inherent dignity and value in the other or in themselves. A healthy sense of self, to use Thurman's language, is garnered out of a balance between self-fact and self-image. The point of balance is in finding the spiritual apex or summit, as in the Gothic design where the lofty idealism and the trenchant desire for recognition come together. In a striking meditation, "Shall I Be Good?" Thurman addresses this need for recognition. He asks, Shall I be good because of some reward? Because the virtuous act pays dividends?

> It is not enough to be good because of some reward, because the virtuous act pays dividends. The virtuous act may or may not pay dividends. In the last analysis, men cannot be persuaded to be good because of the reward either here or beyond this "vale of tears." Men must finally come to the place in their maturity which makes them do the good thing because it is *good*. Not because it is a command, even a divine command, but because the good deed, the good thought, the good life is in *itself* good. This is the strength of the good deed—that it is good. When this is our awareness, then the whole matter of reward and punishment, approval and disapproval, becomes strangely irrelevant.[54]

Respect

Respect is the public analogue of civility. In the perspective of civility I am proposing, respect has to do with the accepted standards of association of free people (citizens) and with social dignity. In this view, respect includes (1) a certain self-referential index that recognizes oneself as inhering and therefore deserving certain acknowledgments of one's human dignity in public space and (2) a responsibility to the other to demonstrate in public space one's obligation to the other as inhering and therefore deserving certain acknowledgments of human dignity. Fundamental to this twofold definition of respect is the relation between empathy and balance. In this view, Sara Lawrence-Lightfoot's excellent and creative exploration of respect as a nonhierarchical expression of human relationship is invaluable for the public task of ethical leadership. Lawrence-Lightfoot notes that respect is often viewed as "a debt due people because of their attained or inherited position, age, gender, class, race, professional status, accomplishments, etc. Whether defined by rules of law, habits, or culture, respect often implies required expressions of esteem, approbation, or submission." By contrast, her "focus is on the way respect creates symmetry, empathy, and connection in all kinds of relationships," which allows leaders to move beyond a strictly hierarchical, rules-based management model, but aspires to the cultivation of a moral ethos that creates balance, creativity, and imaginative enterprise.[55]

Leadership that holds at its center the social practice of civility as a moral and practical goal finds creative resonance with the features of respect cited by Lawrence-Lightfoot. An example from African American women's leadership practices is helpful. At the end of the nineteenth century and through the early twentieth century, one of the most effective communal leadership efforts was the Negro Women's Club Movement, which had its genesis in the black church tradition of protest and struggle. The movement, sometimes called "the politics of respectability," was at once a quest for civic virtue and a call to activism and political engagement. The idea of the politics of respectability is also related to our earlier discussion regarding *social capital*.

From its beginnings, the Negro Women's Club Movement was involved in suffrage, education and training, and social empowerment through its extensive networks of social capital that extended beyond its own communities. Black women leaders like Sojourner Truth, Mary Church Terrell, Frances Ellen Watkins Harper, Ida B. Wells, and Mary McLeod Bethune were able to move between socially constructed worlds of race, class, and gender and to create opportunities for their people. At the heart of their activism was a strident faith in respect as a social good and in respect as a moral and practical obligation.

The Negro Women's Club Movement, like its successors in the modern civil rights movement, created "bridge leaders." According to Belinda Robnett, these women, though excluded from formal leadership roles, formed their own tightly knit corps of leaders who were able to "operate in the movement's free spaces, thus making connections" that could not be made by formal leaders, and had "greater leadership mobility in nonhierarchical structures and institutions." In their capacity as bridge leaders, these "women were not simply organizers in the civil rights movement but were critical mobilizers of civil rights activities."[56] Political scientist Frederick C. Harris refers to this distinctive phenomenon as "the dualistic orientation of black oppositional civic culture." Harris captures in this statement the paradoxical strivings of black leaders that combine the quest for social dignity with political activism. Throughout the modern civil rights movement, this dualistic orientation of black oppositional civic culture provided black leadership with the critical skills and competencies to wage an unorthodox campaign against social inferiority and segregated status. James H. Evans has argued that this quest for respect is part and parcel of the black church tradition and serves as the theological rationale for the larger question of honor and grace.[57]

This view of respectability critiques the ways in which exclusively rules-based ethics violate the fundamental quest for social dignity and empowerment sought by leaders in this tradition. Respect has to do with personal and social boundaries that rest on the moral inviolability of human beings. The famous chant "R-E-S-P-E-C-T, find out what it means to me," made popular by Aretha Franklin, is both an invitation and a warning to those who would dare violate the sanctity of individual and collective space. When people feel disrespected by leaders, they may not respond openly but will find ways to retaliate, often by performing poorly and creating dysfunctional environments. Leaders have the obligation to demonstrate that those with whom they work deserve certain acknowledgments of human dignity in organizational life and culture. Such leadership stresses nonhierarchical associations that breed and nurture equal dignity and freedom of individuals in relationships that perceive power as opportunity for empathy and respect. The implications for creating diversity within organizations and society as a whole are far-reaching and potentially revolutionary.

There are two extremes that leaders must learn to keep in balance as related to respect—*self-respect* and *respect for others*. For leaders in public space, this means learning to respect oneself as part of the larger fabric of civil society—one's gifts, talents, and skills but also one's unique position as a citizen with certain rights and responsibilities to the collective good. Leaders who are engaged in public life, especially political leaders, often see their role in narrow visions of self-interest or group interests. But respect as a civic good also involves the need to understand what values guide decisions and actions as related to one's self-acknowledgment as a citizen, and how these values are related to larger complex issues that collide at the intersection.

Fannie Lou Hamer's activism in the civil right's movement illustrates this idea of balance of self-respect and respect for others. Any small estimate of the indignities she was subjected to as child growing up in the Mississippi Delta and later as an adult would make it difficult for most to understand how she was able to maintain a healthy sense of self-respect and still not only demand her citizenship but also struggle for the dignity and respect of others, both black and white. Poorly educated, living in black tenancy for over forty years, she rose from picking cotton to picking presidents. In Winona, Mississippi, Fannie Lou Hamer, Annelle Ponder, and fourteen year-old June Johnson were jailed and beaten mercilessly after attending a voter registration campaign sponsored by the Student Nonviolent Coordinating Committee in the summer of 1963. Hamer suffered permanent kidney damage and loss of sight in her left eye from the beatings. While white officers looked on, two black male inmates were forced to beat her with a blackjack until they were exhausted. "I had been beat 'til I was real hard, just hard like a piece of wood or somethin'," Hamer would later say. "A person don't know what can happen to they body if they beat with something like I was beat with."[58] Despite concerted and violent efforts to curtail her transformative practices of civility, Hamer became a field secretary for the Student Nonviolent Coordinating Committee and later served as the vice-chair of the Mississippi Freedom Democratic Party. In 1971, six years before her death, she said:

> My whole fight is for the liberation of all people because no man is an island to himself; when a white child is dying, is being shot, there's a little bit of America being destroyed. When it is a black child shot in America, it is a little bit of America being destroyed. If they keep it up, a little of this going, and a little of that going, one day, this country will crumble. But we have to try to see to it that not only the lives of young and adult blacks are saved but also whites.[59]

Ella Josephine Baker's long and fruitful career of organizing and mobilizing groups around issues of justice was rooted in this deep sense of respectability. Heralded by many as the "midwife" of the Southern Christian Leadership Conference (SCLC) and the Student Nonviolent Coordinating Committee (SNCC), Baker's grassroots organizing and leadership in the civil rights movement spanned more than four decades as she participated in more than fifty different organizations and campaigns for freedom and justice. One of the distinguishing characteristics of her philosophy of organizing, which she referred to as "group-centered leadership," was the value she placed on *respect*. Ms. Baker practiced self-respect and demanded respect from and for others. Her work in organizing SNCC was an example of the respect that she insisted upon from and for students in the movement. According to SNCC activists like Bob Moses:

> It was Ella more than anyone else who gave us the space to operate in. As long as she was sitting there in the meetings, no one else could dare come in and say I think you should do this or that, because no one could pull rank on her. Her stature was such that there wasn't anyone from the NAACP to Dr. King who could get by her. I think that the actual course of the SNCC movement is a testimony to the fact that the students were

left free to develop on their own. Baker's support of Moses and other movement leaders proved indispensable on more than one occasion.[60]

In addition to Bob Moses, Baker's leadership and practice of respect found fertile ground in an entire generation of leaders like Julian Bond, Diane Nash, Stokely Carmichael, Curtis Muhammad, and Bernice Johnson Reagon, for whom the principled demand for respect was and, for some, is unmistakably rooted in their public witness and character.

Hamer's and Baker's quests for respect are emblematic of a larger question that confronts leaders in our national life and in the movement for democratization throughout the world. Fundamentalists of all creeds, on the right and the left, demand that there is only one way in which to understand the truth: their way. Much of the debate surrounding large-scale moral issues, such as abortion and gay marriage, emanate from this jostling of positions on what is *right*. Respect and empathy for the other, however, demand that we find common ground. Common ground, however, is not reached by simply arguing for the "rightness" of one moral perspective or the other—there must be inserted into the equation the possibility that one's moral perspective may not be absolutely right—and that perhaps another perspective might add light to a far more complex set of circumstances. Respect for the other demands that leaders assume a posture of humility. Oswald W. S. McCall's meditation on humility is instructive:

> There is humility by which the angels see, and no mind can perceive God, or man, or any truth without it. Eschew contempt. The mind's nobleness never lives where there is not reverence, neither does the mind's light. But reverence has its roots in humility, the last grace and the first essential of the noble mind.
>
> God himself cannot teach a proud man. Conceit would not recognize God if it saw Him.
>
> Pride strode down the middle of the road and met Patience. Pride said, "That fellow has a poor spirit." Pride met Purity, and nodded approval. "A cunning means to an end!" he said. He met Truth. "What deformity is this?" said Pride, and suddenly came upon Love. Then he buttoned up his pockets, edging away with suspicion. But when God Almighty stepped out to tell Pride that he had looked at everything and seen nothing, Pride drew himself up until he towered over God and said, "Who are you, little fellow? Get out of my way."[61]

Senator Barack Obama's speech at the Call to Renewal's "Building a Covenant for a New America" conference is an excellent example of the challenge to reach common ground through respect and empathy for the other. He said, "Democracy demands that the religiously motivated translate their concerns into universal, rather than religion-specific values. It requires that their proposals be subject to argument, and amenable to reason." He closed with a personal account of his own need to listen to the other with empathy and respect. During his bid for the Senate, he received an email from a doctor at the University of Chicago Medical School congratulating him on his primary win and saying that he had voted for him but was considering not casting his vote for Obama in the general election because he had read an entry on his website that said Obama would fight "right-wing ideologues who want to take away a woman's right to choose." The doctor, Obama suggested, was opposed to abortion and gay marriage, but was also against what he called the "idolatry of the free market and quick resort to militarism that seemed to characterize much of the Republican agenda." He felt that Obama had demonstrated a strong sense of justice but that the way in which the website addressed the pro-life question was not fair-minded. Obama said that he reviewed the website and agreed that the words "right-wing ideologues" did appear to be less than fair-minded (at least in the doctor's case). He said, "Re-reading the doctor's letter, though, I felt a pang of shame. It is people like him who are looking for a deeper, fuller conversation about religion in this country. They may not change their positions, but they are willing to listen and learn from those who are willing to speak in fair-minded words. Those who know of the central and awesome place that God holds in the lives of so many, and who refuse to treat faith as simply another political issue with which to score points." So he wrote back to the doctor and thanked him for his advice. The next day, he circulated the email to his staff and changed the language on his website to state in clear but simple terms his pro-choice position. That night, before he went to bed, he said a prayer of his own—a prayer that he might extend the same presumption of good faith to others that the doctor had extended to him. He said, "It's a prayer I think I share with a lot of Americans. A hope that we can live with one another in a way that reconciles the beliefs of each with the good of all. It's a prayer worth praying, and a conversation worth having in this country in the months and years to come."[62]

Similarly, leaders who seek to bring about democratic reform in developing nations learn early that creative change and transformation must be grounded in recognition, and respect for differences inherent in the complex histories and cultures of others. Anthony Appiah has suggested that "a tenable global ethics has to temper a respect for difference with a respect for the freedom of actual human beings to make their own choices. That's why cosmopolitans don't insist that everyone become cosmopolitan. They know they don't have all the answers. They're humble enough to think that they might learn from strangers; not too humble to think that strangers can't learn from them."[63] Ethical leaders like Obama and Hamer teach us that humility is not a liability but the pathway to greatness.

Reverence

Reverence is preceded by loyalty. One of the supreme tests of civility has been and continues to be the question of *loyalty*. Loyalty to a business, organization, bureaucracy, or even to national policy can create serious ethical dilemmas for leaders. The dilemma is how leaders reconcile contending demands for loyalty: the inclusive moral demand of one's own moral vision versus the often contradicting demands of polity, race, ethnicity, sexuality, and nation. Loyalty is not easily defined. Josiah Royce's definition of loyalty as "the willing and practical and thoroughgoing devotion of a person to a cause"[64] captures the basic intent of what is meant here by the term. Nonetheless, *loyalty* is one of those elusive terms like *love* because it is attached to something profoundly spiritual. Notice that Royce speaks of persons as being loyal, but loyalty is also found among animals. We often speak of the loyalty of dogs. As any dog owner knows, the loyalty of a dog is actually more trustworthy and consistent than the loyalty of friends. Is this because dogs tend not to discriminate or lack levels of awareness that humans possess? Perhaps, though some loyal dog owners might disagree.

Loyalty in its most fundamental sense is a discipline of informed consent of the will to a higher cause to which the leader seeks union within the self and with others. But loyalty, for the ethical leader, does not seek confirmation from external events or rewards, but finds its genesis and apotheosis in the integrity of the cause to which the leader is committed. Loyalty begins with the integrity of the act—behavior that is an outflow of one's personal commitment to truth that finds rational correspondence with the vision of the hopeful. At its core are the discipline of freedom—freedom of the will and emotions—and the leader's attachment to the goal or end to be achieved. A quote by Howard Thurman synthesizes the related dynamics of cognitive, affective, and behavioral responses to the role of freedom in the quest for loyalty: "The secret is the quiet inner purpose and release of vitality with which it inspires the act. Achieving the goal is not measured by some external standard, though such must not be completely ignored. Rather, it is measured in terms of *loyalty* to the purpose and the freedom which it inspires."[65]

Personal freedom is a guide to the integrity of loyalty in that it places before the leader the hard work of discipline and mastery of the head and the heart. The critical consideration for our purposes is how loyalty as an ethical principle helps to establish a basis for civility. But civility, as we have noted, can be dysfunctional and destructive. Leaders who have committed their loyalty to a particular belief system, as in religion or nationhood, can do as great harm as good. Much depends on the aim of one's values and hopes. The Hitlers and Mussolinis of the world are easy examples, but in the contemporary contexts of public life, the examples are not easily located. How might we begin to understand the opposing loyalties to the questions of Palestinian homeland and the state of Israel? The historical contingencies of the debate are complex and rife with controversy. But "most conflicts don't arise from warring values,"[66] but from long and complicated histories that converge at the intersection. Questions of loyalty are always particularized in competing visions of the good unless there is an agreement or a commitment to *understanding* that involves looking, listening, and learning from the other. Such a process requires a type of revolutionary patience that is not concerned primarily with time as a measured, calculative constraint. Yet this kind of patience proceeds from another place that transcends loyalty and seeks a spiritual unity of consciousness that serves as a vision of the possible and a critique of present affairs. Such a spiritual unity of consciousness is founded on *reverence for life*.

Albert Schweitzer popularized the idea of reverence for life as an ethical demand. Reverence for life, for Schweitzer, meant a type of ethics that would reconcile egotism and altruism by demanding respect for all human beings and by seeking the highest development of each individual.[67] Schweitzer believed reverence for life was the highest calling of human beings, and because all are a part of life that exhibits what he called "will-to-live," then it is our moral obligation to participate as expressions of that life and to hold in reverence the high calling that life itself has placed upon us. Schweitzer's ethical perspective is born out of a deeply spiritual reflection on and involvement in nature, in which all living beings, human and nonhuman, participate. He writes:

Ethics consist in my experiencing the compulsion to show to all will-to-live the same reverence as I do my own. *A man is truly ethical only when he obeys the compulsion to help all life which he is able to assist, and shrinks from injuring anything that lives.* If I save an insect from a puddle, life has devoted itself to life, and the division of life against itself has ended. Whenever my life devotes itself in any way to life, my finite will-to-live experiences union with the infinite will in which all life is one" [emphasis added].[68]

This insistence on the ethical life begins with the individual's commitment or loyalty to the reverence for life. But in the complex dynamics of social life, how might the leader use this maxim as a guide for decision-making? Jim Wallis speaks to this social, political, and religious ideal in what he calls "the consistent ethic of life" and the dilemma it creates in respect to the question of public values. The question for Wallis is not what political allegiance best serves one's particular conception of values but how one's faith, critically understood, best addresses the larger questions of war, poverty, and race. God, says Wallis, is neither Democratic nor Republican; and on questions of deeply held beliefs about the sacredness of life, one should espouse a "consistent ethic of life."[69]

A "consistent ethic of life," however, is fraught with multifaceted challenges at the intersections of religiously inspired and politically problematic issues like abortion. How does one discern, deliberate, and decide on such issues and maintain a consistent ethic of life? A critical dimension of this problem for leaders is which ethical theories and practices best address the question of consistency. Can one claim to be against abortion and yet ignore weightier issues of war, poverty, and social injustice? Shall one adopt a universal ethic that says that in all cases and at all times, killing is morally wrong? Or should one approach this issue as a utilitarian value that serves the greater good, which implies that in some instances killing is justified? How does one apply sacred scriptures, reason, experience, and tradition in explicating and supporting moral decisions? In my perspective, the challenge of loyalty to reverence must find a home in respect to the morally anchored character of leaders who are part of a certain kind of community of discourse and practice, especially those who will be responsible for helping others think through these delicate and terribly significant public issues. In this sense, ethical decision-making does not rely exclusively on rationalist, realist, retooler, and relationalist perspectives but seeks validation within a community that is "constitutive of the shared self-understandings of the participants and embodied in institutional arrangements" that require *courage* and that aspire to a sense of *justice* and *compassion*.[70]

In summary, the spiritual unity that loyalty seeks finds it fullest expression in reverence for life. Leaders should not, therefore, allow their loyalties to kin, nation, or even religious beliefs to supersede the ethic of reverence for life. But at a deeper level, reverence for life appeals to something that is fundamentally human that seeks ultimate unity with what some mystics have called "the Larger Life."[71] The Larger Life finds affinity with *a sense of community*. As we shall discuss at length, as a rational construct, community is the ideal that serves as the goal of human existence and the norm for ethical judgment. But at the affective dimension, a *sense* of community is the inherent sense of belonging to and knowing that proceeds from the matrix of all things. It is the connectedness with what physicist Fritjof Capra calls "the web of life" and what others have called "deep ecology."[72] We are all caught in the web—no body is free until all bodies are free. Such a vision of community flies in the face of the rationalistic, profit-maximizing individualism that is at the heart of our problematic. In simple terms, leadership at the intersection demands that, as my good friend Malidoma Patrice Somé puts it, "if you want to get home, then you must give the other a ride."

Moreover, to dare to lead at the intersection where worlds collide demands that one embrace a vision of the possible, a hopeful future. There is, quite frankly, no other way to remain sane and humane without a vision of what Abraham Heschel called "the Possibility of Possibility" or what Howard Thurman referred to as "the Growing Edge."[73] Thurman reminds us that always at work, underneath the myriad appearances of failure and tragedy, is a "growing edge" that transcends the contradictions of life and melds them into the harmonious purposes of the universe.

In many respects, Martin Luther King Jr.'s prophetic vision of the World House mirrors what we have in mind with the idea of reverence that sees the interrelatedness and inherent value of all life. It was his sense of community that led him to identify the great new problem of humankind as the challenge of divided loyalties: loyalty to the particularized and local visions of race, ethnicity, and the state versus the demand for global community:

> We have inherited a large house, a great 'world house' in which we have to live together—black and white, Easterner and Westerner, Gentile and Jew, Catholic and Protestant, Moslem and Hindu—a family unduly separated in ideas, culture and interest, who, because we can never again live apart, must learn somehow to live together with each other in peace.[74]

For King, the remedy for this problem of loyalty was a "revolution of values and priorities." At the heart of such a revolution is the question of loyalty. "A genuine revolution of values means in the final analysis that our loyalties must become ecumenical rather than sectional. Every nation must now develop an overriding loyalty to mankind [*sic*] as a whole in order to preserve the best in our individual societies." King suggested that this spiritual revolution would lift us beyond tribe, race, class, and nation to a worldwide fellowship of love.[75] At once, in this singular vision of reverence and possibility, King articulated the dream of the beloved community in which civility was inspired and supported within the context of global communion. Many believe he was speaking in many languages as the Spirit gave utterance— languages that speak in loving and just ways to the agonizing yet redemptive possibilities inherent in recognition, respectability, and reverence toward a beloved community more grand than even the nation can ever hope for—*a new heaven and a new earth.*

Similarly, for Thurman, the question of loyalty finds its fullest expression in the dilemma of nationalism and reverence for life. Stated in social and political terms, the modern state, according to Thurman, has tremendous power over the individuals who make up the common life. It manifests this power in three important ways: the state assumes a transcendent role and becomes an object of religious devotion; it gives the individual citizen an integrated basis for her behavior so that there is always a normative standard that enables her to determine when she is out of community; and the notion of the state carries with it the idea of a collective and transcendent destiny, thus reaffirming during crises the individual's sense of belonging to and participating in something greater than herself.[76] According to Thurman, the transcendent character of the state and the religious loyalty that it inspires and demands have been a major problem for the United States. He felt that the unreconciled conflict between loyalty to God and loyalty to the state is responsible for the American church's silence on issues of racism, segregation, and war. This thesis has serious implications for the American civil religion debate and for Christians who wave the flag higher than they hold the cross.[77]

A critical concern for the state, according to Thurman, is the presence of minorities who exist as "outsiders" in the midst of "insiders." Minorities are required to honor the same demands of sovereignty but are denied the basic rewards of that allegiance. This creates two pressing problems for the state: it creates a condition of guilt in the collective consciousness of the society that threatens the vitality of the body politic; and it fosters an environment of power politics between world states that compete for the loyalties of minority groups.[78] Thurman believed the greatest challenge for the state, particularly the United States, was to create a social environment in which the individual and minorities have an authentic sense of belonging to the society. Such a climate would be one in which each person has the opportunity to actualize his or her potential, "thereby experiencing community within himself as part and parcel of the experience of community within the State."[79] How leaders at the intersection of worlds colliding begin to address these and other concerns of loyalty and reverence as part of our civic life—but, more important, as fellow human beings—is the subject of community.

✦ Chapter Five

COMMUNITY AT THE INTERSECTION

THE QUEST FOR COMMUNITY

The quest for community, like character and civility, has a long and ambivalent history in American society. Since its founding, the nation has struggled with the antagonistic twins of self-reliance and community.[1] Correspondingly, Americans have exhibited schizophrenic behavior regarding what constitutes its primary values: liberty and equality. The language of liberty is generally situated within the moral authority of the individual and self-reliance. Equality, on the other hand, typically emphasizes sociality and the moral authority of the collective. These contending values, however, are not mutually exclusive, but finding the balance between them has been one of the greatest challenges to American democracy. The American obsession with self-reliance, liberty, and individualism has created another dynamic that actually undermines its moral vision of community. During his mid-nineteenth-century observations of a youthful American republic experimenting with democracy, Alexis de Tocqueville noted in *La Démocratie en Amérique* (II 4.6) the irony of individualism and the inbred anesthetizing conformity that would mock the grand dream of community in America in the years to come: "I see an innumerable crowd of similar and equal men who compete among themselves to procure small and vulgar pleasures."

Tocqueville also saw in this early picture of American competitive individualism a paradox of sorts—the spirit of creative individuality that nurtured the moral ethos of democracy also gave birth to another phenomenon that complicated the inherent possibility of democratic culture. Growing alongside this quest for individual fulfillment, exemplified in the

American quest for community, is a kind of servitude:

> ordered, mild and peaceable . . . , a singular power, tutelary, all-encom-
> passing, [acting through] a system of complicated minor rules, minuscule
> and uniform, which do not break the spirit but soften it, bend and direct
> it; it rarely forces action, but continually sets up resistance to action; it
> does not destroy, but prevents birth; it does not tyrannize, but inhibits,
> compromises, enervates, subdues, stupefies, and ends by reducing each
> nation to being nothing more than a herd of timid, industrious animals
> of whom the government is the shepherd.[2]

Ralph Waldo Emerson's 1841 essay "Self-Reliance" echoes a similar pronouncement: "Society everywhere is in conspiracy against the manhood of every one of its members. Society is a joint-stock company, in which the members agree, for the better of securing of his bread to each shareholder, to surrender the liberty and culture of the eater. The virtue in most requests is conformity. Self-reliance is its aversion. It loves not realities and creators, but names and customs."[3] Emerson's and Tocqueville's concern was with the encroachment of a rational bureaucratic culture reinforced and perpetuated by the state. The conformity of the individual to the mass values of the herd was for them both a warning and a prophecy of what was to come.

Closely related to the intrusion of the state was the fusion of religion and bourgeois values that persist in contemporary public debates across political divisions. The "Protestant anxiety" to secure grace and favor from God through self-reliance and industry informed the habits and practices of many loyal citizens. Ronald Takaki describes the development of the dilemma in this manner:

> The fusion of Protestant asceticism and republican theory provided the
> ideology for bourgeois acquisitiveness and modern capitalism in the
> United States. The seventeenth-century belief in the covenant of grace
> had made it possible for the Puritan to affirm God's omnipotence while
> he strived to demonstrate he had outward signs of salvation. This Prot-
> estant anxiety—the need to know how one had been predestined and
> to do good works and diligently follow one's calling—led ironically to
> the erosion of piety itself. Good works resulted often enough in worldly
> goods and a concern for the here rather than the hereafter. Eighteenth
> century republicanism accelerated this thrust toward commodity accu-
> mulation and the primacy of the marketplace, as it disintegrated the

feudal order and freed men as individuals to prove their virtue in the pursuit of possessions.[4]

The rise of the modern state and the ever-incessant quest for the freedom of the individual as a moral and political construction combined to create a rules-based ethic that actually conspires against self-reliance, liberty, and equality. These values are rooted in communities of discourse and practice that are part of lifeworlds, and it is the lifeworlds of connectedness, networks of reciprocity, and social relations that sustain key values of civil society. The moral languages of rights and utility that belong to the systemworlds of politics and markets are totally inappropriate to serve as moral educators for civil society. In real terms, the dire prophecies of Emerson and Tocqueville meant the extinction of civil society.

I agree with contemporary theorists like Jean Bethke Elstain who call for a "revivification of civil society,"[5] not in opposition to or rejection of the state—a tamed government is a good thing to have around—but a civil society that is attentive to and suspicious of the power of the state. As we have discussed, civil society consists of the public space where citizens meet, discuss, and act upon what they know and value. At stake for leaders in the "revivification of civil society" is the need to address the converging languages of "rights" and "utility" at the intersections where worlds collide. But how is this done, given that the languages of rights and utility flow from the common feature of individualism and competitive enterprise mentioned above?

A point of departure is to begin with the moral language of community, which arises from the traditions, institutions, and social practices of civility that have historically nurtured and sustained our democracy but with important twists. Such a departure involves a community of memory, but not necessarily the communities of memory that have been the dominant voices in the making of America. The memories of John Winthrop's "City on a Hill," Thomas Jefferson's "Notes on the State of Virginia," or Walt Whitman's "I Sing America" will not suffice for a fuller and more accurate retelling of the American story. Now more than ever, we need to hear from the underside of our story—the voices and visions, indeed the stories that may provide new insight into the challenges that we face at the intersection. America is a nation of immigrants, people from many different shores, some who arrived voluntarily and others who arrived without choice. (As Sweet Honey in the Rock sings, some of us waved at the Statue of Liberty but she did not wave back at us.) What about these communities whose memories retell stories of yearning and hope in the promise of democracy only to be denied, but who again and again refuse to submit to second-class citizenship? What are the habits and practices of these who speak from the bottom of the well? What have they to say about courage, justice, and compassion as the spiritual bedrock of the democratic life and culture? What do they have to say that might help us to reshape the meaning of America?

Leaders from these traditions have unique stories to tell about the past, present, and future of democracy in America. Leaders who come from places on the periphery with distinctive perspectives provide lenses that dare to see kaleidoscopic visions of America's future in a world where difference and the jagged edges of history collide at the intersection. One of our greatest challenges is that we are continually discovering that traditional understandings of leadership without a diverse community of memory that informs ethical orientation are bereft of authority and influence. Questions of the good, beautiful, and just are spinning at astronomical speeds in our culture, and there is great anxiety about lost values and the need to return to the past for direction. Amid religiously inspired debates about values and political jostling to leverage advantage, Americans are asking, "Which way is north?" But "Which way is north?" is a highly relative question. For those who stand at different places with very different stories, north for some may appear as south. In fact, the ground has shifted with respect to the question of traditional morals and values and how they inform direction at the intersection.

Most of these discussions on the future of America point toward the individual as the source and director of the moral compass,[6] with emphasis on the classical Western tradition as the narrative repository of virtue. William Bennett's companion volumes *The Book of Virtues: A Treasury of Great Moral Stories* and *The Moral Compass: Stories for a Life's Journey* or Michael Mandelbaum's *The Case for Goliath* are examples of this approach. While these are helpful approaches, they also run the risk of insinuating leaders in a normative gaze that is exclusive and antithetical to a diverse, multicultural consideration of values.[7]

There is a story of a new preacher who arrived in town and needed to find a post office. So he stepped out onto the street and discovered two little boys in front of the church shooting craps. He approached them and asked, "Young men, can you direct me to the post office?" One of the young men replied immediately, "Sure, Reverend. Go to the end of the street, turn left, and you will walk right into it. Can't miss it." The preacher thanked the young man for the directions—and then contemplated the situation before him and reasoned that this was an excellent evangelistic prospect. So he turned to the young men and said, "Young men, I would like to show you the way to heaven." One of the little boys responded, "Pardon me, Reverend, but how can you show us the way to heaven and you don't know the way to the post office?"

Asking for direction from faces and places we did not expect is a humbling experience. Leaders at the intersection, however, must become accustomed to and comfortable with asking for help from those who traditionally have been neglected and despised. I am convinced that if there is any hope for the American Tower of Babel, it will come from "the stones that the builders rejected." Implied, of course, in this bold assertion is that the ways we have come to think about leadership need to be redefined. Xenophobic practices have a long and sordid history in our culture. John Hope Franklin, the great historian, reports that as early as the founding of the nation, Benjamin Banneker, the African American astronomer and mathematician, sent Thomas Jefferson a copy of his almanac with a terse reprimand that he and all others must "wean yourselves from those narrow prejudices which you have imbibed."[8] Weaning ourselves from our narrow prejudices and presuppositions about power will require a radical reconstruction of cultural memory with an attendant revolution of values and priorities and a politics of conversion.

One of the challenges we will increasingly face will be how this country accommodates new leadership from places that were not a part of the original blueprint. The contemporary debate on immigration policies provides a sobering look at the deep and abiding fissures that plague narrow and myopic visions of leadership. Immigration is an issue not just of what constitutes citizenship, desert, and entitlement in our democracy, but of who will lead. In the late fifties, John F. Kennedy in *A Nation of Immigrants* wrote, "Immigration policy should be generous; it should be fair; it should be flexible. . . . With such a policy, we can turn to the world and to our own past with clean hands and a clear conscience. . . . The immigrants we welcome today and tomorrow will carry on this tradition and help us to retain, reinvigorate, and strengthen the American spirit."[9]

Our notion of democracy, by its very nature and history, suggests that our borders are always expanding and are ever inclusive. And so it must be with leadership—ever expanding, becoming more and more inclusive and respectful of the other. Leaders at the intersection will need to respond to the question of the other with recognition, respect, and reverence.

Recognition is a critical issue for leaders who are concerned about democracy. In order for a strong, vibrant democracy to exist and to expand, leaders must be willing to see the other in all of his or her differences. More important, recognition of the other begins with recognition of self and our relatedness with the other. History has marked us all in some very strange and trying ways, but to render the other as invisible and to marginalize certain individuals and groups as untouchables speaks volumes about how we see ourselves.

Respect, like recognition, sees difference but accepts its right to peacefully coexist. But respect adds another critical dimension for leaders to ponder. Respect also means the other, however defined, has inherent worth and dignity and consequently deserves treatment as an equal. Respect that does not anticipate justice, as in fairness and equity, does not deserve the name. Human beings can coexist and conduct themselves civilly even if they can't stand one another—this is the nature of our social contract with others in civil society. We can hate, but we do not have the right to exclude, maim, injure, or kill the other because we disagree.

There is yet another step that ethical leaders must be prepared to take in reference to the other. Ethical leaders must come to a place where their relationship with the other extends beyond respect but to a place where they see that the inherent worth and dignity of the other is like their own. In other words, ethical leaders must see the possibility of a human mosaic—in all its difference, like shattered pieces of glass, broken and uneven but beautifully arranged—that allows us to move beyond respect and to seek spiritual unity and reverence for life. As the second-century playwright and former North African slave Terence wrote, "I am human: nothing human is alien to me." This is an important step toward learning reverence for the other. All great religious and moral traditions insist that the other is a precious creation that is interrelated with our own personhood and journey.

What a revelation it is to discover not only the values that we hold in common, but that values that are very different from our own can have their own integrity—and that different values and the conflict they engender can provide new and refreshing ways of seeing ourselves and others as part of a larger experiment in living together. If we are to "retain, reinvigorate, and strengthen the American spirit," there must be an "ethic for strangers" that extends beyond conventional understandings of hospitality.

The old African American spiritual my father loved says, "I'm going to sit at the Welcome Table, I'm going to sit at the Welcome Table one of these days!" Years ago, I was invited to preach at a church, but for some reason, the "word" would not come. Nearly an hour before I was to present, that old song came to me in Daddy's voice: *"I'm going to sit at the Welcome Table one of these days!"* The refrain called me back to memory. I remembered my family's flight from Mississippi. My daddy was a sharecropper, and he had an altercation with his boss-man, Mr. Joe Hand, and had to leave in a hurry. He later sent for my mother and three siblings to join him in the Promised Land of Chicago. The rest of that story was written in the pain and travail of a displaced black Southerner in a hostile urban environment to which he was never reconciled. I sang my sermon that morning in the old way, long meters, dragging the melody until the words bled into one another and rested in the hollow caverns of our throats.

> I'm going to sit at the Welcome Table,
> I'm going to sit at the Welcome Table one of these days.

Far beyond the inherited and distorted Anglo creeds and evangelical formulae of salvation American style, that melody shook up calcified memories and the Spirit walked the aisles and touched two other displaced Southerners sitting in the congregation. At the close of the service, they met me at the door and related to me their story of Frogbottom, Mississippi. They reported that only a week earlier, Daddy's boss-man's son had burned his wife in the fields where my family once worked. Daddy wanted me to remember.[10]

To sit at the Welcome Table requires that the hosts do more than bring out the traditional eating utensils, settings, and arrangements for guests. Rather, it means providing chopsticks and eating tortillas and *injera*, restructuring the seating arrangements, allowing the stranger to participate in constructing the recipe and preparing different dishes—in other words, allowing the other to become a leader with us.

The poet Langston Hughes, while not denying his estrangement from American society, embraces the possibility of the Welcome Table:

> I, too, sing America.
> I am the darker brother.
> They send me to eat in the kitchen
> When company comes,
> But I laugh,
> And eat well,
> And grow strong.

Tomorrow,
I'll sit at the table
When company comes.
Nobody'll dare
Say to me,
"Eat in the kitchen,"
Then.

Besides,
They'll see how beautiful I am
and be ashamed—

I, too, am America.[11]

At the intersection of worlds colliding and values shifting to conspire against the cluster of norms and values we like to remember as once constituting the founding of our nation, we must ask, What is America, after all? Is it the failed chronicle of history-makers credited with the founding of a nation-state—Washington, Adams, Hamilton, Jefferson, and so on, the great white men of the American time-line leading to Ronald Reagan? Or are the true history-makers the marginalized "who stand outside the time-line and every head-line"? Does America go on forever?[12] What is the meaning of America? If we hear only from the great white male leaders, then America means certain ways of living in the world, but if we could hear from the voices of the marginalized, then America might mean something quite different. Hughes speaks again for these voices when he writes, "America never was America to me."

Let America be America again.
Let it be the dream it used to be.
Let it be the pioneer on the plain
Seeking a home where he himself is free.

(America never was America to me.)

Let America be the dream the dreamers dreamed—
Let it be the strong land of love
Where never kings connive nor tyrants scheme
That any man be crushed by one above.

(It never was America to me.)[13]

If we really hear the poet's refrain, then we might better understand the disputed remarks of Michelle Obama during the Democratic primary on February 18, 2008, in Madison, Wisconsin: "For the first time in my adult lifetime, I'm really proud of my country, and not just because Barack has done well, but because I think people are hungry for change." Entangled in the mythology of American progress is the spurious premise that the founders of this nation intended a society that has compassion for all. Part of the reckoning that must take place in the unraveling of this shroud of innocence is to come to grips with our history—the underside of our story, the story of a people as diverse as the world, yet bound by an ethic of exclusiveness and individualism. Leadership in this century cannot repeat this error without dire consequences. Ethical leadership not only recognizes difference but also respects the differences that others present in the larger narrative of democracy. Even more, ethical leadership embraces the possibility of America and the world as a place where reverence for life informs our direction and vision of "north." Reverence for life, as we will discuss, is really about a sense of community, the third component of the Ethical Leadership Model.

A Sense of Community

A sense of community represents the spiritual dimension in the tripartite model of ethical leadership. Community as a rational construction is the ideal that serves as the goal of human existence and the norm for ethical judgment. Concretely expressed, it is the mutually cooperative and voluntary venture of persons in which they realize the solidarity of humanity by freely assuming responsibility for one another within the context of civil relations. The work of ethical leadership, therefore, begins with community as both the source and the end of all practices associated with the development of leaders. As mentioned above, integrity—as a sense of wholeness, integration, and balance—is the work of community within self. One can hardly hope to create community in the world without first looking deeply within the self and discovering the challenges of creating a healthy sense of self. Furthermore, community provides the context for the sensuous articulation of the values of compassion, justice, and courage as dynamic and interrelated practices. As described by Howard Thurman and Martin Luther King Jr., community refers to a sense of unity and interdependence with nature as a whole; the centrality of civil society in the development of self-worth and affirmation; community occurring as a network of extended families; and other institutions as media through which the individual shares his or her sense of self and belonging—a common ground upon which the diversity of people and/or ideas and values can unite in a spiritual reality that is unmarked by separateness and differences.[14]

For our purposes, community refers to *wholeness, integration,* and *harmony.* Fundamental to this definition of community is the goal-seeking nature of life itself. According to Howard Thurman, all of life is involved in goal-seeking. In each manifestation of life, there is potential for it to realize its proper form or to come to itself. The actualization of any form of life is synonymous with community. Community as "actualized potential" is true at all levels of life, from tiny cells to human society.[15]

The significance of community for self and civil society is the primary concern of our model for the development of ethical leadership. A healthy sense of self is intricately related to the interaction between self and society. In respect to this interactive model of self and society, the quest for personal identity is inextricably bound to the quest for wholeness, harmony, and integration in society. Our model seeks to engage participants in the quest for community at personal and social levels through the production of their own rituals or creative exercises. The primary questions are: How do we create and maintain a responsible and respectful relationship with each other in the quest for community, and how does this model relate to the broader and critical issues of ethical leadership that have been already discussed? There are three attendant practices or *virtuosities* that define community: personal and social quests for courage, justice, and compassion.

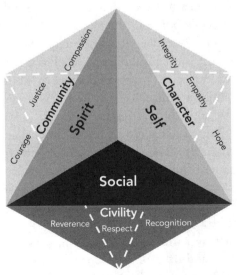

FIGURE 4. THE ETHICAL LEADERSHIP MODEL™

THE DEFINING VIRTUES, VALUES, AND VIRTUOSITIES OF CHARACTER, CIVILITY, AND COMMUNITY

Courage

Courage is considered a virtue by nearly every ancient philosopher. For Plato, courage was rooted in the tripartite construction of the self and the state and it was guided by reason, *knowing* what not to fear. Aristotle wrote that "courage is the first of human qualities because it is the quality which guarantees the others."[16] It is no small accident that the ancients located courage around the heart. Courage is a balanced coordination of both the mind (cognitive) and the will (voluntaristic). While courage has a rational component, as Aristotle pointed out, it requires more than knowledge; it has rather to do with achieving balance between extremes of *foolhardiness* and *fear.* According to Aristotle, a person who fears nothing is not brave but mad, because there are such things as rational fears. Standing in front of an oncoming locomotive without a rational motive is not brave but delusional; but to stand in front of a train in an act of rescue of another is courageous.[17] Leaders must learn to balance these extremes through *practice.*

When my son Clinton was five years old, we moved to Cambridge for a year. Near our apartment was an empty parking lot where I taught him to ride a bicycle. He began with training wheels. Every evening, we would go to the parking lot and he would mount the tiny bike and take off. He was a daredevil on training wheels. But one day, I removed the training wheels and he was terrified. Thus began the process of learning to balance his fears and his fearlessness. What Clinton and I learned from this experience was that as he practiced and negotiated his fears and desire to be Evel Knievel, he soon learned the art of balance, which is essential to staying on a moving bicycle. Leaders who are able to balance their fears and fearlessness are a scarce commodity. Resolving the problem of integrity is one of the challenges of achieving balance in respect to what constitutes courage in various contexts. Leaders who have not devoted attention to the deeper issues of integrity (identity, authenticity, and purpose) are forever at the mercy of the look of the other—or the nagging pursuit of recognition.

Courage is located in the spiritual/personal dimension of our model. It represents the spiritual virtuosity that seeks moral excellence in respect to the self, but it is achieved through practicing integrity and recognition.

As integrity seeks community within self and a sense of wholeness, integration, and harmony, it predisposes the leader to seek balance at this personal level, which is primarily psychological. But as we have seen, it is interrelated with empathy and hope, which are social and spiritual dimensions of character. Creating balance at the personal level also requires work on recognition. As we have stated, recognition is a primary social value that addresses the inner need to be addressed and responded to. Recognition is dialogical in the sense that it seeks the address and response of the other. Practicing self-recognition as an integral part of meeting this very basic human need is indispensable. For ethical leaders, defiant acts of courage are related to the virtue of integrity and recognition. When one responds out of the deepest center of self, not for recognition from others but because one understands that his or her response is appropriate to the challenge at hand—"Here I stand, I can do no other!"—then one is brought back to his or her centermost being, to that which is the meaning of community within self.

During the spring of 2006, I traveled throughout South Africa lecturing on ethical leadership. One of my visitations was in Durban. My hosts took me to Pietermaritzburg, the township famous for an incident early in the career of Mahatma Gandhi. In 1893, Gandhi arrived in Durban to serve as legal counsel to the merchant Dada Abdulla. Early in his employment, he was asked by Dada Abdulla to take a trip to Pretoria in the Transvaal. Traveling by train, Gandhi acquired a first-class ticket and had proceeded to his compartment when a railway official requested that he remove himself to the van compartment, since "coolies" and non-whites were not permitted in first-class compartments. When Gandhi protested and refused to comply, he was thrown violently off the train and his luggage tossed onto the platform. Gandhi stayed at the Pietermaritzburg station in the cold of that winter night and began to reflect on his "duty": Should he stay and fight for his "rights" or return to India? His own "hardship was superficial . . . only a symptom of the deep disease of colour prejudice." His granddaughter, Ella Gandhi, shared with me that this was the defining moment of Gandhi's life as a social activist.[18]

The incident inspired Gandhi to begin his career protesting against laws discriminating against Indians in South Africa. As I stood in the train station, which now has a memorial dedicated to his courageous action after that incident, I reflected on a similar incident that involved an African American seamstress named Rosa Parks, who also had been told to give up her seat to a white passenger. Gandhi used the incident to mount a movement of Hindus and Muslims that sought equal justice in pre-apartheid South Africa; Rosa Parks's legendary refusal to give up her seat became the flashpoint for the modern civil rights movement in America. Both leaders reflect in their actions what we are calling "defiant acts of courage." But their courageous actions were preceded by disciplined lifestyles that had prepared them for the moment.

Courage and Faith

An integral dimension of courage is *faith*. Faith requires risk in the face of the possibility of failure, disgrace, and shame. No great leader who has stood at the intersection and dared to create change has not had to re-examine motives and question the rationality of his or her choice. There are many leaders who subscribe to faith, but true faith includes courage—the power *to be*, to transform, and to create new realities. The great Protestant theologian Paul Tillich said that there is a courage that is faith and a faith that is courage. Courage manifests itself in acts of defiance against life-annihilating factors that are both internal and external to the agent. The internal dimension that courage addresses, however, is the most challenging, because it has to do with the question of anxiety (*angst*), which is more than fear. Tillich makes a critical distinction between fear and anxiety: "A danger, a pain, an enemy may be feared, but fear can be conquered by action. Anxiety cannot, for no finite being can conquer its finitude. Anxiety is always present, although it is latent. Therefore, it can become manifest at any moment, even in situations where nothing is to be feared."[19]

The question of anxiety, our struggle with our limitations as creatures of space and time, is a major struggle for leaders at the intersection. Our deep existential longings, our despair, and our awareness that we are "dying animals"[20] are more than personal issues that we must confront; they also inform our behavior and decisions. Seldom do leaders or most people, for that matter, have the opportunity to confront their anxieties. Courage as "the power of life *to be*" helps leaders to face the experience of dread wrought by our finitude. Courage as self-affirmation despite the threats of destruction, disease, and death enables leaders to move forward with faith in the inherent possibilities of life.

Such faith that is courage requires spiritual discipline that summons the imagination. A meditation from Thurman's collection *Meditations of the Heart* provides a guide for leaders who need courage:

The concern I lay before God today is my need for courage:
I need courage to be honest—
Honest in my use of words
Honest in accepting responsibility
Honest in dealing with my fellows
Honest in my relations with God.

I need courage to face the problems of my own life—the problems of
    personal values:
They are confused
They are often unreal
They are too exacting for comfort.

The problems on my job:
Perhaps I am working at cross-purposes with my own desires, ambi-
    tions, equipment.
Perhaps I am arrogant instead of taking pride in doing work well.
Perhaps I am doing what I am doing just to prove a point—spending
    a lifetime to prove a point that is not worth proving at all.
Perhaps I have never found anything that could challenge me, and my
    life seems wasted.
Here in the quietness I lay before God my need for courage, for the
    strength to be honest, for the guidance to deal effectually with the
    problems of my own life.

O God, thou wilt not despise![21]

Leaders of this century will need the courage that is faith to explore
the unknown and unchartered territories of human imagination. Faith
that is courage takes leaders into strange territory without a map. In medi-
eval times, there were maps of the known world. The maps graphically
described what explorers and cartographers had experienced up to that
time about the world. At the edge of maps were inscribed the words, "Here
there be dragons!" What this inscription meant was that at the limits of
human exploration and experience was the fear of the unknown. We know
now that dragons did not exist beyond these boundaries; rather, there were
other civilizations and peoples. Because of ignorance and fear, most would
never journey beyond what was known and acceptable, but there were
the adventurous spirits who dared to travel beyond fixed constructions of

the mind to discover new worlds. Only the trespassers, the nonconformists, the creative dreamers dared to envision new worlds. But it was costly.
Many paid dearly with their lives. Leaders of the new century must not be
afraid of dragons, dragons within and without—for dragons cannot harm
you unless you give them power over your soul!

There is an oft-quoted story of Thurman's, originally told by Olive
Schreiner, about an old mother duck who had for years led her ducklings
to the same pond. Finally, one day, she led a new batch of ducklings to
the old pond and it was all dried up and nothing was left but baked mud.
Still, she persisted in bringing her younglings down to it and walked about
flapping her wings with an anxious quack, trying to induce them to enter.
But the young ducklings, with fresh young instincts, could hear far off
the delicious drippings from a new dam that was built up higher to catch
the water. When they smelled the chickweed and the long grass that was
growing beside the dam, the young ducklings absolutely refused to disport
themselves on the baked mud and to pretend. And so they set out for new
pastures—perhaps to lose themselves on the way or perhaps to find themselves. "To the old mother duck," Schreiner writes, "one is inclined to say,
'Ah, good old mother duck, can you not see that the world has changed?
You cannot bring water back into the dried up pond! Perhaps it was better
and more pleasant when it was there, but it has gone forever; and, would
you and yours swim again, it must be in other waters.'"

For emerging leaders, who confront the fears of life, it will take courage that is faith if we are to give our world, nation, cities, and communities
a new dream—a dream that is fashioned out of the best insights of the past
and our most critical and informed analyses of the present. The future of
our communities, our nation, and the world depends on a new generation
of men and women who dare to dream creatively and to call forth new
realities based on those dreams.

Courage takes many forms within organizations that seek redress
of ethical improprieties. The recent scandals in major corporations and
large accounting houses provide examples of individuals coming forward
to "whistle blow." I am more concerned, however, with the *pre-whistle-
blowing* stage of organizational ethical decline. Might it not be possible to
create a moral ethos that serves as a protective shield against improprieties?
Instead, most responses have been to rules-based ethics that proliferate
with each surge of new discoveries of ethical failures within organizations.
Courage asks for more than a rules-based response. It asks, "Who is willing to step into the intersection and work on adaptive strategies that lead

to a more refined moral ethos within organizations and government while maintaining respect for rules, protocol, and organizational integrity?" This is the work of leaders who are willing to form communities of discourse and practice at those intersections and work for change within organizations and the larger society. Defiant acts of courage are dangerous and risky by nature, but the power of community serves as the source of motivation and resilience. An integral part of this daring to risk failure and to create community at the intersection is a sense of justice.

A Sense of Justice and Integrity

A sense of justice is the expression of a healthy sense of self, which we have referred to as integrity—a sense of wholeness or community within self. Wholeness within the self begins with the awareness that all dimensions of my self are not equal, but proportionately related. I am a body with intricate and well-defined functions and systems of order. When one part is not functioning to its full potential, it creates disharmony with the others. If I am not breathing properly, it affects the flow of blood, which impacts my immune, endocrine, and central nervous systems, and so on. What I seek to achieve in a well-functioning body, however, is not simply a physical organism that works well but the entire range of my emotional, mental, and spiritual makeup as well. These systems work in respect to an inner harmony that guides and maintains the balance and harmony of the organism. I can be aware of the rules and laws that help to maintain a healthy physical, emotional, and spiritual existence, but if I fail to live by these, it does not matter. The point, of course, is that knowledge of these rules is not adequate in themselves. I must also choose to live by what I know helps to maintain that balance. I must be involved in practices that help to maintain health and harmonious relations among the members of my body.

Thich Nhat Hanh, the Zen Buddhist monk, author, and peace activist, suggests that *mindful breathing and walking* provide an inner balance that creates an internal environment that enables the practitioner to work for justice in the world. Being *mindful* or aware of walking and breathing as essential activities of the body helps "to defuse harmful emotions, calm and concentrate your mind, and bring yourself back to the present moment, where life is truly available."[22] The question of virtuous living is on the same order. I must maintain a habit structure that allows for the free flow of virtuous living as I understand it. Justice is a *virtuosity*—it requires the consistent pursuit of balanced living at the center of my existence in pursuit of excellence at all levels. The challenge, however, is to become mindful, aware that there are parts of my self that are not in order that seek priority and prominence over others. My appetite often calls for delicacies that my body cannot abide, as do my mind and spirit. If I allow toxic elements to enter my body, I have done an injustice to myself. If I imbibe and practice values that war against the noble aspirations of my mind and spirit, I have committed an injustice to myself.

Ethical leaders, therefore, are constantly looking for ways to improve the functioning of the body, mind, and spirit as a personal practice of cultivating personal justice that seeks integration, balance, and harmony within self. Mahatma Gandhi practiced a strict dietary regime and physical exercises as a way of promoting a deeper understanding of truth or *satyagahra*. He was well aware that if justice was the goal that he sought for his people, then his personal existence had to reflect the same discipline and practice that he was demanding in his public life. Gandhi often said, "You must be the change you wish to see in the world."

Social justice refers to the social and public spheres that leaders engage, but it begins with a sense of justice. Human beings, especially children, display what James Q. Wilson calls "the moral sense," certain natural sensibilities that are "formed out of interaction of their innate dispositions and their earliest familial experiences," which "shape human behavior and the judgments people make of the behavior of others."[23] The moral sense of justice, according to Wilson, precedes social constructs of justice as in rules, principles, and laws, yet it informs how certain rational renderings of justice are shaped by traditions and customs of different cultures. Human beings are characterized universally by "the desire for survival and sustenance with the desire for companionship and approval" and are constantly in pursuit of social arrangements that best provide for these basic needs and desires.[24] A sense of justice as fairness arises from this basic human instinct. It has its genesis in early childhood associations with family and kin and is expressed in feelings of *equity*, *reciprocity*, and *impartiality*.[25]

Harvard law professor Lani Guinier tells the story of a discussion that she had with her four-year old son, Nikolas, about a *Sesame Street Magazine* exercise. The exercise pictured six children, four with hands raised, indicating their choice to play tag, and two whose hands were down because they wanted to play hide-and-seek. The magazine asked the readers to count the number of children who wanted to play tag and the number who wanted to play hide-and-seek and to decide on which game the children wanted to play. To his mother's surprise, Nikolas responded, "They will play both.

First they will play tag. Then they will play hide-and-seek." Despite the "rules" implied by the exercise, Guinier says Nikolas was right. It is natural for children to take turns. "The winner may get to play first or more often, but even the 'loser' gets something." Nikolas's wisdom underscores a fundamental issue at stake in respect to justice as fairness. The prevalent practice of "winners take all" flies in the face of the idea of community that we are espousing. But in political elections, corporate takeovers, and the game of nations, this is the norm. In a world of winners and losers, there is little room for principles of equity, reciprocity, and impartiality. The idea of winners taking all also circumvents the project of democracy as embracing difference and inclusion. Losers are the minority and are forever disadvantaged, suggests Guinier, by "the tyranny of the majority." Rather than a zero-sum game where winners take all, we should seek *positive sum solutions* "in which all perspectives are represented and in which all people work together to find common ground."[26]

Howard Thurman suggests that the search for common ground as a sense of justice involves *sympathetic understanding*.[27] In Thurman, the term is borrowed largely from the moral grammar of the social gospel and modernistic liberalism, where the relationist ethic serves as the primary means for the development of an equitable and just society, as opposed to the coercive tactics of the state. In Thurman's later usages, sympathetic understanding provides the vehicle for moral imagination to serve as the basis for empathy, respect, and the development of genuine human fellowship and collaboration across differences. In his earliest published essay, titled "College and Color," Thurman defines "sympathetic understanding":

> By sympathetic understanding I do not mean a patronizing attitude or anything that is cheap and sentimental. Nor do I mean an attitude that is so swollen with condescending pride that its stench is intolerable. But I do mean an attitude which says that a man of another race is essentially myself, and that I feel toward him fundamentally as if he were myself. His needs and cravings and the drives which lie behind his actions are similar to mine in their essentials. It is more or less a truism that an idea held in mind tends to express itself in action. Especially is this true if the idea carries with it an emotional fringe. We cannot properly appreciate and understand what is going on in objective experience unless we somehow get back of it to the great world of ideas—intangible, unseen— which controls human activity.[28]

Leaders who seek community at the intersection need to return to the great world of ideas that are inclusive, dynamic, and imaginative. The visions that we seek, the changes that we envision, and the hope that we wish to inspire come from the deep wells of our own remembering by aligning private visions with public values without recourse to romantic wanderings. We are witnessing in right-wing fundamentalists and Christian nationalists memories of America that hark back to a time of nostalgic innocence that never really existed. The challenge for America and the world is how we remember our stories, because the story of America, in a strange way, is not only the story of the past—it is also the story of the future. And that future depends largely on how leaders envision possibility and courageously re-create the present. These are leaders who dare to envision great ideas that *unify the disparate parts of the human being*; they speak of a social order that is possible *on the basis of an ordering within the individual self*.[29] In our language, they are leaders who *remember*, *retell*, and *relive* their personal stories in the context of the larger human story of great ideas that are rich in sympathetic understanding and a sense of justice.

Thurman relates a story of encounter with a young girl, Ruth, who exhibits this idea of the moral sense of justice as sympathetic understanding.[30] For Thurman, sympathetic understanding begins with primary contact and proceeds with an evaluation that weighs differences and commonalities of experience. He was invited to speak at the church of a friend whose four-year-old daughter, Ruth, found his black skin an object of curiosity. After Thurman made "several friendly overtures," Ruth said, "Have a seat over there," pointing to a large morris chair. As soon as he was seated, she climbed into his lap and began an intricate examination to see if the black color of his skin could be wiped off. When she discovered that it was a permanent feature of his person, she proceeded with a series of innocent questions, "Are you black all over? Are you black under your collar? But I know you don't have black feet. Did you have to be black? Why aren't you white like Daddy?" Thurman suggests that after Ruth's "grilling cross examination" and discovery of the human being under the black skin, she waved a fond good-bye. He reflected:

> Ruth's first reaction was one of shyness mingled with fear. My overtures assured her that I was harmless and friendly in spirit. A relationship of primary contact established, she proceeded to a firsthand investigation of the phenomenon. Her first problem was whether my color was genuine or artificial and whether it covered my entire body. "If he is the same

color all over, he must be different from daddy." The next step was to see if I had chosen my color or if I had no choice in the matter.

Convinced that I was black and had always been black, she dismissed that difference as beside the point and began to appreciate that part of me over which she felt that I had a measure of control. In other words, she judged me by the qualities which I had in common with her father and not by our differences. In a very fundamental way Ruth's attitude was one of sympathetic understanding which led to a very real respect for my personality.[31]

More is at stake in this simple illustration of sympathetic understanding between Ruth and Thurman. As it relates to a sense of justice on the scale of larger public interactions, he argued that the primary issue of concern is the will-to-power among individuals, social groups, and nations. Thurman's suggested solution is the adaptation of a "technique of relaxation," in which individuals and groups stand outside the usual contexts of power relation to seek a new relation and new, creative methods of social interaction. Thurman believed that this technique was a learned response that required discipline and practice—that, indeed, it was a skill that could be learned and carried over into the collective life of groups.[32] He further suggested that meaningful experiences shared among individuals would accomplish that end. "Experiences of meaning which people share are more compelling than the barriers that separate them," Thurman writes. "If such experiences can be multiplied over a time interval of sufficient duration, then any barrier between men, of whatever kind, can be undermined."[33] For him, this was the central ethical imperative of community.[34]

How might Thurman's call for a "technique of relaxation" provide a corrective to the failure of liberal notions of justice that fail to provide a sense of community? For instance, Michael Sandel has argued for a concept of justice that is not limited to the narrow constructs of a theory of right or utilitarianism. Sandel critiques liberal notions of justice as being unable to maintain a sense of community because of an inadequate theory of self and community. He argues that a theory of self that is unsituated and ahistorical cannot provide for the essential connectedness necessary to form bonds of community that are constitutive. This means that theories of justice that are constructed through rational, rules-based ethics create organizations and institutions that are driven by an account of individuals as being essentially self-interested and governed by the will-to-power. Such theories of justice must give way to an understanding of self that is self-reflective and seeks unity with others. In this perspective, the-will-to-power is understood as the central motivating factor of human existence and hence of group and organizational life. Justice, in this view, places emphasis on structure and rules that serve as both a constraint on egotistical tendencies and a guide for conformity. The governing rationale of the rationalist, as we have seen, is to provide a structure that is *external* and *prior* to the agent and, as such, external to the self-centered drives and motivations that are antithetical to cooperation and peaceful coexistence. Through the inculcation of the values of duty and right actions, individuals learn and maintain the prescribed order of the group.

It is in this respect that an ethic of relation highlights a moral sense of justice or sympathetic understanding that can serve as a vital corrective to the tyranny of rules-based ethics by promoting the value of connectiveness for which Sandel argues. The sense of justice that emphasizes self-discovery and community over the will-to-power is a spiritual project that first requires a method for "relaxing the will." It emanates from a perspective that places premium on relationships that are formed through traditions, institutions, and social practices that conspire to create community. Thurman believed that this practice could be utilized by both individuals and groups. Justice, for him, is more than the "artificial equalization of non-equals" promoted by the state.[35] It has to do, rather, with the ways in which communities creatively engage the imagination as a vehicle for empathy and respect wrought by the practice of sympathetic understanding.

The traditional notion of justice, says Thurman, operates on the inherent relationship between deed and consequence, reward and punishment as expressed in *lex talionis* (literally, "the law of retaliation"). Central to the notion of justice is power. Power includes both the *will* and *ability* to effect change in a given situation. Thurman examines two expressions of justice.[36] One type is the justice to which persons appeal when they are dealing with one another from within a context of equality of will when neither has the ability to inflict her will upon the other. This he refers to as "blindfolded justice" or the justice of the law. Here, the notion of justice as the "artificial equalization of unequals" is operative. Justice as such is external to the individual and beyond her power to effect—this is the basic understanding of justice as a principle of rights or what Martin Luther King called "enforceable obligations."

The other idea of justice in Thurman is expressed in structures when individuals are unequal in terms of power. If the person who has the advantage wields power over the other, she strips him of selfhood, of his "private, autonomous existence," and reduces him to a thing. But if the individual who has the advantage refrains from exercising her power over the other, she establishes voluntary distance between her ability and will. In this instance, the idea of justice is not external to the individual, but internal. When one refrains from executing power over the other in such a context, she shows compassion. King called this view of justice "nonen-foreceable obligations."[37]

This idea of justice is synonymous with a moral sense of justice. Inherent in the sense of justice is compassion that fulfills justice by recognizing the inherent worth and equality of the other. Compassion and justice,[38] according to Thurman, are part of the moral integrity of life. The moral order operates on the logic of cause and effect, deed and consequence. Therefore, the unrighteous deed will not go unpunished, but the wronged individual is never the avenger. Judgment for the evil deed is inherent in life itself. He writes, "The moral law is abiding. There is no escape from the relentless logic of antecedent and consequence."[39] Therefore, the individual who shows compassion, even to her enemy, will ultimately be vindicated. Thurman believed that the exercise of vengeance or retaliation is not the individual's, but God's. This is true for Thurman at both personal and social levels:

> There is a judgment which presides over the private and collective destiny of man. It is a judgment that establishes itself in human history as well as in human character. God is the Creator of life, and the ultimate responsibility of life is to God. If there be any government or social institution . . . that operates among men in a manner that makes for human misery . . . to the extent that it is so, it cannot survive, because it is against life and carries within itself the seeds of its own destruction.[40]

Compassion involves imagination. Imagination is an integral dimension of empathy.[41] Through the use of imagination, the individual is able to transcend herself and reach the other at the core of his being, at the seat of "common consciousness." In doing so, the other is addressed at a place beyond all good and evil. This, according to Thurman, is the experience of love. When an individual is addressed at the centermost place of personality, she experiences wholeness and harmony with the other. This is the "common ground" of our relations with others:

I see you where you are striving and struggling, and in light of the highest possibility of your personality, I deal with you there. My religious
faith is insistent that this can be done only out of a life of devotion. I
must cultivate the inner spiritual resources of my life to such a point that
I can bring you to my sanctuary before his presence until, at last, I do
not know you from myself.[42]

Compassion involves redemptive suffering. To demonstrate compassion for the other is to expose ourselves in such a way that the other may
have free access to our inner self. This involves vulnerability and the potential for suffering, but it is only through our willingness to risk suffering that
redemption of the other is achieved. Redemption occurs when one person
becomes for the other what is needed when the need is most urgently and
acutely felt.[43] Compassion as redemptive suffering is not contingent on the
other's response; rather, it is unsolicited and self-giving. It transcends merit
and demerit. It simply loves. Ultimately, compassion is victorious over any
defense, even hate, because it is the creative power of Spirit creating community, the very essence and vitality of all being.[44]

Finally, compassion is synonymous with reconciliation.[45] Reconciliation occurs within the individual when her inner need to be cared for and
understood is met in encounter with God. The experience of reconciliation with God becomes the ground and moral mandate for sharing one's
experience in relations with others and in society. Whatever impedes the
actualization of community at either personal or social levels must be confronted. Thurman, like King, believed that the way to the reconciliation of
society is through redemptive suffering rooted in love.[46]

Awakening to a Sense of Justice

In *The Republic*, Socrates challenges his young interlocutors Cephalus,
Polemarchus, Glaucon, and Thrasymachus to think of justice not merely
as an external property of persons, as in convention, propriety, personal
interest, or might, but as an inner quality of the soul. For Plato, justice
is more than right conduct (duty) or doing good to friends and evil to
enemies (fraternity). It is not the capacity to perform injury and to make
enemies tremble (retributive justice). Nor is it the artificial equalization of
nonequals (social contracts mediated by the State).[47] It has to do first with
a harmonious relationship within the self. For Socrates, this was an exquisite balance of the appetite, will, and reason, with the latter serving as a
charioteer of the other two, which he likened to demanding and passionate

steeds. Like Socrates, we believe that leaders must begin with the self in thinking about justice in respect to community, though they may not subscribe to the grander architecture of *The Republic*.[48] But if knowledge is virtue, as Socrates proclaimed, then knowledge is neither merely related to rationalist perspectives of ethics nor limited to a utilitarian calculus; rather, knowledge as virtue suggests *relation* and draws upon the power of story as the way of discerning appropriate actions and behaviors as in the practice of justice.

One of the stories Socrates used to help his sophomoric band grasp his view of justice is the Allegory of the Cave. Stated simply, he asked them to imagine a dark cave with prisoners who were bound to its floor and facing a wall. All their lives, they have been in this bound position unable to see what was behind them. On the wall, they saw images in varied activities: making love, making war, dancing and singing, crying and laughing, and so on. Little did they know that these images on the wall were only shadows. One day, one of the prisoners was dragged outside the cave into the bright light of the real world and discovered that what he had been looking at all of his life were but shadows on a wall. For Plato, this discovery is related to recollection, or *anamnesis*: remembering the soul's code, its true calling and purpose. External agents play important roles in introducing others to the light.[49] (Might it be that for the first time, he saw his own face mirrored through the eyes of the other — and in facing the other, he knew what he was called to do?) He returns to save the others in the cave and is killed by those whom he returned to rescue.

The Allegory of the Cave is a powerful narrative construction that casts light on the interiority of justice. The point of the story is that the prisoner indeed became conscious; and his *awakening* was the first step in the realization of justice. For ethical leaders, justice first begins with an awareness of self—not an isolated, unanchored self but one who is intricately and intimately related to others as the allegory suggests. Though this enlightened one was liberated, he was aware that he was not free as long as others were bound, hence his return to the cave. Justice begins with awakening to the self and to the other—and realizing that one cannot be free and equal until all are free and equal. For leaders, this is a daring ideal that may never be fully realized, yet it serves as a critique on all existing arrangements that are unjust.

The Allegory of the Cave has its cultural parallels in stories of great spiritual and ethical leaders from many cultures and times. According to legend, Siddhartha Gautama (Buddha) was sheltered from the pain and

suffering that lay just outside of his father's court, but one day he decided
to venture outside the walls of his cave of shadows and discovered dete-
rioration, disease, and death, and he realized that suffering was the common lot of humankind. This revelation set him on a path culminating in
enlightenment. One can see similar parallels in the lives of other spiritual
leaders. Moses witnessed the oppression of his fellow Hebrews, then led
them out of bondage; Jesus returned home to Nazareth as a preacher after
his wilderness encounter; Muhammad received his revelations from the
archangel Gabriel in a cave on Mount Hira, where he fasted and prayed,
lamenting over the troubles of his people. Modern parallels can be found
in leaders such as Gandhi and Rosa Parks, whom I have mentioned.

Howard Thurman suggests that these experiences of awakening to calling and character can be a sudden event that appears like a shaft of light
along one's path; it may be the slow, steady unyielding of self-disclosure; or
it can be that some individuals seem to know early on what their mission
and role will be in respect to justice and the creation of a friendly world
underneath friendly skies. However one comes to self-knowledge, there is
an accompanying call to commitment or what Thurman calls "singleness
of mind." Singleness of mind involves volition, which may be a radical,
self-conscious yielding on the part of the individual or a systematic and disciplined effort over time.[50] The result of the commitment of the individual
is a new, integrated basis for moral action. A new value content and center
of loyalty inform her or his actions in the world.[51] The person's loyalty to
God, which proceeds from the personal assurance of being loved by God,
forms the ground of the moral life. What is discovered in private must be
witnessed to in the world. This "crucible experience" is iconoclastic in that
it breaks the self-images of leaders and gives birth to new names, new faces,
and new possibilities in the struggle for a just and loving human community. According to Warren Bennis and Robert Thomas, it is "the crucible"
that ultimately defines the leader: "Whatever the crucible experience," they
write, "going into battle, overcoming fears, entering unknown territory—
the individual creates a narrative around it, a story of how he or she was
challenged, met that challenge, and became a new and better self."[52]

Compassion

The third and most important dimension of the ethical leader's practice
that anticipates community is compassion. Compassion is the supreme
virtuosity of ethical leadership. Within the Ethical Leadership Model, it is
located on the spiritual side of the triangle and is the culmination of hope

and reverence—and indeed all of the practices. The model begins with integrity and ends in compassion. Compassion is the fulfillment of the *virtues* of character: integrity, empathy, and hope; it provides the moral tissue for the *values* of civility: recognition, respect, and reverence; and the *virtuosities* of courage and justice find their fulfillment in acts of compassion.

Compassion as used in this context is synonymous with love, but it is concerned primarily with the willingness to suffer with the other. According to the Dalai Lama, compassion in the Tibetan language is *shen dug ngal wa la mi sö pa*, which means, literally, "the inability to bear the sight of another's suffering."[53] Compassion calls the leader alongside the other to share in her sorrow and tragedy, but also in her hopes and aspirations. Moreover, it suggests that we are fundamentally interrelated in that all suffering is potentially our own. Buddhists refer to this sense of deep ecology or interconnectedness as "dependent origination"; that is, all of reality is a matter of cause and effect, and any existing phenomenon is actually dependent on seemingly unrelated ingredients. Nothing in its final analysis is discrete, independent, or solid but is actually the composite of all existence. The South Vietnamese Buddhist monk Thich Nhat Hanh calls this fundamental sense of interrelatedness "interbeing." He suggests that when we "look deeply" into a phenomenon or experience, we discover its interbeing, so that "the distinction between observer and the observed disappears" and we see the true nature of the object—and our relatedness to it.

> When we look into the heart of a flower, we see clouds, sunshine, minerals, time, the earth, and everything else in the cosmos in it. Without clouds, there would be no rain, and there would be no flower. Without time, the flower could not bloom. In fact, the flower is made entirely of non-flower elements; it has no independent, individual existence. It *inter-is* with everything else in the universe.[54]

Compassion and Character

Compassion, writes Thomas Merton, is the keen awareness of the interdependence of all things.[55] This awareness begins at a level of consciousness wrought by a sense of wholeness in respect to the self. To be aware of oneself is to be conscious of the fact that I am also a composite being whose inner life is an exquisite network of affective, cognitive, and physical elements that are wholly dependent on each other for the development of a healthy sense of self. Demonstrating compassion for the self begins with an understanding that my character is interrelated both to my own personal stories and to the stories of others. The stories of my personal development are inextricably related to who I am and what I am called to be and do. The answers to the critical questions of identity (Who am I?), purpose (What am I to do?), and method (How do I realize my purpose?) are found in a compassionate understanding of ourselves. It is through remembering, retelling, and reliving my story that I develop a sense of compassion for myself and others who are a part of my story. Leaders who seek wholeness, integration, and harmony at the personal level of character must be attentive to dangerous memories that have settled in subterranean wells and often show up unannounced and inform behavior. Leaders who are unaware of deep pain and hurt that still linger in places that we choose to forget are candidates for tragedy.

Some years ago, while serving as a dean at my seminary and launching new projects that were not well received by some members of the community, I discovered how early childhood experiences of being "bullied" were playing out in my role as leader. During our early years in Chicago, my family moved constantly, and consequently my sister, brother, and I were placed in new schools with each move. In each new neighborhood and at each new school, I had to contend with bullies. For some reason, I was the object of the bullies' concern. I had to fight in the streets, on the way to school, at recess, after school, on the playground, and sometimes in the classroom. There was always someone who wanted to challenge my manhood—and the etiquette of the culture demanded a response in kind. Sometimes I was the victor but ultimately the loser. I didn't enjoy the fighting. It made me feel awful—my clothes would be dirty and torn, but more deeply, I felt dirty and conflicted after the fights. As a forty-year-old, I had no idea that these experiences were still lingering and contributing to the way that I felt in this new role at the seminary. I was angry and felt like I was being challenged again on the playground.

One day, on an airplane flight returning from a conference in Myrtle Beach, South Carolina, I meditated on those childhood conflicts and my deep feelings of intimidation and rage. As I reflected on these feelings in my journal, I began writing a poem that was later published in an anthology titled *From Brother to Brother: Voices of African American Men*:

bright, sunny day
                              i felt the sun
                              inside me
                              smiling

all dressed up in white jeans and white t-shirt
                              gaily clad
                              my heart danced   like a feather on the
                              wind
11 years old
                              and too young to know
                              and too innocent to deserve
                              the way robert and bay' broh . . .

teddy taunted me
in the fourth grade
he was the baddest—
in the school
we fought at recess
and i kicked his—
              i was scared
              with a trembling that is still here
                    my heart cracked in
                              zigzagged patterns
                                    like fresh concrete
                                              under the jackhammer

i lost parts of me
that teddy never knew

now i cry
when i watch
movies with my children
and when karate kid
does that one-legged kick
in the bully's face

dear teddy and robert and bay' broh
i know now

30 years later
that the sun still shines

> on my white clothes
> and my heart is still gay
> my steps dance to melodies
> in broken places that
> jackhammers and fists
> can never destroy[56]

This was one of my earliest experiences of consciously remembering my story as a way of understanding how these early experiences of fear, pain, and rage were determining my response to what I perceived as being bullied in the context of leadership. I had to return to these memories and forgive myself for being afraid, intimidated, and angry. I also had to forgive my tormentors. Compassion for them and for myself meant forgiving by first understanding what was going on inside of me and how these dangerous memories were impacting my role as a leader. Retelling my story meant that I had to reframe the dynamics of the context in which I found myself and to find reasonable ways to negotiate the conflict in interests among others who were engaged. Because of my willingness to forgive and to become more compassionate and understanding of my own controlling dramas, I was able to see others in a new light—and able to see that many of them like Teddy, Robert, and Bay' Broh had brought their controlling dramas into this context as well.

Compassion at the level of character demands careful attention to and practice of integrity, empathy, and hope as defining virtues. Compassion helps us to understand that no one ever wins a fight. In fact, no one ever *wins* anything in this world. Leadership is not about winning and losing; rather, it is about growing and stretching, becoming better and better, more balanced and harmonious as we seek wholeness within ourselves and with others. Our greatest triumphs and tragedies from childhood are normally associated with winning or losing. But these dangerous memories often disguise themselves and prevent us from seeing the profound and central meaning of our existence: that we are here to grow in excellence, to become conscious of our own beauty and greatness as creations of a wise and benevolent source from whom we originate and to whom we return.

The awful scars and lingering fears perpetuated by the violence of our environment and the devastating rage that erupts from within play out in scenarios that prevent us from "looking deeply" into this marvelous truth of our existence—that we are interrelated and dependent on one another. We have resources that are imminently present like bountiful streams of life just below the surface of our day-to-day interactions. These streams of life—the memories, dreams, and aspirations—are present as veritable tutors that can be summoned through "looking deeply" and "listening intently" to our inner lives. In quieting the mind and spirit, we make space for their emergence. Often they come when we are engaged in long thoughts and soul-searching about our destinies, when we have reached the limits of our understanding, when we have emptied all of our normal resources and our regular routines are no longer able to provide the specific answers we desire for the next step of our journey. It is then, in the moment of crisis, that the angel appears with a message of hope that sheds light on our dimly lit paths and old, worn, and broken mirrors of ourselves.

Compassion for ourselves and others involves empathy or sympathetic understanding that reaches beyond the fabricated lines of difference to see that the other is like ourselves—that her face is like our own, searching, inquisitive, and driven to places of loneliness and despair that require healing from within and from the touch of the other. Ethical leaders understand that this healing comes only through integrity, empathy, and hope from the outstretched hand and *the open heart*. Howard Thurman writes, "There is a profound ground of unity that is more pertinent and authentic than all the unilateral dimensions of our lives. This a man discovers when he is able to keep open the door of his heart. This is one's ultimate responsibility, and it does not depend upon whether the heart of another is kept open for him." Thurman reasons that "if sweeping through the door of my heart there moves continually a genuine love for you, it bypasses all your hate and all your indifference and gets through to you at your center." This is so, he believes, because "it is impossible to keep another from loving you."[57]

Compassion and Civility

The lessons of creating a compassionate character have direct implications for how leaders perform in public space. For leaders who must negotiate the traffic at the intersection where worlds collide, compassion must of necessity be a suffering love that seeks the redemption of the other. By redemption, I mean the ability and willingness to stand in the other's place and to become a *sacrifice* for his or her highest good. The language of sacrifice has become an anathema in our culture. It is normally associated with servility and powerlessness, as in *scapegoating*. The theorist Reneé Girard suggests that all violence arises from the human need for recognition, to be seen as powerful and beautiful and special. I somehow believe that you possess something that I do not have—and that I need to take it from you, which results in violence, and that violence becomes contagious until it reaches beyond individuals to clans, tribes, and nations. Girard suggests that in all cultures where the contagion of violence has reached its apotheosis, there is a need for a ritualistic scapegoat to bring the envy, rage, and violence to an end. Scapegoating, in this sense, provides a remedy or a therapeutic intervention for the suffering of the people by the killing of an innocent victim. Scapegoating can also serve more sinister purposes. The Negro served as scapegoat in American society, according to Thurman, as a way of maintaining segregation as a source of loyalty to a cause that was transcendent. "Segregation is the status that keeps a group available for sacrifice and thus keeps the cult of the South intact and in health."[58]

But compassion that seeks the redemption of the other has to do with the conscious and deliberate decision to be for the other what she cannot be for herself, even at risk of endangering oneself. The question of redemptive suffering for the other in this perspective proceeds from an understanding of the dependent origination or fundamental interrelatedness of existence. In this sense, it can be inferred that all suffering is potentially redemptive because evil is not an intruder in the universe but a vital, integral part of life.[59] For Thurman, the suffering of the innocent must be viewed from this perspective. There are two ways in which the suffering of the innocent is redemptive. One way involves the innocent person who is simply caught in the onslaught and perplexities of existence. Thurman suggests that this suffering of the innocent minority is propitiatory in that it restores the balance or equilibrium in humanity that is offset by moral evil. "Their shoulders hold the sky suspended. They stand, and earth's foundations stay."[60] Although the innocent sufferer, in this sense, is not conscious of her redemptive role, she still participates in the broader purposes of a creative, harmonious universe.[61]

The other form of redemptive suffering of the innocent is a conscious, deliberate act on the part of the individual.[62] Here the suffering is characterized by the discovery of ultimate confirmation that the individual experiences as part of the movement of life. For leaders who are concerned about the creation of community, this insight is most important. The leader understands her life as being a part of the very rhythm and flow of life itself, which includes good and evil. Therefore, all the vicissitudes of existence, including death (the ultimate logic of suffering), have inherent meaning and value in the higher purposes of life itself. The fundamental experience that the leader realizes in her self-validation is deep compassion. The leader not only experiences compassion but is moved to show compassion for others. It is in her response to this deep compassion that she is enabled to suffer willingly for others in light of a higher cause or purpose. Thurman says, "It is only for love of someone or something that a man knows that because of the confirmation of life in him, he can make death an instrument in his hands."[63]

Redemptive suffering in compassion for the other, therefore, becomes the means of removing barriers that inhibit the actualization of community.[64] Unlike the former dimension, where the redemptive suffering of the innocent is unconscious, in this dimension it is a moral action involving the will and freedom. The ethical leader consciously participates in the collective destiny of the human community. She acknowledges the dynamic tensions and crises wrought in life by destructiveness and violence but refuses to ascribe normalcy to this state of affairs. The leader's vision is set rather to an ideal of harmony, integration, and wholeness that is always in the future. The compassionate leader never accepts "the absence of community as his destiny."[65] In redemptive suffering, therefore, the leader is driven by her identification with the movement of life toward community. For such a person, "to be confirmed in life is to make even of death a little thing."[66]

Unmerited suffering gives valuable insight into the power and miracle of compassion in creating community. Thurman argued that the lives of great historical personages (Jesus, Socrates, John Brown, Galileo, etc.) attest to this fact. The loving, sacrificial death of Jesus is but one illustration of the profound truth that the contradictions of life are not final.[67] The contradictions of life are not final because, while evil feeds on life and gains its validity from the same source as goodness, the weight of the universe is ultimately against any ongoing dualism.[68] This is the "growing edge" of hope for the leader who chooses to suffer redemptively for the actualization of human community.[69]

In this sense, redemption has to do with atonement—not for the sins of the other, so to speak, but to bear in one's own body and existence the pain and suffering of the other that are consequences of confronting unjust and destructive forces that militate against his existence. In a revealing personal testimony, King writes:

My personal trials have taught me the value of unmerited suffering. . . .
I have lived these past few years with the conviction that unearned suffering is redemptive. There are some who still find the cross a stumbling
block, others consider it foolishness, but I am more convinced than ever
before that it is the power of God unto social and individual salvation.
So like the Apostle Paul I can now humbly say, "I bear in my body the
marks of the Lord Jesus."[70]

Our world is filled with instances of injustice and destructive forces
that rally against the life chances of the "least of these." These instances
are reflected in the criminal justice system and the horrendous plight of
young black males, the woefully inadequate resources of educational systems for the urban underclass, intergenerational poverty, the depletion of
our natural resources, global warming, the political and economic issues
associated with HIV/AIDS, the suffering of animals, and so on. Compassion at the intersection goes beyond the virtues of character and requires
another dimension of practice that has to do with what we have called
civility—recognition, respect, and reverence for the other. It also builds on
the defining virtuosities of community, which we have discussed as courage and a sense of justice.

In an era when compassion has been linked to conservatism, it is
important that we look again at its relationship with civility and community. Transformative acts of civility that are rooted in defiant acts of
courage, a sense of justice, and deep compassion actually demand more
than conservative values of family and "sexual morality." Civility also raises
deeper questions than liberal preoccupation with diversity and multicultural rights and entitlements. Leaders at the intersection must ask the prior
question, "What is a compassionate society?" It has become increasingly
difficult to speak about compassion in the midst of all the violence, abandonment, fears, and pains that beset our society. When most conservatives
speak of compassion, they speak to the role of individuals who are Good
Samaritans who find creative ways to respond to suffering but often without
serious regard to the larger issues of structural justice. Liberals tend to ask the
question in reverse, by raising the issues of structural justice without serious
regard to the spiritual dimension of values. But neither side has asked the
deeper question of "the redemption of the soul of America." An authentic
language of civility and community in America will require deep compassion
that issues forth in redemption.

This language of community, however, must not be reserved only for those who are a part of our tightly knit communities of kin, class, and nation; it must also extend to the stranger. When Martin Luther King Jr. and other leaders began their campaign for civil rights, the language they spoke went beyond the languages of rights and utility. It was a language that called for redemptive suffering for those who had been denied participation in the destiny of America. More fundamentally, it was a call to a new kind of communal ethic that placed character and civility at the center of their campaigns for justice. The Southern Christian Leadership Conference, which King led, called for voting rights for African Americans, but the organization's ultimate goal was "to foster and create 'the beloved community' in America where brotherhood is a reality." The method they chose to bring about this goal was nonviolent direct action, which held as it core value redemptive suffering for the other.[71] In King's last years, the vision of the beloved community extended beyond the plight of African Americans and white Americans to a global vision of community. The language of community expressed deep compassion for the stranger.

King often used the story of the good Samaritan to illustrate this point. The good Samaritan, who rescued a stranger who had been beaten and left for dead on the side of the Jericho Road, was moved beyond charity to action. He showed compassion for the stranger even at the risk of his own safety. But King takes the story beyond an individual act of compassion to address the larger structural concerns of justice as fairness. In his April 6, 1967, speech at Riverside Church titled "Beyond Vietnam: A Time to Break Silence," he declared:

> A true revolution of values will soon cause us to question the fairness and justice of many of our past and present policies. On the one hand, we are called to play the Good Samaritan on life's roadside, but that will be only an initial act. One day we must come to see that the whole Jericho Road must be transformed so that men and women will not be constantly beaten and robbed as they make their journey on life's highway. True compassion is more than flinging a coin to a beggar. It comes to see that an edifice which produces beggars needs restructuring.[72]

Leaders in this century are called to be more than charitable actors who respond only to the needs of individuals; they must be willing to stand at the intersection where worlds collide and create communities of justice and compassion. How is this done? Who dares to stand in the place of redemption

and suffer with strangers? One of the most significant spiritual and intellectual resources of the young Howard Thurman was Olive Schreiner.[73]
Schreiner, an Englishwoman who lived in South Africa, was a witness to
the widespread atrocities of war (the Boer War and World War I), a fear-
less champion of racial justice, and an outspoken feminist who critically
engaged the male-dominated hierarchies of her day. She was also a deeply
sensitive individual, gifted with second sight in matters of the heart. For
Schreiner, the private life represented the intersection of spiritual enlightenment and public engagement. Because of her belief in the unity of all
life, she could not make a radical distinction between spirituality and social
transformation. This is the essential message in Thurman's collection of
her writings, *A Track to the Water's Edge*.[74] Schreiner's writings also reveal a
profound understanding of the place of courage, justice, and compassion
in creating the beloved community.

In an excerpt from Schreiner's "Three Dreams in the Desert," the
story is told of a woman who is seeking the land of freedom. In her quest,
she meets an aged man who personifies Reason. Reason points her to the
land of freedom, which is beyond a "dark, flowing river." He informs her
that the journey will involve great suffering and sacrifice. The woman first
has to sacrifice her child, whom she has concealed beneath her clothing,
before she makes her "track to the water's edge." Finally, when she reaches
the bank of the river, she says to Reason:

> "For what do I go to this far land which no one has ever reached? *Oh, I
> am alone! I am utterly alone!*"
>
> And Reason, that old man, said to her, "Silence! What do you
> hear?"
>
> And she listened intently, and she said, "I hear a sound of feet, a
> thousand times ten thousand and thousands of thousands, and they beat
> this way!"
>
> He said, "They are the feet of those that shall follow you. Lead on!
> Make a track to the water's edge! Where you stand now, the ground will
> be beaten flat by ten thousand times ten thousand feet." And he said,
> "Have you seen the locusts, how they cross a stream? First one comes
> down the water-edge, and it is swept away, and then another comes and
> then another, and then another, and at last with their bodies piled up, a
> bridge is built and the rest pass over."
>
> She said, "And, of those that come first, some are swept away, and
> are heard of no more; their bodies do not even build the bridge?"

"And are swept away, and are heard of no more—and what of that?"
he said.

"They make a track to the water's edge."

"They make a track to the water's edge—"

And she said, "Over that bridge which shall be built with our bodies,
who will pass?"

He said, "*The entire human race.*"

And the woman grasped her staff.

And I saw her turn down that dark path to the river.[75]

In a world threatened by the onslaught of disease, poverty, and war,
we need more than ever a new generation of leaders who will embrace *the
strangeness of compassion* that creates a new language of community for
America and the world. How strange would it be to see a new cadre of
leaders who are spiritually alert and ethically centered who dare to make a
track to the water's edge? These leaders must take as their moral compass a
renewed vigor in the struggle for justice and a heart filled with compassion
for the stranger—the radically different other in whose face we see our
own and the face of the new world that calls us. These are the leaders who
stand at the intersections of character, civility, and community and dare to
reimagine the world.

Chapter Six

STAYING AWAKE AT THE INTERSECTION

Among the many challenges that leaders will face in the twenty-first century, the greatest of all is the challenge to *stay awake*. The opening chapter of Thomas Friedman's *The World Is Flat* is titled "While I Was Sleeping." His inference is that while Americans were sleeping, the *round* world of Christopher Columbus changed dramatically through a series of "flatteners" that have created our present state of affairs nationally and globally. Friedman's much-discussed treatment of the flat world is both a warning about and a summons to new ways of thinking about how we relate to one another on a planet that is becoming increasingly small. Friedman's warning, however, is not the first.

Nearly forty years earlier, Martin Luther King Jr. also warned us of the danger of falling asleep. He told a story of Washington Irving's classic about Rip Van Winkle, who slept through the American Revolution. When Rip Van Winkle fell asleep, the sign at the inn in a little town on the Hudson Bay had a picture of King George III of England. When he awakened twenty years later, the picture was of the first president of the United States, George Washington. King suggests that "the most striking thing about this story is not that Rip slept twenty years, but that he slept through a revolution that would alter the course of human history. . . . One of the great liabilities of history is that all too many people fail to remain awake through great periods of social change."[1]

Leaders of the new century must not only be aware of environmental realities that shape the challenges and issues they must confront—they must also be aware of the inner environments that shape character, civility, and a sense of community. Leaders who are not awake, that is, aware of the interiority of experience, the often deep subconscious elements that drive behavior and action, are increasingly in very vulnerable circumstances and can endanger the mission of a team, an organization, and even, as we have witnessed too many times to ignore, very large numbers of people.

What are the critical resources and methodologies at our disposal to develop a new generation of emerging leaders who are *awake*—physically and emotionally whole, spiritually disciplined, intellectually astute, and morally anchored? Leadership studies abound with various approaches to this question. Among the most popular are theories of adaptive strategies, authenticity, personal efficacy, and character development and, more recently, a growing literature on emotional intelligence, connectivity, and resonance.[2] Absent from many of these approaches is the question of spirituality and ethics and how these interrelated themes inform and transform human consciousness so that the leader is predisposed to make the fitting decision and enabled to carry out the appropriate ethical action among competing claims and a cacophony of voices and visions.

As a new generation of seekers experiment with New Age spiritualities, ancient esoteric traditions, and more traditional religious beliefs and practices, America is caught in a deluge of corruption, debates about morality, and the failure of leadership. Television talk shows regularly feature New Age gurus sharing the most recent formulas on how to get rich and be successful. Busy Wall Street executives can even cram in "spirituality seminars" while they complete the latest blockbuster mergers. Wherever camouflages are needed for the weightier ethical issues related to power and money, talk about spirituality seems to get the job done. But while the new spirituality offers a "quick fix," it won't cure the spiritual malaise that abounds in America. The time is ripe for a different kind of discussion on spirituality that includes ethics and leadership.

BEWARE OF UNICORNS!

Some years ago I was traveling on a country road in Richmond, Indiana, where I noticed an unusual sign at the entrance of an old farm. It read "Beware of Unicorns!" At first, I was struck by the incongruity of this language against the backdrop of our postmodernist culture: a crazy time filled with displacement and ambiguity, mocked by the marred marvels of scientific technology and the ancient dilemmas of human existence. "What in the world," I asked myself, "is a unicorn doing out here?" This imaginary creature, with one spirally horn protruding from its head, seemed out of place in the picturesque American Gothic countryside. "Beware!" the sign read, signaling caution and danger to anyone who dared trespass beyond the weathered white-picket fence. I remembered once when I was eleven years old, a friend and I climbed a huge fence with a sign that said "Beware" and a leaping Great Dane greeted us. I shall never forget how quickly our young agile bodies, without thought, literally jumped backwards over the fence out of harm's way. "But this is different," I said to myself. "A unicorn doesn't bite. Its huge horn is magical—it can either hurt or heal. The unicorn guards the secrets of the imagination, and the imagination both blesses and curses; it can bring freedom or bondage—it all depends on what we do with it. In fact, the sign, while signaling caution and danger, is really an invitation to the freedom of the imagination." The unicorn represents that ever-thin line between realities as they are given to us and the realities we dare to bring into being through the power of imagination.

We may never know whether there is a "real unicorn" behind the fences of an old Indiana farmhouse or in the enchanted environments of the soul unless we dare trespass into forbidden territory. Yes, trespassers beware of unicorns—mythical animals born of the creative imagination hiding in the protective venues of lonely Midwestern landscapes and in the deeper recesses of the human spirit.

"How shall I meet the unicorn?" I thought to myself. "How shall I meet my freedom?" These are also questions born of imaginative journeying and are at the heart of spirituality, ethics, and leadership. Ethical leaders, therefore, are seekers who search for unicorns in the vast, often cold and impersonal worlds of modernity. Empowered by imagination, leaders become visionaries who are willing to enter the no-trespassing zones of systemworlds and to recognize the inherent potential for transformation within and around them. In fact, the practice of imagination is a summons to leaders who dare to go beyond white-picket fences into dangerous territory without a map. In remembering, retelling, and reliving personal narratives, leaders are also empowered to think, feel, and create new possibilities within organizations, teams, and other structured environments that call out for courage, creativity, and hope.

The power of *systemworlds* that intersect with our *lifeworlds* cannot be underestimated. At the intersection, where leaders face continual change, rapid innovation, and increasing globalization, complexity has become the norm. The complex demands leaders encounter today, in both their work and their personal lives, call for forms of self-development that many people are only in the process of achieving. Individuals must develop an enhanced capacity for dealing with increasingly complex challenges, whether on the job or in their personal lives. Individuals or, more important, leaders must become comfortable with the perspective of a lifelong process of self-development, a process that allows for the continual evaluation of the basic beliefs leaders hold about the nature and source of the self.

I wish to be immediately clear that the critique on the absence of the spiritual in leadership discourse and practice is not necessarily an issue of religion. It is centrally an issue of attending to the human spirit, with emphasis on what it means to be human. Critical to the Ethical Leadership Model of transformation is the solicitation and utilization of stories in nurturing the human spirit. Stories provide the vehicles through which leaders come to appreciate and empathize with others. The remembering, retelling, and reliving of stories encourage the cultivation of listening, or what scholars like Stephen Carter have called "civil listening."

IMAGINATION, CHARACTER, CIVILITY, AND COMMUNITY

The imagination is engaged in story discourse at two levels. One is the narrative level, where the hearer is engaged in *second-order discourse* that is primarily descriptive and easily accessible. At a deeper level, however, there is a dimension of story that scholars have called *first-order language*, which is primal and primordial and invites the listener into the sphere of possibility.[3] Storytelling is the prime vehicle for transmission of the wisdom, habits, and practices that fund the moral character (character), transformative civil discourse (civility), and reconciling acts of community (community) of ethical leaders. When revitalized with imagination, tradition becomes a discourse (oral, written, rite, or sacrament) that is able to bring revelation at the intersection of lifeworlds and systems.[4] However, imagination without the input of tradition fails to inculcate habits of conduct within leaders that preserve their sense of continuity with the past.

Imagination empowers leaders to remember and even relive past moments of joy and pain, of deep love and of sorrow. As character is formed and informed by particular stories or sociohistorical narratives, leaders are provided with opportunities to remember, retell, and relive their own stories. Thus, the process of remembering, retelling, and reliving personal narratives is key to the transformation of their emotional and affective centers and the organizational life of which they are a part.

Critical to our approach is the assumption that leaders who are awake are best prepared to handle the dangers of the intersection. Models for the transformation of individual awareness or consciousness, however, often fail to consider the role of spirituality and ethics in human development. The basic argument underlying our interventive strategy is that human development requires an ethical anchor, a structure in which leaders themselves must be central participants. Self-destructive behaviors, poor decision-making, diminished life skills, arrested development in emotional intelligence, faulty communication skills, severe limitations in conduct, and the absence of trust, duty, and responsibility to others are all signs of a ruptured ethical center. The ethical center both forms and informs the leader's sense of self in relation to others and the universe as a whole. Any leadership model that seeks to spark a transformation of consciousness must first help leaders engage and repair their ethical centers. The calls for ethical compliance and more rules-based moral approaches to repair and correct ethical lapses and corruption are necessary but insufficient conditions to address a more fundamental issue, which we are referring to as the ethical center.

The ethical center represents the seat of consciousness or *reflexive consciousness*, that is, the thought that "I am not only conscious, aware, and knowing; I am also *aware* that I am conscious. In other words, I am awake!" There is a dimension of the self that is not only engaged in experience but also aware that it is *experiencing*. When I am reading a great novel and become engrossed in the reading, I literally identify with the characters—and if interrupted, I become aware that I was reading. Becoming aware of the moral life is much the same. The philosopher Laurence Thomas makes this point in respect to the moral life. He differentiates between *morally autonomous* character and *morally nonautonomous* character. The nonautonomous character's moral life and its modes of moral deliberations are based on rules, customs, and traditions that have been given by the society or culture of which he or she is a part. The morally autonomous character, on the other hand, is concerned with moral rules and codes of conduct that are traditional, but insists on being able to justify *why* he or she is moral. In other words, both may be persons of good moral character, but unlike the morally nonautonomous character, the morally autonomous character asks *why* it is important to seek excellence in moral living. Thomas calls these "morally anchored" individuals, whom he likens to virtuosos who display great technical skill in their craft and, while understanding the basic rules of their art, are also able to transcend these in quest of excellence.[5] Such individuals, suggests Thomas, are characterized by three salient features: they have an altruistic nature, they are proficient at monitoring social behavior, and they are equally proficient in moral deliberation. Therefore, leaders who are "morally anchored," that is, who are aware of the challenges and risks associated with responding from this center of consciousness, are prepared to engage in the task of social engagement and reconstruction.

The premise contained in this perspective is that ethical leaders arise from a certain *moral ethos* or *community of discourse and practice*. Organizations, like individuals, need a moral ethos out of which critical actions, behaviors, and decisions are made for the collective good. As defined by Robin S. Snell:

> Moral ethos is a set of force-fields within organizations, comprising everyday norms, rules-in-use, social pressures and qualities of relationships, all of which impinge on members' understandings, judgements and decisions concerning good and bad, right and wrong. As a hidden curriculum of morality in the workplace, moral ethos is synonymous with moral or ethical climate, i.e., shared member perceptions about how ethical dilemmas are to be viewed and resolved—atmosphere, culture and milieu.[6]

Robert Jackall warns that moral ethos in managerial circles is not fixed, but rather flexible. He notes:

> In the welter of practical affairs in the corporate world, morality does not emerge from a set of internally held convictions or principles, but rather from ongoing albeit changing relationships with some reason, some coterie, some social network, some clique that matters to a person. Since the relationships are always multiple, contingent and in flux, managerial moralities are always situational, always relative.[7]

In order to create and sustain a moral ethos in these "flexible moral environments," there must be leaders within the organization who are morally anchored and committed to the maintenance and continuation of a moral ethos through the continual pursuit of excellence in all aspects of the organization's culture. These leaders must stay awake at the intersection where worlds collide.

Imagination and Character

Marianne Williamson's edited volume *Imagine What America Could Be in the Twenty-first Century* is a great example of what is at stake for leaders across various disciplines and domains who dare to use imagination as a tool for envisioning possibility. In one of the articles written by Peter Senge, he suggests that imagining new futures allows us to see possibility beyond the fixed patterns of the "machine system," which has been the dominant paradigm since the Industrial Age. He suggests three ways of thinking about the future: (1) to conceive of the future as an extension of the past (extrapolation), (2) to imagine what might be, independent of what is, or as free of the influence of the present as one might become, and (3) to cultivate awareness and reflectiveness—to become open to what is arising in the world and in us and continually ponder what matters most deeply to us. The third option, he thinks, is the way of the future and requires creative use of the imagination.[8] *Awareness* and *effectiveness*, or heart and head, are both integral to the practice of imagining. The cognitive faculty is not in alien territory in imaginative adventures, as is often thought; rather, it is a key asset. But the domination of calculative and technical reason without the affective, emotional centers out of which we also think, feel, and work prevents the opportunity to envision possibility at the intersection where worlds collide. The imagination calls both the heart and the head into action—it is also a summons to meet the unicorns within us.

One's character and horizon of meaning and the way one understands his or her life and role in the larger whole are related in large part to the ways in which one has been shaped by early childhood experiences, family, significant others, traditions, institutions, and the society of which he or she is a part. In fact, most of our moral outlooks and actions derive from early childhood memories or "scripts" that have been handed down by lifeworlds and systemworlds. Howard Gardner writes:

> By the age of four or five, most youngsters have constructed dozens of scripts based on daily experience; moreover, they have heard dozens of stories from their elders and perhaps scores from the communications media that happen to be prevalent in their societies. No doubt, the number of scripts and stories continues to mount in the years thereafter; and . . . these narratives become more complex, subtle and ambiguous. I would not be surprised if more adults in Western society possess a hundred or more regular scripts and have internalized several hundred stories.[9]

One cannot underestimate the power of media to shape stories, beliefs, habits, and practices. In 1998 I lectured in an area outside of Johannesburg at an HIV/AIDS conference. After the lecture, a young black South African male approached me with an exaggerated swagger in his walk. His cap was turned backwards, and he was dressed in typical hip-hop attire. His greeting, however, both surprised and instructed me on how the power of story communicated through various media informs behavior. He said, "What's up, my nigger?" After pausing and gently reflecting on the question, I responded: "I know what's up. You are standing at the intersection where worlds collide and you don't even know what hit you!"

Character, as "the unity of a narrative quest,"[10] is related to traditions and how the stories of those traditions shape leaders' understanding of civic responsibility and sense of community. For it is in the interlocking stories of a people that ethical leaders acquire their sense of values and an understanding of their place in the world. Interestingly, the words *character* and *ethos* in the Greek are spelled alike with one small inflection that determines their distinction. In fact, Aristotle noted the common roots of *character* and *ethos* (habit) in his *Nicomachean Ethics*.[11] Leaders find their sense of identity and purpose within the context of traditions that are the bearers of memory and stories that fund moral wisdom.

Consequently, the leader understands that morals have much to do with the lifeworld or lifeworlds that precede and determine her perspectives. The world that one encounters is arranged, fabricated, and designed before she becomes conscious that she is a part of it—and before she realizes that she is also part of how it will continue to be and to perpetuate itself. But the world that we encounter is not fixed and static; rather, it is flexible and its "reality" depends in large part on our interaction with it. James Baldwin, the great African American writer and cultural critic, writes, "Nothing is fixed, forever and forever and forever, it is not fixed; the earth is always shifting, the light is always changing, the sea does not cease to grind the rock."[12] Baldwin was well aware of the power and the danger of meeting the unicorn within us, for it is in the shifting of the world and the reimagining of possibility that the ethical leader finds his or her character.

Imagination and Civility

Imagination allows leaders to empathize with the other. Empathy, trust, and a sense of responsibility for the other are essential to the development of a code of civil conduct. By providing leaders with opportunities to use their imaginations to enter the stories of the other, the public construct of an ethical center—civility—is funded with empathy, trust, and a sense of responsibility for the other. *Civility* is the psychosocial ecology of an individual; it is a certain understanding or self-referential index of the individual's place within a democratic social system as it relates to individual character. In a sense, civility is character in public space. How one understands herself and her place in the larger whole determines largely how one responds to public life and practices. The *public* is the space where citizens meet and engage in meaningful discussion and action about values and where they hold one another accountable for what they know and value. Leaders must be aware of the intersection of public and private spaces as they interact with others about the future and destiny of democracy—democracy, after all, is fundamentally an ethical practice, a contentious debate about goods (values) that define our larger social vision of equality and freedom.[13]

Stephen Carter compares civic life to a train ride with many passengers with competing needs and interests. He argues:

> Civility . . . is the sum of the many sacrifices we are called to make for the sake of living together. When we pretend that we travel alone, we can also pretend that these sacrifices are unnecessary. Yielding to this very human instinct for self-seeking . . . is often immoral, and certainly should not be done without forethought. We should make sacrifices for others not simply because doing so makes social life easier (although it does), but as a signal of respect for our fellow citizens, marking them as full equals, both before the law and before God.[14]

The empathy and respect that Carter calls for in this imaginative analogy is wrought by bringing to consciousness our interrelatedness or *sense of community*. Imaginative projection that puts one in another's place becomes central to a leader's repository of tools that allows him or her to maintain an ethic of balance and justice in public life. Again what is at stake in this imaginative use of story is the appeal to the leader's ethical center, his or her awareness that sacrifices must be made for the sake of the whole.

Imagination and Community

Imagination has the potential to empower leaders to transcend damage wrought by powerful systems of injustice through a sense of community. A contemporary example of ethical leadership, in this respect, is the story of

Nelson Mandela. Though he was physically imprisoned, his sense of character imbued with an imaginative quest for human community allowed him to survive and transcend the political bondage meted out against him and his people. Much of this power, Mandela suggests, was rooted in the combination of moral will and imagination. Perhaps the greatest contribution of Nelson Mandela for the future of ethical leadership was his ability to hold in critical relief the vision of a community wrought by courage, justice, and compassion.

During the summer of 2005, I led a delegation of students sponsored by Oprah Winfrey to South Africa to study ethical leadership within the context of the South African democratization process. After a visit to Robben Island, the prison facility where Mandela spent most of his twenty-seven years incarcerated, one of the students wrote in his diary:

> The impact was strongest when I stood directly in front of Nelson Mandela's cell, number five in the B section, which was reserved for political prisoners. Sections A and C housed criminal prisoners. What affected me most was to hear how these prisoners were actually treated. It was heart-breaking to look at the cement floor where Mr. Mandela slept without a cot or anything for cushion. It was enormously troubling to look at the five-gallon bucket that Mr. Mandela had to use for a bathroom because there was no toilet in his cell. Who can imagine having to smell something like that two feet away from you all night long until the following morning when you were allowed to empty and clean your waste bucket?[15]

Leaders who are able to stand at the intersections of personal reality and possibility (character), social reality and possibility (civility), and spiritual reality and possibility (community) and consciously set goals and objectives and implement life-affirming resolutions are what we are terming ethical leaders. Training a new generation of leaders will require a methodological emphasis on the power of story and the practice of remembering, retelling, and living these stories through imaginative journeying to meet the unicorn. Such an undertaking will require a discussion of the place of spirituality, ethics, and leadership as a broader interpretative framework for a kind of training essential to stimulate consciousness and mold character, civility, and community as three principal dimensions of the work of ethical leadership.

Chapter Seven

REMEMBERING, RETELLING, AND RELIVING OUR STORIES

REMEMBERING OUR STORIES

Remembering personal and collective stories of which one is a part allows leaders to experience a sense of wholeness, harmony, and integration, or better, a sense of *integrity*. In ancient Egypt, there was the wonderful story of Isis and Osiris. While there are many versions of this story, I first heard the one that is shared here from an Egyptologist while on a study tour in that beautiful land.[1] Like many cosmogonic myths,[2] the story begins with two gods: Nut, the sky god, and Geb, the earth god. In this story of beginnings, Nut and Geb had two sets of twins, male and female respectively. One couplet was named Osiris and Isis; the other Seth and Nephthys. Each couplet was husband-wife and sister-brother to each. Isis was the sister-wife to Osiris; and Nephthys, the sister-wife to Seth. Osiris was powerful and the legendary leader of all human beings, and Isis was the most beautiful of the goddesses and the most powerful. What a pair!

Now, their brother and sister, Seth and Nephthys, were a different story. Nephthys, like her sister, was beautiful, but her husband-brother, Seth, was not as powerful or as virile as Osiris. In fact, Seth was impotent. This made for an interesting drama in the beginnings of the world because one day Seth discovered that Nephthys was with child. Of course, the only possible suspect was his brother, Osiris. All Egyptian heaven broke loose! Various versions tell different stories, but in this one, Seth secretly plots and eventually murders Osiris, dismembers his body parts, and hides each part under the sands throughout Upper and Lower Egypt.

When Isis discovers the murder of her lover, she sets out on a long journey to find each part of Osiris's body. She is accompanied by her sister,

Nephthys, who is also in love with Osiris. It is because of Isis's great love for Osiris that when she finally finds each part of his *dismembered* body, she *remembers* him. Finally, after she *remembers* him, she takes the most precious part, the sexual organ, and conceives a son, Horus, who is the resurrected Osiris, the avenger of his father's death.

This story is an example of the process of *remembering* that is a vital dimension of the transformation of consciousness that leaders must explore as an exercise in self-discovery. Remembering acts to re-collect, reassemble, and reconfigure individual and collective consciousness into a meaningful and sequential whole through the process of narrativization. The significance of remembering is the narrativization of the past, the reclaiming of bodies of disparate and disconnected meaning lodged in the unconscious matrices of the soul.[3] It is not merely a return to intellectual excavation of historical data, but is associated with deep emotional energy, which is spiritual and emphatic. Remembering our stories offers entrée into forgotten worlds of meaning that allow recovery of dismembered bodies of experience otherwise invisible to consciousness. They help us to better understand and respond to the questions of character: *Who am I, really? What do I really want? And how do I propose to get what I really want?*

Every story has a plot, and so do our personal stories. A plot can be a story or sequence of events in a narrated or presented work, such as a novel, play, or movie. A plot can also be a small piece of ground set aside for planting. I am using the word "plot" in both senses. In the latter, I am suggesting, along with James Hillman, that each life is like a tiny acorn that contains within itself an oak tree. The *acorn theory* holds that we come into the world with a blueprint, so to speak, of who we are and what we are "called" to do. The plot, therefore, is an image of our destiny. Hillman writes:

> Sooner or later something seems to call us onto a particular path. You may remember this "something" as a signal moment in childhood when an urge out of nowhere, a fascination, a peculiar turn of events struck like an annunciation: This is what I must do, this is what I've got to have. This is who I am.[4]

Early childhood memories help us to gain some sense of the dreams, ideals, and imaginings that literally call us to our destinies. Leaders must begin by asking and seeking answers to several primary questions: What is the *plot* of my personal story? What are the initial dramatic resources that contribute to my life story? What was my environment like in my early stories (the feelings, the textures, the mood, the pathos, the ethos of early memories)? What is at stake, or what really matters in my story? Who are the other characters in my story? How are they alike and how are they different? Who am I in my story? What *character* do I play in the story? What are the dreams, imaginings, and ideals that literally grabbed my sensibilities at an early age?

RETELLING OUR STORIES

Leaders must not only remember their stories through the process of storytelling; leaders must interrogate belief systems that have been handed down to them by tradition, mores, and customs. Leaders must ask, "What beliefs does one use to form a sense of self and sense of his or her place in the world?" This process of retelling and reframing stories involves three interrelated steps of *self-reading*, *self-authoring*, and *self-revision*. This process corresponds respectively to three views of the moral agency: *heteronomy* (the rule or law of the other), *autonomy* (the rule or law of self), and *relationality* (the rule or law of relations).[5]

Self-reading suggests that a person's core identity is determined by what certain people and ideas, the people and ideas that are most important in his life, tell him about who he is. While it is important to observe the contributions of others, of customs, mores, and traditions, leaders who are stuck in the stage of self-reading are vulnerable to what others think about them and often fail to exercise what they believe is the appropriate decision in ethical situations that require their response. They become prisoners to *heteronomous* ethics, or the rule of the other. Philosopher Jean-Paul Sartre once said that "hell is other people." The insatiable demand for recognition from others at this stage can be detrimental to the leader's personal growth and ethical life.

Self-authoring, on the other hand, refers to the leader's *autonomous* response to ethical situations that arise. In other words, at this stage, the leader "authors the book of her identity" by paying close attention to her own insights, independent of the responses and judgments of others and independent of external ideas and values. Such a person understands the value of self-regulation, or what has been referred to earlier as "morally anchored character." Who can deny that independence is a laudable attribute of leaders? Leaders, however, who fail to pay attention to practices that have preceded them run the serious risk of making isolated judgments, that is, without feedback from experience, tradition, and customs that have protected and guided the community in the past.

Self-revision requires a relational ethic that takes into account views and judgments other than the leader's own. Leaders who make ethical judgments that will impact others must learn to *self-revise* within the context of relations with other people, ideas, and values. One of the greatest challenges of leaders is the ability to look, listen, and learn from others who share a common vision and mission within organizational and communal structures that work for change. One great example of Martin Luther King Jr.'s method of decision-making was his ability to hold in creative tension conflicting views and to find a third way that combined the best of the *thesis* (values from the past) and *antithesis* (conflicting views) in the construction of a *synthesis* (a view that is substantively different and qualitatively new). In this sense, self-revision is synonymous with retelling or reframing our stories.

Reframing our stories is less about making sacrosanct a particular set of beliefs than it is about finding *common ground* with others. Discovering the limits of one's beliefs can be painful, but it provides one with opportunity for growth and respect among peers and team members. Reframing our stories results in forming a new habit structure that accommodates the ethical choices with which one is confronted in the context of relations with others. Finally, reframing our stories gives us power over our moral outlook and development; it helps to heal and repair ruptures that have grown deeply over time and that often distort moral vision and action. Remembering our story is not enough; one must also retell the story. This requires *critical reframing* of the materials of our story that need addressing in the present.

Related to retelling our stories is the role again of the imagination— our ability to envision the future. I am not suggesting that we pull out a crystal ball and see into the future but rather that we engage possibility. At the intersection, leaders must dare to reimagine themselves and their stories in the context of relations with others. "Who am I?"—the question of identity and character—is related to "Who will I become?" As I have suggested, character is related to "calling."

A graduate student approached Howard Thurman seeking advice on what needed to be done in the world. Thurman interrupted him and said, "Don't ask yourself what the world needs. Ask yourself what makes you come alive, and go and do that, because what the world needs is people who have come alive."[6] The calling of character or the character that calls comes to us from both the past and the future—in remembering our stories and in imagining the possibility inherent in our stories. What makes us *come alive* nudges us from both dimensions. Imagining grants permission to come alive. In this sense, the question of calling or purpose is related to *identity*. To know oneself, one's uniqueness in respect to gifts, talents, and skills, is to have a clue as to who one is and what one's purpose is in the world. Vocation, as it is used here, refers to "purpose." It is derived from the Latin verb *vocare*, "to call." What one is called to do is predicated on a number of factors in respect to natural endowments and social configurations, but the ultimate choice rests upon what one comes to understand about oneself in the midst of a number of claims presented to the self in the course of life. In this respect, what is commonly referred to as *fate*, the family and social environment one inherits, may provide the context for discovery of vocation, but ultimately one's destiny is determined by what one does with the inner will, desires, and signals that come from a healthy sense of self or a morally anchored character. Vocation, in this sense, has much to do with the pivotal concepts of freedom and imagination. Vocation goes beyond career choices and asks the moral questions, What end does my career seek? and How does my choice of vocation contribute to integration, wholeness, and harmony in society and the world?

Leaders who retell their stories with an imaginative eye for calling, purpose, and character might begin by answering these questions and performing these simple exercises: How do I want my story to end? What do I want others to remember about me? Why is it important to me that I am *remembered* in this way? Begin with the end in mind. Fast-forward to your "golden years." A respected publisher wants to publish your story. What will it say? Write your obituary. What will others say about you?

RELIVING OUR STORIES

Leaders at the intersection must not only remember and retell their stories; they must also live their stories within the context of the *present*. The stories in the past and the imaginative quests for the future find their realization in the present. Leaders must make decisions that proceed from a center of wholeness out of which they are able to speak with authenticity and integrity. This cannot be done without plumbing the depths of who we really are—and this is only discovered in the present. This perspective grows out of the affirmation that pure experience is all there is and that experience is simultaneously *acting* and *relating*. Therefore, agency—what we are doing—precedes the self as agent. In other words, I am who I am because of what I am doing in relation, and all mind-body functions are derived from relating.[7] Hugh Prather in *Notes to Myself* describes poetically the nature of acting and relating in the present:

> My prayer is: I will be what I will be
> and I will do what I will do.
>
> All I want to do, need to do, is stay in
> rhythm with myself. All I want is to do
> what I do and not try to do what I
> don't do. Just what I do. Just keep
> pace with myself. Just be what I will be.
>
> I will be what I will—but I am now
> what I am, and here is where I will
> spend my energy. I need all my energy to
> be what I am today. Today I will work
> in rhythm with myself and not with what
> I "should be." And to work in rhythm
> with myself I must keep tuned into myself.
>
> God revealed his name to Moses, and it
> was: I AM WHAT I AM.
> . . . .
> *I am holding this cat in my arms so it can sleep,*
> *and what more is there.*[8]

There are several questions that leaders must answer at this stage of reliving the story. How then do I make what I remember and envision about my story real? This is a double-edged question, because sometimes what is remembered and envisioned creates challenges for leaders. Often leaders are called to address complex personal ethical issues that crowd the intersection of their stories and render them immobile. Years ago, I was struggling with some difficult decisions that would determine the course of my professional career. I asked a close colleague and friend to help me navigate these decisions. He responded with a clarity and vision that interrupted the noisy internal voices that competed at the intersection of my past and the future that was beckoning. He said, "Be here now!" I had become perplexed by the chronicles of my past that were damning and humiliating and the possibilities of the future that were equally daunting and laced with fear of failure. The energy behind the words "Be here now" provoked a change in my consciousness. I realized that the residual fears lurked in a past that no longer held claim over me and in a future that had not come. I had to come to grips with my present, which owed allegiance neither to the past nor to the future but simply made demands upon my deepest sense of who I was. "Be here now" is a summons to be aware of the inherent grace of the present. After I have remembered and reframed my story, I can then make it real or bring the new insights and revelations to fruition.

To whom or with whom do I want to share my story? The remembering, retelling, and reliving of our stories are not a set of soliloquies that we perform alone. Leaders must identify those to whom they will share their stories. Often those with whom we share are mentors, professionals, family, or esteemed members of our community of work and practice, but that need not be the case. Those with whom we share must first exhibit a sense of openness to listening to our stories. It is counterproductive to share our stories with those who cannot listen without judgment and blame. Equally important, we should share stories with those who are able to ask the hard questions that we find convenient to avoid.

Who are the other stakeholders in my story? I am never the lone actor in my story; I am in relation with others. Therefore, my story must acknowledge others who have made it possible and still others who make my vision of my self come alive. These important others—stakeholders—have value for and in the successful completion of my story. These are often coworkers and fellow team members, but there exists another important dynamic in reliving our stories that should not be overlooked. We must always allow for the *stranger*. Clearly, in organizational life, especially in business, one is taught to be wary of strangers—but strangers can be the ones who make your deepest dreams and aspirations come alive.

Broken and humiliated because he did not have the money to pay for the shipment of a trunk to attend high school in Jacksonville, Florida, a thirteen-year-old Howard Thurman sat on the steps outside of a railroad station in Daytona and wept. Suddenly, he heard a gruff and unfamiliar voice: "Boy, what in the hell is wrong with you?" Thurman says he slowly raised his head and saw a tall black man standing before him dressed in long overalls with a bandana around his neck. He told his story to the stranger, who responded, "Anybody who is trying to get out of this damned town, the least I can do is help." Thurman says he watched as the man deftly opened his coin purse, pulled tobacco from his pouch, rolled a cigarette, struck a match, and lit the cigarette all with one hand, then gave him the money he needed to ship his trunk. He says that it was this stranger who made all the difference for a dream that had been shattered. His autobiography, *With Head and Heart*, is dedicated "to the stranger in the railroad station in Daytona Beach who restored my broken dream sixty-five years ago."[9]

Reliving the story and inviting the stranger to share in your story also involves a shift in traditional sources of authority, which has powerful implications for questions of knowledge and approach. Asking for direction from faces and places we did not expect is a humbling experience. Leaders at the intersection, however, must become accustomed to and comfortable with asking for help from those whom we have traditionally neglected and despised.

Chapter Eight

ETHICAL DECISION-MAKING AT THE INTERSECTION WHERE WORLDS COLLIDE

WHAT'S GOING ON?

At the height of the anti-war movement in 1971, the late R&B singer Marvin Gaye asked a provocative lyrical question that became the standard for a generation of frustrated youth who sought answers beyond nightly media reports and press conferences from politicians. Gaye combined the intimacy of personal narrative with the larger public issues of war and injustice. In this song, Gaye raised the primary ethical question in public life: *What's going on?*[1]

Gaye was not the first to ask the question. Christian ethicist H. R. Niebuhr posed this question as the sine qua non of the ethical life. In discerning the fitting response to actions upon ourselves in private or public, prior to the questions "What shall I do?" or "What is right or good?" Niebuhr suggests that the critical ethical question is, "What is going on?"[2] Our response to the question, however, is always an *interpreted* response that leads one to the larger questions of personal and public accountability within a particular community of discourse and practice. In other words, one raises the ethical question within the context of particular assumptions, beliefs, and values. The fitting ethical response to "What shall I do?" is rooted in the quest to understand our own personal and social narratives that call for responsible action in public life. For historically marginalized communities of color, gender, and sexuality, this problem is particularly acute and demands critical analysis and deliberation on the appropriate response to the question.[3]

However one is situated, she cannot ethically respond, engage, and act without first answering this question. A simple story illustrates this point.

Two people were standing by a river one day when they noticed a baby being carried by the rushing waters toward the falls. They jumped into the water and daringly swam to the child's rescue. As soon as they were settled onshore, they looked and noticed that another child was being carried downstream. Again they dove into the water and rescued the child. But no sooner had they rested for a moment than they looked and saw that the current was carrying yet another child away. This time, only one of them dove into the water, and when he noticed that the other was not attempting to swim to the rescue, he cried out, "Hey, what's going on? Are you going to help?" The other person responded, "Yes, I am going upstream to find out who is throwing babies into the river!" This is the import of the question. It is not enough to ask the question of morals and values as isolated, unrelated, individualistic phenomena, but one must inquire upstream as to what is going on. A threefold process ensues from this initial question: *discernment*, *deliberation*, and *decision*.

DISCERNMENT

Discernment involves *looking*, *listening*, and *learning*. It is synonymous with intuition—seeing clearly what is already *present* (the present as that which *presents* itself to us). Discernment requires paying close attention to the relationships around the object of concern. One must always ask, "What's going on?" and then inquire by paying close attention to the environment and relationships. Daniel Pink calls this sense of discernment "symphony." Like a conductor in an orchestra, one sees the big picture, the many different musical instruments playing together in order to create a fluid, coherent movement of sound. It is a highly improvisational performance that emanates from the ability to observe and sense patterns that are hidden within the musical score and revealed in the very movement of the phenomena. How one becomes proficient in this ability to sense the relationships and patterns among seemingly unrelated and disparate entities has a lot to do with "emotional aptitude," emphasizing looking, listening, and learning as an authentic quest for knowledge.[4]

Looking Around

There are two steps involved in looking: *looking around* and *looking deeply*. Looking around involves *tacit knowing*. Michael Polanyi made this insight early in his work on personal knowledge. Malcolm Gladwell calls this innate capacity "blinking."[5] Key to this idea of looking around is the view that there is something that is hidden in the environment which is discoverable and which calls to the discoverer, but one cannot experience it without *looking* for it, which is simultaneously a process of personal knowledge and an act of faith.[6]

One of my favorite examples of this ability to look around is the athletic artistry of Ervin "Magic" Johnson. Magic was a master of seeing the whole court and being able to get the ball to other players in spaces that did not exist at least to the normal eye. Leaders who are able to discern and create opportunities from places and spaces that do not readily appear are what we are calling *virtuosos*. They possess a sense of the moment; they feel an opening and are attuned to creative opportunities that occur to them while they are in movement themselves. They take risks that often appear to others as risky and dangerous, but they dare the improbable because they have become one with "what's going on."

Looking Deeply

Discernment also involves *self-reflection*, looking deeply into our private lives. Leaders must learn to look deeply into themselves and there discover the wonderful gifts of freedom, imagination, and creativity that neither demon nor angel can conquer or destroy.[7] To look deeply involves more than a visit to the therapist or browsing the self-help section of Barnes & Noble. To look deeply within the self is to ponder the hard questions related to our stories. The public issues of justice and peace have their genesis, development, and maturation in the dramatic resources of our own lives. To look deeply demands that leaders remember, retell, and relive stories that cry out for resolution. Beyond strictly therapeutic investigations of the self, this is a spiritual exercise that requires the discipline, practice, and hard work of *inward journeying*. Leaders who look deeply participate in an inward journey in which they are simultaneously the observers. This dimension of the self that serves as observer becomes conscious of consciousness and connects with a larger consciousness.

In many respects, this movement of consciousness or tacit knowing mirrors the playing of a piano. Nina Abraham Palmer suggests that

> knowing, to begin with, involves tacitly connecting two entities—that *from* which we attend (such as our sense of music or pressure of the muscles in our fingers), and that *to* which we attend (playing a simple tune). It does not take a stretch of imagination to see that continued

learning or increased knowing depends on our conscious focus shifting
further to the bigger and yet bigger picture; and our increasing ability
to depend subsidiarily on more of what at first were the specifics of our
focus. Our making more meaningful the tacit connection between what
we subsidiarily know and what we are attending to.[8]

This notion of discernment, moving from the specific to the larger
picture, becomes more important in high-tech global cultures where
knowledge-based business cultures rely more and more on *design* than
function. The rallying point of technological expertise depends more
on the point of subsidiary knowing that integrates known variables into
larger functions and that creates new models for the transfer of knowledge in existing systems in need of constant innovation. In specific organizational settings, leaders learn that designing the appropriate response
to new knowledge requires less focus on the known and more on what
presents itself as new and possible. W. Chan Kim and Renée Mauborgne
call this approach "blue ocean strategy." The basic idea is that most business strategies are based on a competitive model that competes in existing
market spaces with the intent to beat the competition, exploit the existing
demand, and align the business's activities with a strategic choice of differentiation or low cost which the authors call "red ocean strategy" ("red"
because everybody gets bloodied in the harsh competition). They argue
that this traditional business strategy is really based on a military model
that values confrontation and battling over land that is limited and constant. But in a bold new world, "blue ocean strategy" posits the opposite:
instead of defending and attacking one's market space, the emphasis is
now on creating new market space and making competition irrelevant,
which allows the business to create new demand and to align the whole
system in pursuit of differentiation and low cost. An example of this creative and innovative outlook is the recent history of Cirque du Soleil. In
a shrinking industry, it did not confront or compete with Ringling Bros.
and Barnum & Bailey. "Instead it created uncontested market space that
made the competition irrelevant."[9] Cirque du Soleil reconstructed the
boundaries of circus, theater, ballet, and cinema and designed new space.

A corollary to this perspective takes place in organizational life. Systems that have worked efficiently in the past are constantly in need of
new adaptive strategies that require creativity, evaluation, and monitoring.
Leaders who are able to make the personal connection to knowledge, as
described above, see the advantages in creatively engaging other personnel

in the discernment process, each bringing an angle of vision to the problem or need that was not necessarily apparent at the beginning. Discernment in this sense is a community of explorers in search of possibility—a whole new mind that is communal and open-ended.

To *look deeply* also involves the question of *values*. Leaders who look deeply ask fundamental questions about the defining values that provide for them the resources and the boundaries for their private and public deportment. Values determine, in large measure, what it is that needs changing. If one is unable to name for oneself the defining values of one's own life, then he or she will not be able to authentically speak about change anywhere else. Albert Camus said once, "I realize that it is not my role to transform either the world or man: I have neither sufficient virtue nor insight for that. But it may be to serve, in my place, those few values without which even a transformed world would not be worth living in, and man, even if 'new,' would not deserve to be respected." What are the values that you serve?

Finally, discerning what's going on also requires reexamination of the core values and assumptions about identity (character), relationships with others in my environment who are involved in and will influence my discernment (civility), and my primary network of discourse and practice (community). Leaders who fail to consider their own core values and assumptions in the discerning process, along with the others in their environment of interpretation and meaning, often make decisions that are either inadequate or disastrous to their primary communities of responsibility.

In decision-making situations where leaders are often called upon to make clear choices among competing values, the plethora of information can become confusing and distracting. Remaining focused and yet discerning the larger picture is imperative. Consider the story of the man who was driving rather fast down a country road and met, almost head-on, a car coming from the opposite direction. The woman driving the other car screamed, "Pig!" And the driver promptly retorted, waving his hands and shouting at the top of his lungs, "The nerve—you are the pig! You drive like a maniac! If I had my way, I would blankity-blank your blankity-blank!" As he rounded the curve, he crashed into a huge pig standing in the middle of the road. He failed to pay attention to what was going on around him and the signals from his environment. There are always pigs in the road—learning to interrogate long-held beliefs, assumptions, and practices and to pay close attention to signals from oneself, others, and the environment can save leaders from tragedies at the intersection. Malcolm Gladwell suggests that in such situations there are two indispensable practices: one is maintaining balance between deliberative and instinctive thinking; the other is learning that good decision-making requires frugality in situations with competing choices. Both practices require an attunement to disciplined reflection learned over a lifetime of practice and a sense of guiding values.[10]

Listening Intently

To look deeply into the self also demands that we *listen intently* for *the sound of the genuine* that surrounds us and that is within the other and ourselves. Howard Thurman said, "There is something within every person that waits and listens for the sound of the genuine within herself. . . . There is something in everybody that waits and listens for the sound of the genuine in other people."[11] The sound of the genuine refers to the common consciousness that exists among people and the ways in which listening deeply to the other with empathy and respect allows for *discovery* and *possibility.* Similarly, as stated above in the discussion on empathy, Thurman provides a key in what he calls "sounding," which is "to inform one's self of the view from 'the other side.'"[12] To sense not only the mood and tone of the other but to call into play the entire environment and context where one makes a sounding and ascertains a sense of what is going on.

If I put myself in the place where I am willing to *look deeply* and *listen intently*, then I am in a position to *learn* from my environment and myself. I can begin to discern what is possible and to discover the potential inherent in the many possibilities that present themselves to me at the intersection. I can also begin to answer the primary ethical question of "What is going on?" Before I rush to affix moral rules, codes of conduct, and rigid guidelines for action, I must answer the question "What is going on?" which is related to recognition.

DELIBERATION

The second step involves *deliberation*. Deliberation suggests that there are options to be explored. Considering the options in a situation requires both *analysis* and *interpretation*. Clifford Geertz's example is helpful here: A beautiful woman walks into the room and your eyes are glued to her. She winks at you and you are truly focused on her. She only has eyes for you, so you think. But upon further analysis, as you look deeply at the situation, you discover that she is really winking at the guy behind you or that she has a nervous twitch and so on. There are different levels of meaning and interpretation.

In ethical situations, one must weigh options not just in terms of the consequences for action; if we only use this utilitarian mode of thinking, we miss the point entirely. Rather, far more is at stake—it has to do with character: integrity, empathy, and hope—in sum, one's soul. According to a saying of Jesus, "What shall it profit a person if he or she gains the whole world and loses his or her soul?" (Matthew 16:26; Mark 8:36). The soul—one's essence, the distillation of one's meaning and value—is, in the final analysis, the basis of identity, purpose, and destiny if one is willing to look at oneself long enough to recognize one's potential; it is also the seat from which the leader evaluates and make judgments about self and the world.

Deliberation involves the exploration of options: What is really here that is of value to my vision, mission, goals, and objectives? Does this reading of the situation conspire with or against my highest goals and aspirations? Deliberation also involves *bricolage*: the process of inclusion, exclusion, and reconfiguration. In metallurgy, this is standard practice. The elements of a particular compound are blended in such a way that something qualitatively new and substantively different is created from the transformation of materials at hand. In other words, I begin with the material at hand, that which presents itself as potential to fulfill my highest values and noblest aspirations. I ask, "What is of value here that should be kept? What needs to be excluded? What must I bring in that is new?"

In businesses and organizations, this is especially important. Restructuring is one of the ways we talk about creating change, but what if we decided that instead of restructuring, we would first imagine possibilities inherent in the environment? Maybe the answer that we seek is not in changing the business structure, but in first rethinking the values that will define our purpose, goals, and objectives. What if we were to conclude that the quality of life among those who make the vision real is just as important as the bottom line? Could we begin to ask those who are related, "What are the possibilities that you see in reimagining ourselves and our organization and in creating alignment with values?" The future of successful movements and organizations will be dependent on leadership that emphasizes shared vision and values. No longer can we function in this fast-changing environment with dysfunctional leadership practices that dismiss, undermine, and destroy the wisdom of the community.

One of the most courageous and compassionate acts in the annals of modern business practices took place shortly after the Malden Mills factory in Lawrence, Massachusetts, burned down on December 11, 1995. Instead of subscribing to the popular options of restructuring, shutting down, downsizing, and perhaps moving overseas, CEO Aaron Feuerstein rebuilt an environmentally safe and worker-friendly factory at his own expense, spending $300 million of the insurance money and borrowing an additional $100 million. He kept all three thousand employees on the payroll with full benefits for six months. He credited his actions to the values he learned from the Talmud. "You are not permitted to oppress the working man, because he's poor and he's needy, amongst your brethren and amongst the non-Jew in your community," said Feuerstein.[13]

> I have a responsibility to the worker, both blue-collar and white-collar. I have an equal responsibility to the community. It would have been unconscionable to put 3,000 people on the streets and deliver a death-blow to the cities of Lawrence and Methuen. Maybe on paper our company is worthless to Wall Street, but I can tell you it's worth more.[14]

DECISION

Related to discernment and deliberation is *decision*. "To decide" comes from the Latin *decidere*, which means "to cut off." After exploration and investigation of options, which are the ones that I need to cut off? Some paths will not allow this organization to achieve its shared vision and values. All of my choices must be informed by certain values and shared visions. Leaders involved in discernment, deliberation, and decision often encounter what Joseph L. Badarraco calls "defining moments." Unlike purely ethical decisions that ask questions of right and wrong, "defining moments" ask us to choose between competing values and ideals in which we intensely believe. Hence, "defining moments" ask leaders "to dig below the busy surface of their lives and refocus on their core values and principles. Once uncovered, those values and principles renew their sense of purpose and act as a springboard for shrewd, pragmatic, politically astute action." Badarraco suggests three primary steps as guides for discernment concerning appropriate actions and strategies for leaders confronted with "defining moments":

1. Who am I?

   What feelings and intuitions are coming into conflict in this
   situation?

   Which of the values that are in conflict are most deeply rooted in my
   life?

   What combination of expediency and shrewdness, coupled with
   imagination and boldness, will help me implement my personal
   understanding of what is right?

2. Who are we?

   What are the other strong, persuasive interpretations of the ethics of
   the situation?

   What point of view is most likely to win a contest of interpretations
   inside my organization and influence the thinking of other people?

   Have I orchestrated a process that can make manifest the values I
   care about in my organization?

3. Who is my community?

   Have I done all I can to secure my position and the strength of my
   organization?

   Have I thought creatively and boldly about my organization's role
   and its relationship to stakeholders?

   What combination of shrewdness, creativity and tenacity will help
   me to transform my vision into reality?[15]

A Defining Moment: The Case of Ladan and Laleh Bijani

"Defining moments" do not always call for "shrewd, pragmatic, and politically astute action." Sometimes they require gentleness, humility, and
compassion. In July 2003, I walked into a Delta Crown Room and noticed
an advertisement by a well-known accounting firm with a background
that was one-half black and one-half white. The caption underneath read,
"This is the way we see our ethics." The assumption, of course, was that
ethical questions for this company were clear-cut, right or wrong. In the
complex world of ethical decision-making, we do not have such a luxury.
Earlier that month, a team of neurosurgeons headed by Dr. Ben Carson,
the famous neurosurgeon and director of the Division of Pediatric Neurosurgery at Johns Hopkins in Baltimore, was part of a prestigious medical
team that had performed surgery on twenty-nine-year-old twins Ladan

and Laleh Bijani, who were craniopagus twins, conjoined twins connected at their heads. Craniopagus twins occur once in every two million live births. Successful separation is rare.

In an interview with National Public Radio, Carson explained why he proceeded with the surgery despite his and the team's reservations. The delicate procedure was risky and fraught with many ethical concerns. He explained, "They [the twins] were intensely interested in being separated. They both had law degrees. They were way outside the norm in terms of people who understood where they wanted to go and had informed consent. Nevertheless, the complexity of their situation dictated to me in my normal decision-making process that the likelihood of success would be no greater than 50 percent and that that was too high a risk. Usually when we're looking at risk of 10 percent or more, we're thinking that that's too high." Although the twins seemed to see the issue in black and white, Dr. Carson suggested that he and his team did not. From the very beginning, he said that he was reluctant to perform the surgery because of the attendant risks—but the two sisters persisted. Despite the odds, Laden and Laleh, according to Carson, were clear: "Doctor, we would rather die than spend another day together."[16]

Integrity demanded that the surgeons share with the sisters the high risks involved—but was there more? Was there any point along the way from preliminary observations and during the surgery when they could have simply decided not to perform the risky surgery, or were there other motivations—their contributions to science, hubris, and recognition? Dr. Carson, a leader with impeccable credentials and known for his honesty and integrity, indicated that just the opposite was true. He said that though he was reluctant to proceed with the surgery, he also empathized with them as individuals. "But then I put myself in their place and I said what if you were stuck to the person you liked the most in the world 24/7 and you could never get away from them for even one second? And I realized what they were going through."[17] What must it be like to be joined to another in such an intimate way that their individuality was never given a possibility? He mentioned the way in which they had to share everything—even going to the restroom together. What must it be like to exist in this state their entire lives and not experience the freedom of individuality? Even during the surgery and after the neurosurgeons had opened the joined skulls and were trying to ensure blood supplies to both brains by fashioning a bypass from a vein taken from Ladan's right thigh, he thought they should stop the procedure. But Dr. Keith Goh, the lead surgeon, and Dr. Loo Choon

Yong, the administrative chair of Singapore's Raffles Hospital, reminded him of the sisters' request that no matter what happened they wanted him to proceed. Carson went a step further and insisted that he speak with the twins' appointed guardian; but the guardian refused to grant permission to stop the surgery because of her vow to Laden and Laleh to proceed no matter what the outcome.

Carson indicated that his emotional identification with them impacted his decision-making.

> Once it became clear that they were going to proceed, then I felt an obligation to help because I had a fair amount of experience with this, and if things had not come out well, I would have felt very guilty for not at least having helped with the effort. . . . Well, I must admit that I liked them a great deal. They had terrific personalities. They had a sense of humor. They had learned to speak English in only seven months. Does that impact upon one's decision-making? Absolutely. And one of the things that they said is that they'd rather die than continue living in that fashion.

Carson's empathy with the twins' desire to proceed with the surgery despite the attendant risks, even death, is an example of the role that the affective dimension plays in such situations. However, his normal decision-making process, which was basically utilitarian and pragmatic, was informed by years of experience.

> Most of the time I'm going to ask myself what's the best thing that happens if I do something? What's the worst thing that happens if I do something? What's the best thing that happens if I do nothing? And what's the worst thing that happens when I do nothing? And when I answer those four questions and I also go through those four questions with the patient, or with their parents, everybody has a very clear understanding.[18]

Beyond deliberation, there was also the important step of discernment. Carson asked the primary ethical question, "What's going on?" He consulted with Dr. Goh and other neurosurgery colleagues, some who had refused to accept the case and emphatically disputed the Singapore team's decision to perform the surgery,[19] but Carson suggested:

First of all, when you talk about trusting your gut, a lot of people think of that in a negative sense. But you know, our subconscious is extraordinarily powerful and has the ability to draw on our lifetime of experience. What we may be talking about here is wisdom, and that's not something that can be taught. I personally believe it comes from a higher source. Some people have three Ph.D.s behind their name, but don't have it. Other people have no letters behind their names and have it in spades. I think that has a lot to do with success that people have.

Finally, after they spoke with the twins' guardian and she insisted that they go forward with the operation, he proceeded in hope—though he knew then that it was likely that at least one of the twins would die. What does hope mean in this context? How does hope function as an operative concept in moral reasoning through the complex web of discernment, deliberation, and decision? What is the meaning of hope after the failed procedure? Hope is genuine anticipation of the future. James Gustafson's description of hope discussed earlier applies to Carson's attitude in this difficult situation: "Hope is carried by the confidence that life is more reliable than unreliable, that the future is open, that new possibilities of life exist, that the present patterns of life are not fated by the blind god Necessity, but are susceptible to change, to a recombination of aspects and elements of the world."[20] Carson could have succumbed to the extremes of *despair* and *a sense of fatedness*, but he answered that hope is beyond the moment— what is learned through scientific experimentation will benefit others in the long run. Simply a utilitarian argument based upon an experimental calculus? No, he chose to believe that there is a "growing edge" that reaches beyond our temptation to despair and our inclinations to fatalism. Like Thurman, Carson reminds us that always at work, underneath the myriad appearances of failure and tragedy, is a "growing edge" that transcends the contradictions of life and melds them into the harmonious purposes of the universe. "Such is the growing edge! It is the extra breath from the exhausted lung, the one more thing to try when all else has failed, the upward reach of life when weariness closes in upon all endeavor. This is the basis for hope in moments of despair, the incentive to carry . . . the source of confidence when worlds crash and dreams whiten into ash."

Carson's decision-making process underscores the messiness of ethical decision-making at the intersection. Moreover, it illustrates the related variables of recognition, respect, and reverence for life. At stake for this altruistic and self-giving humanitarian was even more. Carson, as this case demonstrates, represents the moral virtuoso who constantly monitors and evaluates his own self-conscious needs, but does not allow them to overcome the ethical demand to take the risks of courageous leadership in the most trying of situations—the question of human life.

As we observed in our discussion on a sense of justice, neither rationalist nor realist perspectives adequately address the deeper questions of human desire and need to be connected with others in acts of empathy, respect, and justice. In determining the appropriate action among competing interests, the ethical leader is faced with the need to balance rationalist and realist claims with a sense of justice as fairness that seeks connectivity and community. This balancing act, however, can be fraught with perilous consequences. Carson's and his team's sense of justice as fairness was informed by their need to empathize with and respect the decision of the twins and their family. Perhaps the ultimate measure of justice, in this respect, is how one's decision is aligned with compassion. Demonstrating compassion for the self begins with an understanding that character is interrelated both to one's own personal story and the stories of others. The Dalai Lama's definition of compassion, *shen dug ngal wa la mi sö pa*, "the inability to bear the sight of another's suffering," speaks to the reverence for life of all sentient beings.[21] Compassion calls the leader alongside the other to share in her sorrow and tragedy, but also in her hopes and aspirations. Carson and the entire medical team showed compassion, the highest and noblest expression of ethical leadership.

KATRINA: A DEFINING MOMENT

Katrina was a defining moment in our nation's history. One cannot begin to understand the aftermath of Hurricane Katrina without noting the failure of leadership at federal, state, and local levels in regard to the questions of race and class. As the many critics emerged to speak about the damage wrought by the hurricane, few spoke to the larger question of ethical leadership and how the failure of leadership played out in the Gulf Coast. The questions of race and class loom large in any intelligent appraisal of that tragedy, revealing a conglomerate of competing interests, narrow visions, and indifference. Shortly after the hurricane swept through New Orleans and surrounding areas, I listened to conservative talk-show hosts discussing the claims of a number of prominent African Americans, who suggested that the slow response by the federal government was an indication that

America does not care about its black and poor citizens. I was struck by the responses of the talk-show hosts and their callers, who dismissed these claims as paranoia, race baiting, and superfluous. It has become clearer now that race played a major role in the poor preparedness of disaster organizations and the lackadaisical reaction of officials at all levels. But I quickly add that, while this is true, it does not help us as citizens deal with a more immediate and fundamental issue: there is a failure of ethical leadership in American society that crosses racial, political, social, and cultural lines. The failure of ethical leadership is far more dangerous and costly and, in the end, more damaging than even the worst hurricanes that wreak devastation on our shores. How a nation with the vast material and technical resources that we possess could allow two days to pass before responding to such an enormous national crisis is not only a racial or political problem, but a problem of leadership—ethical leadership, which rests upon an understanding of character, civility, and community that goes beyond family values and political expediency.[22]

Much of the public debate that has emerged around the crisis is emblematic of the demise of the kind of leadership that is so sorely needed at this critical juncture in our history. Far beyond the blame-shame game that played out in the aftermath of Katrina, questions of race, ethnicity, and class were not adequately addressed. It is the critical task of leaders to infuse the ethical dimension into any inquiry, so that objective, historical, and subjective questions are systematically explored. The ethical question asks more than "What went wrong?" and "Who was accountable?" It asks, "What is going on?" "What are the rules?" "Who makes the rules?" and "Who enforces the rules?" It asks the question of character. Honest, forthright answers to these questions should come not only from elected or appointed officials, but from informed leaders who care deeply about the future of American society.

The Bush administration, the Department of Homeland Security, the Federal Emergency Management Agency, the governor of Louisiana, and the local officials deserve varying levels of criticism and blame for the failure to respond quickly and efficiently. Survivors of this catastrophe and an outraged citizenry have had much to say about how leaders made decisions, but any critique that does not raise the ethical questions of character surrounding these issues—questions of integrity, empathy, and hope—misses the point entirely.

Where was integrity in the decision-making to prepare for and respond to Hurricane Katrina? We expect leaders to demonstrate integrity with respect to public trust. Before August 29, 2005, public officials knew the risks associated with a Category 4 hurricane hitting New Orleans, yet race, economics, and politics overruled good science, common sense, and moral judgment. Now the social and fiscal costs far outweigh the initial investment in sound levees and disaster-preparedness education that could have been put in place before the storm. The question of empathy demands that leaders empathize with the other—beyond family, tribe, clan, class, or political affiliation. Learning to empathize with others before tragedy is just as important as the public grief that occurs after the fact. Beyond the promises from the president, Congress, and state and local governments to rebuild New Orleans and the other affected areas along the Gulf Coast, leaders must instill hope—not the vacuous sentimentality that disguises itself as hope for political advantage, but hope demonstrated through concrete, long-term proposals that address the larger structural and cultural issues that contributed to the tragic aftermath of Katrina. These virtues of character (integrity, empathy, and hope) are related to public values of civility and spiritual virtuosities of community outlined in the Ethical Leadership Model—questions of recognition, respect, and reverence (civility) and questions of courage, justice, and compassion (community).

In the years ahead, America will be engaged in rebuilding the stricken areas along our beautiful Gulf Coast. The larger task of rebuilding, however, will be to develop a new generation of ethical leaders who possess competencies and skills rooted in character, civility, and community—leaders who dare to stand at the dangerous intersection where vast, impersonal systemworlds meet and often collide with our fragile and precious lifeworlds and who help us to negotiate the traffic.

NOTES

Preface

1. Ronald A. Heifitz and Martin Linsky, *Leadership on the Line: Staying Alive through the Dangers of Leading* (Boston: Harvard Business School Press); Bill George with Peter Sims, *True North: Discover Your Authentic Leadership* (San Francisco: Jossey-Bass/Wiley, 2007); Warren Bennis and Robert Thomas, *Geeks and Geezers: How Era, Values, and Defining Moments Shape Leaders* (Boston: Harvard Business School Press, 2002) 101–106; Ronald Heifetz, *Leadership without Easy Answers* (Cambridge, Mass.: Belknap / Harvard University Press, 1994); Daniel Goleman, Richard Boyatzis and Anne McKee, *Primal Leadership: Realizing the Power of Emotional Intelligence* (Boston: Harvard Business School Press, 2002); Manfred F. R. Kets De Vries, *Leaders, Fools and Impostors: Essays on the Psychology of Leadership* (San Francisco: Jossey-Bass Publishers, 1993); Rob Goffee and Gareth Jones, *Why Should Anyone Be Led by You? What It Takes to Be an Authentic Leader* (Boston: Harvard Business School Press, 2006).

2. Walter Earl Fluker, ed., *The Papers of Howard Washington Thurman*, Volume I (University Press of South Carolina, 2009); Walter Earl Fluker, ed., *The Stones That the Builders Rejected: The Development of Ethical Leadership from the Black Church Tradition* (Harrisburg, Penn.: Trinity International, 1998), 8–9; and Walter Earl Fluker and Catherine Tumber, eds., *A Strange Freedom: The Best of Howard Thurman on Religious Experience and Public Life* (Boston: Beacon, 1998).

3. See, for instance, the collected volume of essays on the subject edited by Joanne B. Ciulla, *Ethics, The Heart of Leadership,* 2nd ed. (Westport, Connecticut and London: Praeger, 2004).

4. Walter Earl Fluker, "Somewhere, Sometime, Someplace: The Call to Ethical Leadership," *Convergence* 4, no. 1 (Spring 2005): 120–23 and Walter Earl Fluker, "Beware of the Unicorns! Ethical Leadership and the Power of Imagination," *Convergence* 7, no. 3 (Fall 2006): 1–4.

Introduction: At the Intersection Where Worlds Collide

1. Thomas E. McCollough, *The Moral Imagination and Public Life: Raising the Ethical Question in Public Life* (Chatman, N.J.: Chatman, 1991), 19.

2. Ronald Heifitz and Martin Linsky, *Leadership on the Line: Staying Alive through the Dangers of Leading* (Boston: Harvard Business School Press, 2002).

Chapter 1: Howard Washington Thurman and Martin Luther King Jr.

1. Barack Obama, "A More Perfect Union," speech given at Constitution Hall, Philadelphia, Pa., March 18, 2008.

2. Toni Morrison, *Playing in the Dark: Whiteness and the Literary Imagination* (Cambridge: Harvard University Press, 1992).

3. James Melvin Washington, ed., *A Testament of Hope: The Essential Writings and Speeches of Martin Luther King Jr.* (San Francisco: Harper and Row, 1986), xi.

4. Peter J. Paris, *The Social Teaching of the Black Churches* (Philadelphia, Pa.: Fortress, 1985), 10–12.

5. Lawrence N. Jones, "Black Christians in Antebellum America: In Search of Beloved Community," *The Journal of Religious Thought* 12, no. 2 (1985): 12, 19.

6. Stacey Floyd Thomas et al., *Black Church Studies: An Introduction* (Valley Forge, Pa.: Judson Press, 2007); Peter J. Paris, *The Social Teaching of the Black Churches* (Philadelphia: Fortress Press, 1985), 10–12; C. Eric Lincoln and Lawrence Mamiya, *The Black Church in the African American Experience* (Durham, N.C.: Duke University Press, 1990). Alasdair MacIntyre has suggested that "a living tradition . . . is an historically extended, socially embodied argument, and an argument precisely in part about the goods which constitute that tradition." Alasdair MacIntyre, *After Virtue: A Study in Moral Theory* (South Bend, Ind.: University of Notre Dame Press, 1984), 222. *A Testament of Hope: The Essential Writings of Martin Luther King, Jr.* James Melvin Washington, ed. (San Francisco: Harper & Row, 1986), xi; see also Cornel West, "The Prophetic Tradition in Afro-America," in *Prophetic Fragments: Illuminations of the Crisis in American Religion and Culture*. Grand

Rapids, Mich.: Eerdmans; Trenton, N.J.: Africa World, 1988), 38–49. Lawrence N. Jones, "Black Christians in Antebellum America: In Quest of the Beloved Community," *Journal of Religious Thought* 12, no. 2 (1985): 12. See Evelyn Brooks Higginbotham, *Righteous Discontent: The Women's Movement in the Black Baptist Church, 1880–1920* (Cambridge: Harvard University Press, 1993); Delores S. Williams, *Sisters in the Wilderness: The Challenge of Womanist God-Talk* (Maryknoll, N.Y.: Orbis, 1993); Emile M. Townes, *Womanist Justice, Womanist Hope* (Atlanta: Scholars Press, 1993); and Emile M. Townes, ed., *A Troubling in My Soul: Womanist Perspectives on Evil and Suffering* (Maryknoll, N.Y.: Orbis, 1993); Marla F. Frederick, *Between Sundays: Black Women and Everyday Struggles of Faith* (Berkeley: University of California Press, 2003); Marilyn Richardson, *Black Women and Religion: A Bibliography* (Boston: G. K. Hall, 1980). Other texts include Jacquelyn Grant, *White Women's Christ and Black Women's Jesus: Feminist Christology and Womanist Response* (Atlanta: Scholars Press, 1989); Carolyn Rouse, *Engage Surrender: African American Women and Islam* (Berkeley: University of California Press, 2004); Bettye Collier-Thomas, *Daughters of Thunder: Black Women Preachers and Their Sermons, 1850–1979* (San Francisco: Jossey-Bass, 1998); Rosetta E. Ross, *Witnessing and Testifying: Black Women, Religion, and Civil Rights* (Minneapolis: Fortress, 2003; Stephanie Y. Mitchem, *African American Women Tapping Power and Spiritual Wellness* (Cleveland, Oh.: Pilgrim, 2004); Marcia Riggs, *Plenty Good Room: Women versus Male Power in the Black Church,* (Cleveland, Oh.: Pilgrim, 2003); and *Can I Get a Witness? Prophetic Religious Voices of African American Women: An Anthology* (Maryknoll, N.Y.: Orbis, 1997).

7. See Edward O. Jones, *A Candle in the Dark: A History of Morehouse College* (Valley Forge, Pa.: Judson Press, 1967).

8. Howard Thurman, *With Head and Heart: The Autobiography of Howard Thurman* (San Francisco: Harcourt Brace Jovanovich, 1979), 35.

9. David L. Lewis, *King: A Critical Biography*, 2nd ed. (Urbana: University of Illinois Press, 1978), 25.

10. James D. Anderson, *The Education of Blacks in the South, 1860–1935* (Chapel Hill: University of North Carolina Press, 1988). See also Robert Michael Franklin, *Crisis in the Village: Restoring Hope in African American Communities* (Minneapolis: Fortress, 2007).

11. Barack Obama, from *Howard Thurman: Spirit of the Movement*, a documentary film by Arleigh Prelow (Inspirit Communications, 2006).

12. See my earlier work on Thurman and King. Walter Earl Fluker, *They Looked for a City: A Comparative Analysis of the Ideal of Community in Howard Thurman and Martin Luther King, Jr.* (Lanham, Md.: University Press of America, 1988).

13. The "modern civil rights movement" is the designation offered by Aldon D. Morris, *The Origins of the Civil Rights Movement: Black Communities Organizing for Change* (New York: Free Press, 1984). Morris dates the movement from June 1953, the date of the Baton Rouge protest against the city's segregated bus system. The significance of the Baton Rouge movement, for Morris, lies in its impact upon the strategic maneuvers of African Americans "directly involved in economic boycotts, street marches, mass meetings, going to jail by the thousands, and a whole range of disruptive tactics commonly referred to as nonviolent direct action" (ix). This confrontation marks a significant moment in a long tradition of protest by masses of African Americans predating the Civil War. See John Hope Franklin, "The Forerunners," *American Visions* 1, no. 1 (January–February 1986): 26–35; and Adam Fairclough, *To Redeem the Soul of America: The Southern Christian Leadership Conference and Martin Luther King Jr.* (Athens and London: University of Georgia Press, 1987), 11–35.

14. The phrase "the underside of history" is borrowed from Gustavo Gutierrez's insightful critique of the Eurocentric domination of history. See "Theology from the Underside of History," chap. 7 in *The Power of the Poor in History* (New York: Orbis, 1984), 169–214. He writes: "The history of humanity has been written 'with a white hand,' from the side of the dominators." But history, where God reveals Godself and is proclaimed by the poor, "must be reread from the side of the poor . . . from a point of departure in their struggles, their resistances, their hopes" (201). In this respect, Thurman is representative of a rich and vibrant tradition of African American theologizing, which has as its initial problematic the oppressive interaction of race and class in American society. See Fluker, *They Looked for a City*, 3–77.

15. A "site of memory" is "where memory crystallizes and secretes itself . . . at a particular historical moment, a turning point where consciousness of a break with the past is bound up with the sense that memory has been torn—but torn in such a way as to pose the problem of the embodiment of memory in certain sites where a sense of historical continuity persists. There are *lieux de memoire*, sites of memory, because there are no longer *milieux de memoire*, real environments of memory." Pierre Nora, "Between Memory and History: *Les Lieux de Memoire*," *Histriography: Critical Concepts in Historical Studies* by Robert M. Burns (London, New York: Routeldge, 2005), 284; see Walter Earl Fluker, "Dangerous Memories and Redemptive Possibilities: Reflections on the Life and Work of Howard Thurman," in *Black Leaders and Ideologies in the South: Resistance and Nonviolence*, ed. Preston King and Walter Earl Fluker (Oxfordshire: Taylor and Francis, 2004), 147–76.

16. Mozella Gordon Mitchell, *Spiritual Dynamics of Howard Thurman's Theology* (Bristol, Ind.: Wyndham Hall, 1985), 52. See also Luther E. Smith, "Black Theology and Religious Experience," *Journal of the Interdenominational Theological Center* 7, no. 1 (Fall 1980): 59–72; and Walter Earl Fluker, "Dangerous Memories," 147–76.

17. Sue Bailey Thurman, "Response to Tribute by Beth Rhude," Thurman Convocation Commemorating the Fortieth Anniversary of *Jesus and the Disinherited*, Vanderbilt Divinity School, October 26, 1989.

18. George K. Makechnie, dean emeritus of Boston University's Sargent College of Allied Health Professions, has compiled many of these tributes to Thurman's legacy in *Howard Thurman: His Enduring Dream* (Boston: Howard Thurman Center, Boston University, 1988). See also Ricardo A. Millet, ed., *Debate and Understanding* "Simmering on the Calm Presence and Profound Wisdom of Howard Thurman," Special Edition (Spring 1982), Martin Luther King Jr. Afro-American Center, Boston University, 71–90.

19. See Millet, *Debate and Understanding*, 83.

20. Interviews with Anne Spencer Thurman, Sue Bailey Thurman, Joyce Sloan, and Marvin Chandler, Howard Thurman Educational Trust, San Francisco, August 11, 1982.

21. Vincent Harding, introduction to *For the Inward Journey: The Writings of Howard Thurman* by Howard Thurman and Anne Spencer Thurman (San Diego: Harcourt, 1984), xiv.

22. Marian Wright Edelman, *The Measure of Our Success: A Letter to My Children and Yours* (Boston: Beacon, 1992), 69–70.

23. Arthur Ashe and Arnold Rampersad, *Days of Grace: A Memoir* (New York: Knopf, 1993), 286.

24. Vernon E. Jordan Jr. with Annette Gordon-Reed, *Vernon Can Read! A Memoir* (New York: Public Affairs, 2001), 53, 70–71, 287–88.

25. Quoted in Makechnie, *Howard Thurman*, 79.

26. "The reshaping of one's belief system in light of the identification with the indwelling intelligence that is at the center of our mental and bodily processes is called the Opening of the Way. It is important to learn that in reality we don't learn how to grow spiritually. We learn how to remove the impediments to the coming to the foreground of our submerged divine Self. I.e., wrong ideas close the door to the full operation of the Self in the life of the individual. One cannot overstate the fact that the indwelling intelligence was not intended to be limited to operating your background mental process and involuntary bodily functions. And as it is omniscient, it cannot be taught. The reformed Sebekian faculty reflecting rationalization based on one's true self (Ausar) is called Ap-Uat (the Opener of the Way).

The 'way' is a symbol for our beliefs and ideas as conduits of the course of our lives. As we believe, so we act. As we act, so goes our destiny. According to our unreformed Sebekian faculty (Set) we are in the habit of rationalizing our actions according to our identification with our person. We would, for example, firmly believe that we could not help doing so and so because of the way we felt (emotional influence) or didn't feel, etc. Can you imagine the indwelling Self running the body according to the whims and feelings? Surely, its functions must be based on divine law and order (Maat, the 4th Sphere)." Metu-Neter, 142–43. Ra Un Nefer Amen, *Metu Nete, vol. 1: The Great Oracle of Tenuti and the Egyptian System of Spiritual Cultivation* (Bronx, N.Y.: Khamit Corporation, 1990), 142–43.

"The positive thoughts (rationalizations of our actions based on our identity with Ausar) are symbolized by the deity Anpu (Anubis), the *Guide of the Dead*. I.e., it corresponds to the positive thoughts that must guide us when we are in the grips of the emotion; our only guide at such moments are the thoughts reprogrammed into the behavioral patterns. Once the work of this stage of the initiation is completed (which takes place at the 8th stage, sphere 2, Tehuti), the initiate will be impervious to the visitation of any emotion, craving or temptation. This is why it is said that Anpu (Anubis) is the embalmer of Ausar. I.e., he renders him incorruptible" Metu-Neter (145).

"Anpu—called Anubis by the Greek—and Ap-uat (opener of the way), two aspects of the mercurial principle Sebek, shared the duty of guiding the deceased in the underworld of Maat's Hall of Justice, where the heart (will) is weighed. The deceased in this case are symbols of the person undergoing spiritual initiation, as it results in dying to certain things in the world, as well as to the personality (see Seker). This is why 'reformed' Christians say that they are 'born again.' The 'underworld' (tuat, Amenta, etc.) corresponds to the 'subconscious,' to which focus of consciousness is transferred during trance.

"Anpu and Ap-uat are depicted as canine-headed men, because the faculty of cleverness, among others that they represent, is the dominant trait in dogs, foxes, jackals, etc. The ability of canines to learn to respond to a large number of verbal commands is also well known" (233).

27. *The Search for Common Ground* should be understood within this framework. What is not so well known about this mystical spirit is that he was a keen interpreter of the American democratic dogma. Examples of his wrestling with the American democratic experiment can be found in a number of unpublished sermons preached at the Church for the Fellowship of All Peoples from July 29 to August 26, 1951. In these sermons, Thurman gave a decidedly religious interpretation to the

founding principles of democracy, addressing the themes of equality; the right to life, liberty, and the pursuit of happiness; and their significance for the oppressed. "The Declaration of Independence," taped sermon series, Church for the Fellowship of All Peoples, San Francisco, Special Collections, Mugar Memorial Library, Boston University. See also "The American Dream," taped sermon, Marsh Chapel, Boston University, July 6, 1958, Special Collections, Mugar Memorial Library, Boston University; "America in Search of a Soul," Robbins Lecture Series, University of the Redlands, Redlands, Calif., January 20, 1976, Howard Thurman Educational Trust, San Francisco; and "The Fascist Masquerade," in *The Church and Organized Movements* (Interseminary Series), ed. Randolph Crump Miller (Harper & Row, 1959), 82–100.

28. Mozella G. Mitchell, "Techniques of Myth and Ritual in Thurman," in Millet, *Debate and Understanding*, 28. Mitchell claims that "most of Thurman's power stems from his mythical-ritual technique combined with the use of powerful intellect in phenomenological explorations and religious and cultural studies. In his functions as a religious authority and in his mythic-ritual technique, Thurman shares much in common with the shaman of archaic societies. I maintain that his appropriation and use of such techniques is conscious and deliberate, a natural outgrowth of his style of practical mysticism. He becomes in large measure a sophisticated modern-day shaman, and he does so in order to penetrate behind the wall of Christian orthodoxy and to get at and utilize genuine religious experience as a cure for many of the ills of our day. He becomes, then, a self-styled sophisticated shaman." See also Mitchell, *Spiritual Dynamics*, 88; and Stephen Larsen, *The Shaman's Doorway: Opening the Mythic Imagination to Contemporary Consciousness* (New York: Harper & Row, 1976), 9–10. Along with Mircea Eliade and Stephen Larsen, Mitchell makes a distinction between the role of the "priest" and "shaman," in that the former is concerned primarily with "traditional mythological forms" through which members of the community are periodically reawakened to the awareness of the sacred. The shaman, however, "is not satisfied celebrating encounter with the sacred that happened in the long ago but rather develops an affinity for renewing regularly the contact in his [*sic*] own person" (Mitchell, "Techniques," 29).

29. Mitchell, *Spiritual Dynamics*, 88.

30. Joyce Elaine Noll, *Company of Prophets: African American Psychics, Healers, and Visionaries* (St. Paul: Llewellyn, 1991); Malidoma Patrice Somé, *Of Water and the Spirit: Ritual, Magic, and Initiation in the Life of an African Shaman* (New York: Putnam, 1994).

31. James Weldon Johnson, *God's Trombones* (New York: Viking, 1927), 2.

32. W. E. B. DuBois, *The Souls of Black Folk*, with introductions by Dr. Nathan Hare and Alvin F. Poussaint, M.D., New American Library (New York: Signet, 1989), 216. DuBois observed that "it was under the leadership of the priest and medicine man" that the Negro church preserved remnants of African tribal life. *Some Efforts of the American Negroes for Their Own Betterment* (Atlanta, 1898), as quoted in E. Franklin Frazier and C. Eric Lincoln, *The Negro Church in America/ The Black Church Since Frazier* (New York: Schocken Books, 1974), 13. See also Benjamin C. Ray, *African Religion* (Englewood Cliffs, N.J.: Prentice Hall, 1976). Ray discusses archetypal symbols as sacred images: gods, ancestors, sacred actions, or things that make up the traditional African cosmology. He writes, "Ritual specialists, priests, prophets, diviners, and kings are the servants of the community and their role is to mediate the sacred to their people. The life of priests and kings is bound up with the societies they serve; rites which strengthen them, strengthen the people as a whole. . . . In times of colonial oppression and rapid social change, ritual symbols also served to create and reinforce new religious and political movements" (17). Other references to the role of the "priest" and "medicine-man" can be found in Gayraud S. Wilmore, *Black Religion and Black Radicalism: An Interpretation of the Religious History of Afro-American People*, 2nd ed., rev. and enl. (Maryknoll, N.Y.: Orbis, 1986), 19; Lawrence W. Levine, *Black Culture and Black Consciousness: Afro-American Folk Thought from Slavery to Freedom* (New York: Oxford University Press, 1977), 55–88; Albert J. Raboteau, *Slave Religion: The "Invisible Institution" in the Antebellum South* (New York: Oxford University Press, 1980), 43–92, 211–88; and Sterling Stuckey, introduction, "Slavery and the Circle of Culture," *Slave Culture: Nationalist Theory and the Foundations of Black America* (New York: Oxford University Press, 1987), 3–97. See especially Theophus H. Smith's discussion of shamanism and Afro-American spirituality in *Conjuring Culture: Biblical Formations of Black America* (Oxford: Oxford University Press, 1995), 159–76. His insightful depiction of Sojourner Truth as shaman and conjure-woman is a salient feature of "black social prophetism for human transformation on a global scale" (173–74).

33. Thurman, *With Head and Heart*, 265.

34. Ibid., 263; see also Mircea Eliade, *Shamanism: Archaic Techniques of Ecstasy*, Bollingen Series 76 (Princeton University Press, 1964), 16; and Clarence E. Hardy III, "Imagine a World: Howard Thurman, Spiritual Perception, and American Calvinism," in *Journal of Religion*, 81, no. 1 (January 2001): 78–97.

35. Reinhold Niebuhr, *The Irony of American History* (New York: Scribner's, 1952). Charles Long suggests that Thurman "resituate[s] the problematic [of race] within the structures of inwardness as the locus for a new rhythm of time." Charles Long, "Howard Thurman and the Meaning of Religion in America," in *The Human Search: Howard Thurman and the Quest for Freedom: Proceedings of the Second Annual Thurman Convocation*, ed. Mozella G. Mitchell, vol 2, Martin Luther King Jr. Memorial Studies in Religion, Culture and Social Development (New York: Peter Lang, 1992), 141. According to Long, Thurman's investigation of the spirituals represented the appropriation of a *mythos* that provided meaning and affirmation of dignity to an otherwise meaningless existence: "The slaves who lived both within and outside of history, created historical structures but having no power to determine the locus of their meaning found a spiritual locus outside the body of historical time in which to save their bodies and to give meaning to their communities. The spirituals were their myths, and . . . the affirmation of a historicity is an affirmation of the non-modern, [non-Western] peoples" (41). For an exposition of "the terror of history," see Mircea Eliade, *Cosmos and History* (New York: Harper & Row, 1954, 1959), 156–57.

36. Howard Thurman, *The Search for Common Ground* (New York: Harper & Row, 1971).

37. Darrell J. Fasching, "Holy Man for the Coming Millennium," in Mitchell, ed., *The Human Search*, 2:191–203; Walter E. Fluker and Catherine Tumber, introduction to *A Strange Freedom: The Best of Howard Thurman on Religious Experience and Public Life* (Boston: Beacon, 1998); Jan Corbett, "Howard Thurman: A Theologian for Our Times," *American Baptist Quarterly* (December 1979): 9–12; Lerone Bennett, "Howard Thurman: Twentieth Century Holy Man," *Ebony* (February 1978), 68–70, 72, 76, 84–85. Howard Thurman is not a new name in theological discourse. See John Mangram, "Jesus Christ in Howard Thurman's Thought," in *Common Ground: Essays in Honor of Howard Thurman on the Occasion of His Seventy-fifth Birthday, November 18, 1975*, ed. Samuel Lucius Gandy (Washington, D.C.: Hoffman, 1975), 65. J. Deotis Roberts places Thurman's contribution to African American religious thought in the category of mysticism and religious philosophy. "In this category," he writes, "Howard Thurman has no rival and no second among his black brothers. It is surprising to me that he has been ignored almost completely in anthologies and works on mysticism. He is, indeed, one of the great mystics of all times. His mysticism is not 'introverted,' nor is it a mysticism of withdrawal from human problems. His social and ethical issues are at stake." J. Deotis Roberts, "The American Negro's Contribution to Religious

Thought," in *The Negro Impact on Western Civilization*, ed. Joseph Slabey Roucek and Thomas Kiernan (New York: Philosophical Library, 1970), 87. See also Martin Marty, "Mysticism and the Religious Quest for Freedom," in *God and Human Freedom*, ed. Henry J. Young (Richmond, Ind.: Friends United, 1983).

38. With the publication of the forthcoming volume *The Collected Papers of Howard Washington Thurman,* there will for the first time be a documented record of the historical context and the long train of fellows who deeply influenced his thinking and involvement in theological and religious discourse of the first half of the twentieth century. Luther E. Smith early identified Thurman's intellectual sources within the stream of American religious liberalism. A number of dissertations, essays, and books followed Smith's seminal work. Alton Pollard correctly observes that although Howard Thurman embraced the modernistic claims of the liberal school, he took exception to its infatuation with the inherent notions of progress and positivism and the almost total denial of the question of race as a determinant in theological and ethical discourse and practice. Walter Earl Fluker, ed., *The Sound of the Genuine: The Collected Papers of Howard Washington Thurman*, 4 vols. (University Press of South Carolina); Luther E. Smith, *Howard Thurman: The Mystic as Prophet* (University Press of America, 1981; repr., Richmond, Ind.: Friends United, 1992); Alton B. Pollard III, *Mysticism and Social Change: The Social Witness of Howard Thurman*, New York: P. Lang, 1992), 32.

39. Gary Dorrien, *The Making of American Liberal Theology: Idealism, Realism and Modernity, 1900–1950* (Louisville and London: Westminster John Knox, 2003), 558.

40. James Baldwin, *The Fire Next Time* (New York: Vintage International, 1993), 98.

41. See Bernice Johnson Reagon's interesting assessment of Martin Luther King Jr. and other marginalized intellectuals who "straddle" and renegotiate worlds of common practice and tradition with foreign worlds of meaning. The outcome, for Reagon, is a new situation, a synthesis of sorts that allows for creativity, lance, and sanity. See Reagon, "Nobody Knows the Trouble I See"; or "By and By, I'm Goin' Lay Down My Heavy Load," *Journal of American History* 78, no. 1 (June 1991): 111–19. See also David Thelen's discussion of Reagon in "Becoming Martin Luther King Jr.: An Introduction," *Journal of American History* 78, no. 1 (June 1991): 15.

42. See Walter Earl Fluker and Catherine Tumber, eds., *A Strange Freedom: The Best of Howard Thurman on Religious Experience and Public Life*, (Boston: Beacon, 1998), 2–3; 313 n. 2.

43. Thurman, "When Knowledge Comes," in *The Inward Journey* (New York: Harper & Brothers, 1961), 16–17.

44. Thurman, "He Looked for a City." taped sermon, Marsh Chapel, Boston University, January 2, 1955, Special Collections, Mugar Library, Boston University.

45. Ibid.

46. See Thurman, *Disciplines*, (New York: Harper & Row, 1963), 26–37, where he discusses three primary questions related to the discipline of commitment: "Who am I?" "What do I want?" and "How do I propose to get it?"

47. Thurman, "He Looked for a City."

48. Howard Thurman, *With Head and Heart*, 208.

49. Howard Thurman, *Meditations of the Heart* (Richmond, Ind.: Friends United, 1976), 15.

50. Robert N. Bellah et al., *Habits of the Heart: Individualism and Commitment in American Life* (New York: Harper & Row, 1985), 256.

51. In his sermon by the same title, one first notices King's improvisational play with great ideas, borrowed from the critique of social conformity by Henry Emerson Fosdick and Eugene Austin and other sources. See Keith D. Miller, *Voice of Deliverance: The Language of Martin Luther King Jr. and Its Sources* (New York: Free Press, 1992), 105–8, 110–11, 164.

52. Miller, *Voice of Deliverance*; James Cone, *Martin and Malcolm and America: A Dream or a Nightmare* (Maryknoll, N.Y.: Orbis, 1991); Clayborne Carson, *Martin Luther King Jr., Called to Serve, January 1929– June 1951*, vol. 1 (Berkeley: University of California Press, 1992); John Ansbro, *The Making of a Mind* (Maryknoll, N.Y.: Orbis, 1982); Kenneth L. Smith and Ira G. Zepp Jr., *Search for the Beloved Community: The Thinking of Martin Luther King Jr.* (Valley Forge, Pa.: Judson Press, 1974); Adam Fairclough, *To Redeem the Soul of America: The Southern Leadership Conference and Martin Luther King Jr.* (Athens and London: University of Georgia Press, 1987); David Garrow, *Bearing the Cross: Martin Luther King Jr. and the Southern Christian Leadership Conference* (New York: Morrow, 1986); Lewis, *King*; Stephen Oates, *Let the Trumpet Sound: The Life of Martin Luther King Jr.* (New York: New American Library, 1982); Taylor Branch, *Parting the Waters: America in the King Years: 1954–1963* (New York: Simon & Schuster, 1988). See especially Branch's treatment of Vernon Johns, *Parting the Waters*, 1–26. William D. Watley, *Roots of Resistance: The Nonviolent Ethics of Martin Luther King Jr.* (Valley Forge, Pa.: Judson Press, 1985). See especially chap. 1, "Formative Influences: Black Religious Experience, Evangelical Liberalism, and Personalism," 17–46. Fluker, *They Looked for a City*; Lewis V. Baldwin, *There Is a Balm in Gilead: Understanding Martin Luther King Jr. within the Context of*

Southern Religious History (Minneapolis: Fortress Press, 1991); Lewis V. Baldwin, *To Make the Wounded Whole* (Minneapolis: Fortress Press, 1991). For examples of articles that address the impact of the African American church on King's intellectual and social development, see Cornel West, "Prophetic Christian as Organic Intellectual," in *Prophetic Fragments*, 3–12; James H. Cone, "Martin Luther King, Jr., Black Theology—Black Church," *Theology Today* (January 1984), 409–20; and Paul R. Garber, "King Was a Black Theologian," *Journal of Religious Thought* 31 (Fall–Winter 1974), 16–32.

53. With the notable exceptions of Peter J. Paris, Lewis V. Baldwin, Vincent Harding, and, to some extent, Michael Eric Dyson, very little scholarship has been devoted to the spiritual biography of Martin Luther King Jr. and the ways in which it shaped his role as a leader.

54. King, "Unfulfilled Dreams," 6.

55. King, "Transformed Nonconformist," 23.

56. These "faces" refer, respectively, to the early stages of King's development. "Little Mike" refers to his early formation under the shadow of a powerful father figure; "Tweed" was the nickname of his teenage years at Morehouse College; and "the Philosopher King," as he was dubbed, is a reference to his university days in Boston.

57. Don Helder Camara, "Lord Guide Me" in *The Desert Is Fertile* (Maryknoll, N.Y.: Orbis, 1974). Used by permission.

58. King, *Stride toward Freedom: The Montgomery Story* (New York: Harper & Row, 1958), 58–63. See also David Garrow, *Bearing the Cross*, 57–58; David Garrow, "Martin Luther King Jr. and the Spirit of Leadership," in *We Shall Overcome: Martin Luther King Jr. and the Black Freedom Struggle*, ed. Peter J. Albert and Ronald Hoffman (New York: Pantheon Books, 1990): 11–34. I agree with Lewis Baldwin and Preston Williams that this vision, while important, should not be considered as an isolated phenomenon but should be understood as one among other experiences in King's spiritual odyssey and as an example of black church's belief in the intimacy of the divine in struggles for justice. Lewis Baldwin, *There Is a Balm*, 189; and Preston N. Williams, "The Public and Private Burdens of Martin Luther King, Jr.," *Christian Century* (February 25, 1987): 198–99.

59. Quoted in Garrow, *Bearing the Cross*, 58.

60. King, "Transformed Nonconformist," 19.

61. King, *Where Do We Go from Here: Chaos or Community?* (Boston: Beacon, 1967), 172–91.

62. King, "Pilgrimage to Nonviolence," in *Strength to Love* (Philadelphia: Fortress Press, 1963), 154.

63. Several writers have made reference to the influence of Thurman on his younger visionary. See Lerone Bennett, *What Manner of Man*, 2nd rev. ed. (Chicago: Johnson, 1976), 74–75; John Ansbro, *The Making of a Mind* (Maryknoll, N.Y.: Orbis, 1982), 27–29, 272; "Dr. King's Mentor Remembered," *Boston Globe*, January 15, 1982, 13–14; Lewis V. Baldwin, "Understanding Martin Luther King Jr. within the Context of Southern Black Religious History," *Journal of Religious Studies* 13, no. 2 (Fall 1987): 19; Lewis V. Baldwin, "Martin Luther King, the Black Church and the Black Messianic Vision," *Journal of the Interdenominational Center* 12, nos. 1–2 (Fall 1984–Spring 1985): 1; and Larry Murphy, "Howard Thurman and Social Activism," in *God and Human Freedom: A Festschrift in Honor of Howard Thurman* (Richmond, Ind.: Friends United, 1983), 154–55. Perhaps Thurman's own accounting of his relationship with King is sufficient for our purposes: "I am one of a few and maybe the only person who was a member of the faculty of the Graduate School of Theology at Boston University when Dr. King took his doctorate degree who did not have him in the classroom. I think this is a mark of distinction. We had contacts, but our primary contact was sitting around my television watching the World Series. . . . I've known him and his family, his mother and father for many years. And Mrs. Thurman's and my relationship to those two young people (Martin and Coretta King) was a personal and primary one. It was not involved in the light and the drama. *My concern was always about the state of his spiritual life all the time*. And I felt it was my relationship with him that gave me the right to do it, while Mrs. Thurman's interest was always in the little things involving the children and the wife of a man who had to live his private life in public. And this is a great agony. I understand from one of his biographers that a book that I wrote in 1949 was very influential on his thinking: *Jesus and the Disinherited*. But I did not hear this from him and I do not make a claim of it; but lest someone may know that it is in this biographical statement you will think that I am trying to be falsely modest by not mentioning it; so I've done it and now I can go on with my work." Howard Thurman, "Litany and Words in Memoriam for Martin Luther King Jr.," Church for the Fellowship of All Peoples, San Francisco, April 7, 1968, Howard Thurman Educational Trust, San Francisco. Emphasis added.

64. Thurman, *With Head and Heart*, 254–55.

65. Ibid., 255. Thurman recommended an "additional four weeks to those that the doctor felt you [King] needed for complete recovery." "Howard Thurman to Martin Luther King Jr.," October 20, 1958, King Papers, Special Collections, Mugar Memorial Library, Boston University.

66. Branch, *Parting the Waters*, 245.

67. Oates, *Let the Trumpet Sound*, 140. See also Garrow, *Bearing the Cross*, 111–13.

68. "Martin Luther King Jr. to Dr. Howard Thurman," July 7, 1958; "Howard Thurman to Martin Luther King Jr.," July 18, 1958; "Howard Thurman to Martin Luther King Jr.," October 20, 1958; "Martin Luther King Jr. to Howard Thurman," November 8, 1958; "Howard Thurman to Martin Luther King Jr.," November 19, 1958; "Howard Thurman to Martin Luther King Jr.," September 11, 1959; and "Martin Luther King Jr. to Howard Thurman," September 30, 1959; King Papers, Special Collections, Mugar Memorial Library, Boston University.

69. Letter from Martin Luther King Jr. to Howard Thurman, November 8, 1958, from The Howard Thurman Papers Collection, Boston University.

70. Martin Luther King Jr., *Stride toward Freedom*; King, *Where Do We Go from Here?*

71. Thurman, *Disciplines*, 19.

72. Ibid., 34.

73. Thurman, *With Head and Heart*, 255.

74. "Spirituality Out on the Deep," unpublished manuscript, original paper presented at "America in Search of a Soul," Howard Thurman Convocation, Vanderbilt University Divinity School, October 26, 1989.

75. Mitchell, *Spiritual Dynamics*, 52; and Fluker, *They Looked for a City*, 174.

76. Thurman, *Creative Encounter* (Richmond, Ind.: Friends United, 1972), 67–71, 121.

77. Ibid., 81.

78. Ibid., 124.

Chapter 2: What Is Ethical Leadership?

1. Walter Earl Fluker, ed., *The Stones That the Builders Rejected: The Development of Ethical Leadership from the Black Church Tradition* (Harrisburg, Pa.: Trinity Press International, 1998).

2. Howard Thurman, "The Kingdom of Values," in *For the Inward Journey: The Writings of Howard Thurman* (New York: Harcourt Brace Jovanovich, 1984), 54.

3. See Parker Palmer, *Let Your Life Speak: Listening for the Voice of Vocation* (San Francisco: Jossey-Bass, 2000), 75–76; quotations from Havel are taken from Václav Havel, *The Art of the Impossible*; trans. Paul Wilson et al. (New York: Knopf, 1997), 17–18. "Material reality is not the fundamental factor in the movement of human history," but conscious awareness, thought, and spirit are taken from Palmer's commentary on the speech.

4. Kate Marks, comp., *Circle of Songs: Songs, Chants and Dance for Ritual and Celebration* (Lenox, Mass: Full Circle Press, 1993).

5. David Bohm, *Wholeness and the Implicate Order* (New York and London: Routledge, 1980), 55; see esp. chap. 3, "Reality and Knowledge Considered as Process," 48–64.

6. Joseph Jaworski, *Synchronicity: The Inner Path to Leadership* (San Francisco: Berrett-Koeheler, 1996, 1998), 45.

7. "The face of man is the medium through which the invisible in him becomes visible and enters into commerce with us." Emmanuel Levinas, *Difficult Freedom*, trans. Sean Hand (Baltimore: Johns Hopkins Press, 1990), 140.

8. James Hillman, *The Force of Character and the Lasting Life* (New York: Random House, 1999), 142.

9. Emmanuel Levinas, *Totality and Infinity*, trans. Alfonso Lingis (Pittsburgh: Duquesne University Press, 1969), 201. The question "Can things have a face?" is important for the definition above. Levinas suggests that art may be an appropriate lens through which to identify "being" in the face of a thing. He asks, "Is not art an activity that lends faces to things? Does not the façade of a house regard us? . . . We ask ourselves all the same if the impersonal but fascinating and magical march of rhythm does not, in art, substitute itself for sociality, for the face, for speech." Emmanuel Levinas, "Is Ontology Fundamental?" in *Basic Philosophical Writings*, ed. Adriaan T. Peperzak, Simon Critchley, and Robert Bernasconi (Bloomington: Indiana University Press, 1996), 10. An important source for this reading of Levinas has been James Hillman, *The Force of Character and the Lasting Life* (New York: Random House, 1999).

10. C. S. Lewis, *Till We Have Faces: A Myth Retold* (Grand Rapids: Eerdmans, 1956).

11. Examples of the first perspective on spirituality are those promoted within established religious institutions. Here there is a vast array of definitions and approaches to the subject. See, for instance, Felix M. Podimattam, *Global Spirituality: Ecumenical, Inter-religious, and Continental Spirituality* (Delhi: Media House, 2005); Arthur W. Chickering, *Encouraging Authenticity and Spirituality in Higher Education* (San Francisco: Jossey-Bass, 2006); Cathy Ota and Clive Erricker, eds., *Spiritual Education* (Brighton, Portland: Sussex Academic Press, 2005); Robert Fuller, *Wonder: From Emotion to Spirituality* (Chapel Hill: University of North Carolina Press, 2006); Ravi Shankar, *Wisdom for the New Millennium* (Mumbai: Jaico, 2005); James A. Wiseman, *Spirituality and Mysticism: A Global View* (Maryknoll, N.Y.: Orbis, 2006); Cheslyn Jones, Geoffrey Wainwright, and Edward Yarnold, eds., *The Study of Spirituality* (New York and London: Oxford University

Press, 1986), esp. "Note on Spirituality," xiv–xvi. Emphasis is placed on traditions of contemplation, reflection, and mystical life practices within institutionalized religious forms. In recent years, there has been growing interest and awareness of ecumenical and interfaith practices of spiritualities that enhance understanding of respective religious traditions through common dialogue and sharing. See Pujan Roka, *Bhagavad Gita on Effective Leadership: Timeless Wisdom for Leaders* (Lincoln, Neb., iUniverse, 2006); Thich Nhat Hanh, *Living Buddha, Living Christ* (New York: Riverhead, 1995); Dalai Lama, *Ethics for the New Millennium* (New York: Riverhead, 1999); and Fluker and Tumber, *A Strange Freedom*. African Americans tend not to place emphasis on "formalized structures" of spirituality. However, there is a significant presence and a growing literature that suggest that the place of liturgy, ritual, and inherited practices have long standing in the life of African American churches. In this perspective, one finds the recent writings of Peter J. Paris, Cheryl Sanders, Carlyle Fielding Stewart III, Dwight Hopkins, and Renita Weems very helpful.

In respect to the second usage of spirituality, a stream of public conversations from Parker Palmer to Deepak Chopra, which incorporates therapeutic and self-actualization discourses, has found audiences beyond the traditional academic and ecclesiastical institutions that have long dominated the contest. African American women writers, theologians, preachers, clairvoyants, movements like the broadly defined New Age spirituality, and Promise Keepers are among the many who compete for voice and place on a quickly changing playing field. See Deepak Chopra, *How to Know God: The Soul's Journey into the Mystery of Mysteries* (New York: Harmony, 2000); and *The Seven Spiritual Laws of Success: A Practical Guide to the Fulfillment of Your Dreams,* New World Library (San Rafael, Calif.: Amber-Allen Publishing, 1994); Herbert Benson, *Timeless Healing: The Power and Biology of Belief* (New York: Scribner's, 1996); Larry Dossey, M.D., *Healing Words: The Power of Prayer and the Practice of Medicine* (San Francisco: HarperSanFrancisco, 1993); Larry Dossey, M.D., *Prayer Is Good Medicine: How to Reap the Healing Benefits of Prayer* (San Francisco: HarperSanFrancisco, 1996); Parker Palmer, *Let Your Life Speak: Listening for the Voice of Vocation* (San Francisco: Jossey-Bass, 2000).

The third area refers to the broader philosophical and ethical notions of "spirit." Here, spirituality is discussed as a source of authority for private and public discourse that again is located across the spectrum of conservative, liberal, and progressive ideologies. William Bennett, ed., *The Moral Compass: Stories for a Life's Journey* (New York: Simon & Schuster, 1995); Steve Barboza, ed., *The African American Book of Values: Classic Moral Stories* (New York: Doubleday, 1998); Marianne Williamson, *Healing the Soul of America: Reclaiming Our Voices as Spiritual Citizens*, Touchstone Books (New York: Simon & Schuster, 1997); and Michael Lerner, *Spirit Matters* (Charlottesville, Va.: Hampton Road, 2000) may well represent the broad social and cultural context for the language game of spirituality in this perspective. See also Sara Lawrence-Lightfoot, *Balm in Gilead: The Journey of Healer* (Reading, Mass.: Addison-Wesley, 1988); James M. Washington, *Conversations with God: Two Centuries of Prayers by African Americans* (San Francisco: Harper Collins, 1997). Michael Dash, Jonathan Jackson, Stephen Rasor, Peter Paris, Robert Franklin, and Stephen Carter are outstanding exemplars of theologians, ethicists, and educators who have done significant work in the area of African American spirituality.

12. Peter J. Paris, *The Spirituality of African Peoples: The Search for a Common Moral Discourse* (Minneapolis: Fortress Press, 1995), 22.

13. Robert Michael Franklin, *Another Day's Journey* (Minneapolis: Fortress Press, 1997), 86. See also Franklin's taxonomy in "The Spiritualities of the Black Church," where he places King in the social justice tradition (42).

14. Arising here is whether we must become "ethical" in order for society to exist or we are necessarily "ethical" insofar as we enter into the makeup of any actual society. The latter, of course, means that society is always, already directed by "ethical"—technically directive—principles and could not otherwise exist. But this forces us to distinguish between the "ethical" principles that happen to exist and competing ethical principles that come after. Hence, ethical principles are always embedded in actual practice, which means that leadership principles are necessarily based on ethical guides. In this view, the problem cannot be to categorically intrude ethical guides that did not previously exist but rather, first, to disengage the guides we know must be there and, second, to confront these with alternatives, which we seek to demonstrate to be better. This is another way of saying there is always room for argument and discovery in ethics as a science, and that we must press on with counterarguments and open ourselves to its inherent possibilities if we are to make spiritual progress. (Many thanks to Preston King for this observation.)

15. The quotation is taken from *The African American Pulpit*, Judson Press, Winter 1997–1998 Premier Issue.

16. Thomas E. McCollough, *The Moral Imagination and Public Life: Raising the Ethical Question in Public Life* (Chatman, N.J.: Chatman House, 1991), 6–7.

17. As I write this book, federal responses to major corporate and nonprofit accounting scandals (for example, the U.S. Sentencing Guidelines for Organizations in 1991, the creation of ethics officers in most Fortune 1000 U.S. corporations, the Sarbanes-Oxley Act of 2002, and a number

of legislative recommendations and actions to strengthen governance, transparency, and accountability in the independent sector) have not been successful in stemming greed and ethical improprieties. The recent corporate failures and the controversial bailout package of $700 billion to Wall Street are evidence of what is at stake in reexamining the necessary, but insufficient conditions of rules-based ethical compliance. See Weaver, G., Trevino, L. K., and Cochran, P. (1999), "Corporate Ethics Practices in the Mid-1990s: An Empirical Study of the Fortune 1000," in *Journal of Business Ethics*, 18 (3): 283-294. "The Sarbanes-Oxley Act and Implications for Nonprofit Organizations" *BoardSource and Independent Sector* (January 2006) (http://www.independentsector.org/PDFs/sarbanesoxley.pdf); The Sarbanes-Oxley Act of 2002 (http://fl1.findlaw.com/news.findlaw.com/hdocs/docs/gwbush/sarbanesoxley072302.pdf); The Ethics Officers Association EOA (April 2005) http://www.eoa.org/AboutEOA.asp). Steve May provides an excellent conceptual framework for the problem of transparency and accountability that takes into account other important organizational practices that inform healthy ethical organizations: alignment, participation, dialogic participation and courage. Steve May ed., *Case Studies in Organizational Communication: Ethical Perspectives and Practices* (Thousand Oaks, London, and New Delhi: Sage Publications, 2006), 35–47, and Ethics Officers Association with membership of over 1,000, including representatives from a large sector of the Fortune 1000 (EOA, 2005).

18. Unfortunately, utilitarianism has come to be identified with utilitarian individualism. This identification obscures the complexity of the various ethical theories of this school of moral reasoning. For instance, Jeremy Bentham's utilitarianism does not necessarily promote the individual over the collective. On the contrary, "the greatest good for the greatest number" can be viewed as a corrective to *my* self-interest. Bentham and John Stuart Mill, as well as contemporary ethicists like Peter Singer, are concerned with egalitarian formulations that seek a rational calculus for moral disagreements. For instance, the greatest good or pleasure for the greatest number does not necessarily refer to physical pleasure. Mill valued intellectual over physical enjoyment. His famous statement that he would rather be "Socrates dissatisfied, than a pig satisfied" is suggestive of the point that pleasure is not merely quantitative, but qualitative as well. Singer takes this argument further by applying it to the suffering of all sentient beings, including animals. Speciesism, the "prejudice or attitude of bias in favor of the interests of members of one's own species and against those members of other species," according to Singer, violates the moral idea of equality. Quoted in Peter Singer, *Writings on an Ethical Life* (New York: Ecco Press, 2000), 33.

19. Steve May, ed., *Case Studies in Organizational Communication: Ethical Perspectives and Practices* (Thousand Oaks, Calif.: Sage, 2006), 29.

20. Chantell Ilbury and Clem Sunter, *Games Foxes Play: Planning for Extraordinary Times* (Cape Town, South Africa: Human and Rousseau Tafelberg, 2005); see especially their discussion on strategy and tactics, 7–22.

21. The realist leader is also confronted with how to measure "the good" and to ensure equal distribution. John Rawls, articulating a rationalist critique of utilitarianism, says, "The striking feature of the utilitarian view of justice is that it does not matter, except indirectly, how the sum of satisfaction is distributed among individuals" because there are not adequate principles to determine how the rules for distribution are made. John Rawls, *A Theory of Justice* (Cambridge, Mass.: Belknap Press of Harvard University Press, 1971), 26.

22. *Constructive rationalism* posits that human beings by nature are self-interested and if given opportunity will choose options that enhance their own needs and desires. But this is not the only way to view human agency. Human beings can also be altruistic and sympathetic to others' needs and desires. Witness the response of individuals to natural catastrophes like Katrina, the Indonesian tsunami, and the Myanmar and Chinese earthquakes where they performed acts of courage and compassion even at risk to their own safety. In cases such as these, rules and procedures for the distribution of goods are suspended for an ethic of cooperation that is rooted in what James Q. Wilson calls the "moral sense of justice," *The Moral Sense* (New York: Free, 1993). The moral sense of justice, according to Wilson, precedes social constructs of justice as in rules, principles, and laws, yet it informs how certain rational renderings of justice are shaped by an innate moral sensibility. Human beings are characterized universally by "the desire for survival and sustenance with the desire for companionship and approval" and are constantly in pursuit of social arrangements that best provide for these basic needs and desires (122–23). The moral sense of justice as fairness arises from this basic human instinct. It has its genesis in early childhood associations with family and is expressed in feelings of equity, reciprocity, and impartiality. See Wilson's chapter, "Fairness," 55–78. See the later discussion on a sense of justice.

23. Utilitarian individualism is characterized by values of autonomy: the right to be different, the primacy of the individual over the collective, the right to pleasure, the right to be one's own judge of one's own ends, and the right to submit all authoritarian norms and values to a rigorous evaluation on the basis of one's own standard. John G. Strelan, "The Privatisation of the *Cultus Publicus*," *Lutheran Theological Journal* 27, no. 1 (1993): 13–22;

quoted in N. A. Chagnon, *Yanomamö: The Fierce People* (New York: Holt, Rinehart and Winston, 1968). See chapter 1, "Doing Fieldwork among the Yanomamö." The authors of *Habits of the Heart* identified two types of utilitarianism: instrumental and expressive. Instrumental individualism expresses itself in the pursuit of personal success and one's own interests. The focus of concern is not the common good but private comfort, that is, the belief that "the individual has a primary reality, whereas society is a second-order, derived or artificial construct." Robert Bellah et al., *Habits of the Heart: Individualism and Commitment in American Life*, Perennial Library (New York: Harper & Row, 1986), 334. Expressive individualism, the second form of individualism, highly values personal experience and feeling. Because of its emphasis on feelings, sympathy, and personal development, expressive individualism can be highly effective in making connections with smaller groups and communities, but for leaders it runs the risk of a soft response to larger structural issues that maintain order, discipline, and goal attainment. Richard Sennett calls it the "ideology of intimacy," the conviction that "social relationships of all kinds are real, believable and authentic the closer they approach the inner psychological concerns of each person." Richard Sennett, *The Fall of Public Man* (New York: Knopf, 1977), 259. Quoted in John G. Strelan, "The Privatisation of the *Cultus Publicus*," 1.

24. Bellah et al., *Habits of the Heart*.

25. An important resource for ethical leadership is Jeffrey Stout's pragmatist approach, which he calls "moral bricolage," a reconfiguration of the disparate moral languages that serve as means of speaking to the contemporary debates of public life. This method upholds the process of inclusion, exclusion, and reconfiguration of the various moral traditions that make up the common life. According to Stout, this process is the most viable candidate for retrieving, reappropriating, and reconstructing the varied moral strands that comprise the national life. He points to leaders like Thomas Jefferson and Martin Luther King Jr. as *bricoleurs par excellence*. Moral bricolage, according to Stout, is "the process in which one begins with bits and pieces of received linguistic material, arranges some of them into a structured whole, leaves others to the side, and ends up with a moral language one proposes to use." See Jeffrey Stout, *Ethics after Babel: The Language of Morals and Their Discontents* (Boston: Beacon, 1988), 191–242, 292; for a detailed account of Stout's argument, see 74ff.

26. See discussion on "adaptive capacity as applied creativity" in Warren G. Bennis and Robert J. Thomas, *Geeks and Geezers: How Era, Values, and Defining Moments Shape Leaders* (Boston: Harvard Business School Press, 2002), 101-6.

27. Ronald Heifetz, *Leadership without Easy Answers* (Cambridge, Mass.: Belknap Press of Harvard University Press, 1994).

28. Quoted in Joseph L. Badaracco Jr., "The Discipline of Building Character," in *Harvard Business Review on Leadership* (Boston: Harvard Business Review Publishing, 1998), 89–113.

29. See note 25 above on Jeffrey Stout, *Ethics after Babel.*

30. This question predates our modern situation and was introduced as early as nineteenth-century sociologist Ferdinand Toinnes's *Community and Society* (*Gemeinschaft und Gesellschaft*), trans. and ed. Charles Loomis (East Lansing: Michigan State University Press, 1957).

31. Robinson Jeffers, "The Inhumanist," in *The Double Axe and Other Poems*, part 2 (New York: Random House, 1948), 52–54.

32. Alasdair MacIntyre, *After Virtue: A Study in Moral Theory* (South Bend, Ind.: University of Notre Dame Press, 1984).

33. Michael J. Sandel, *Liberalism and the Limits of Justice*, 2nd ed. (New York: Cambridge University Press, 1998), 173.

34. Jan Assmann writes, "The term 'cultural memory' is merely a translation of the Greek name Mnemosyne. Since Mnemosyne was the mother of the nine Muses, her name came to stand for the totality of cultural activities as they were personified by the different Muses. By subsuming these cultural activities under the personification of memory, the Greeks were viewing culture not only as based on memory but as a form of memory in itself." He connects cultural memory with the history of discourse. "The memory-line I am concerned with is, however, much more specific. It is just one of the many *Wanderstrassen* of cultural memory, as Aby Warburg called it. Further, its investigation involves a methodology of its own that must not be confounded with the much more general concerns of mnemohistory. This is the history of discourse. By 'discourse' I understand something much more specific than what this term has come to refer to in the wake of Michel Foucault and others. I am referring to a concatenation of texts which are based on each other and treat or negotiate a common subject matter. In this view, discourse is a kind of textual conversation or debate which might extend over generations and centuries, even millennia, depending on institutionalizations of permanence such as writing, canonization, educational and clerical institutions, and so forth." Jan Assmann, *Moses the Egyptian: The Memory of Egypt in Western Monotheism* (Cambridge: Harvard University Press), 14–17.

35. Claude Levi-Strauss, *Structural Anthropology* (New York: Basic, 1963), 179.

36. "This conquest of myth as myth is only one aspect of the recognition of symbols and their power to reveal. To understand the myth as myth is to

understand what the myth with its time, its space, its events, it personages, its drama, adds to the revelatory function of the primary symbols." Paul Ricoeur, *The Symbolism of Evil* (New York: Harper & Row, 1967), 162.

37. See Mircea Eliade, *Myth and Reality* (New York: Harper & Row, 1963), 17–18; and Robert Graves, ed., *New Larousse Encyclopedia of Mythology* (New York: Hamlyn, 1982), v.

38. Alasdaire MacIntyre, "Myth," in *The Encyclopedia of Philosophy* (New York: Macmillan, 1967), 5:436.

39. Lawrence Levine, *Black Culture and Black Consciousness* (New York: Oxford Unversity Press, 1977), 90; Sterling Stuckey, "Through Prism of Folklore: The Black Ethos in Slavery," in *Going through the Storm: The Influence of African American Art in History* (New York: Oxford University Press, 1994), 4; also in Eric Foner, *America's Black Past* (New York: Harper & Row, 1970), 111. Rosetta Ross's treatment of "witnessing" and "testifying" as black church practices rooted in the "ritualized mundane" provides the context for both the understanding of narrative and the social construction of traditional knowledge that conspire in the identification of black women's public performance of defiance and resistance. Her treatment of figures like Septima Clark, Fannie Lou Hamer, and Ella Baker are examples of the way in which she historically situates these important figures and offers a fresh perspective on the ways in which the civil rights movement developed as an organic moral and spiritual force through women's agency. Rosetta E. Ross, *Witnessing and Testifying: Black Women, Religion and Civil Rights* (Minneapolis: Fortress Press, 2003).

40. Lawrence Levine comments on this peculiar quality of story: "The nature of their content and delivery . . . allowed slave tales to evoke the past and make it part of the living present." Levine, *Black Culture*, 90.

41. Alex Haley, "Alex Haley Discovers His Roots," in *The African American Book of Values: Classic Moral Stories*, ed. Steve Barboza (New York: Doubleday, 1998), 372.

42. MacIntyre, *After Virtue*, 216.

43. Fluker, *Stones That the Builders Rejected*.

44. Edward Shils, "Tradition and Liberty: Antinomy and Inter-dependence," in *The Virtue of Civility: Selected Essays on Liberalism, Tradition, and Civil Society*, ed. Steven Grosby (Indianapolis: Liberty Fund, 1997), 106–7, emphasis added.

45. Bellah in *Habits of the Heart* defines a community as "a group of people who are socially interdependent, who participate together in discussion and decision making, who share certain practices . . . that both define the community and are nurtured by it. Such a community is not quickly formed. It almost always has a history and so is called a

community of memory, defined in part by its past and its memory of its past" (33).

46. See the excellent argument by Jeffrey Stout, *Democracy and Tradition* (Princeton, N.J.: Princeton University Press, 2004). Stout responds to the impasse created by introducing religious premises into political debates by recommending that parties engage in public *conversation*, by which he means "an exchange of views in which the respective parties express their premises . . . try to make sense of each other's perspectives, and expose their own commitments to the possibility of criticism" (10–11); see also H. Richard Niebuhr, *The Responsible Self: An Essay in Christian Moral Philosophy* with an introduction by James M. Gustafson (New York: Harper & Row, 1963, 1978).

47. William James, *The Principles of Psychology*, vol. 1, chap. 5, "Habit" (New York: Dover, 1890; repr., 1950), 105.

48. "Excellence," writes Aristotle, "is an art won by training and habituation. We do not act rightly because we have virtue or excellence, but rather we have those because we have acted rightly. We are what we repeatedly do. Excellence, then, is not an act but a habit." "Excellence . . . but a habit." This is a quote often attributed to Aristotle, but it actually comes from Will Durant, *The Story of Philosophy: The Lives and Opinions of the Greater Philosophers* (New York: Simon and Schuster, 1926), 61.

49. Diane Dreher, *The Tao of Personal Leadership* (New York: Harper Business, 1996), 23.

50. See chapter 7, "Remembering, Retelling, and Reliving Our Stories."

51. Marla F. Frederick, *Between Sundays: Black Women and Everyday Struggles of Faith* (Berkeley: University of California Press, 2003), ix.

52. Ibid., 8. Carolyn Rouse's excellent text *Engage Surrender: African American Women and Islam* (Berkeley: University of California Press, 2004) is similar in the sense of ethnography and how these women understand and transform themselves.

53. For example, see my treatment of King's dialectical methodology in Walter Earl Fluker, "Transformed Nonconformity in the Thought of Martin Luther King Jr.," *Princeton Theological Bulletin*, Spring 2004; Cornel West, *Prophesy Deliverance! An Afro-American Revolutionary Christianity* (Philadelphia: Westminster, 1982), 108–9.

54. Gustavo Gutierrez wrote a powerful treatise titled *We Drink from Our Own Wells: The Spiritual Journey of a People*, trans. Matthew J. O'Connell (Maryknoll, N.Y.: Orbis, 1984).

55. Robert McAfee Brown, *Spirituality and Liberation: Overcoming the Great Fallacy* (Philadelphia: Westminster, 1988), 118.

56. Jacob Needleman, *The American Soul: Rediscovering the Wisdom of the Founders* (New York: Jeremy P. Tarcher/Putnam, 2002), 10.

Chapter 3: Character at the Intersection

1. Walter Earl Fluker, "At the Intersection Where Worlds Collide: The Quest for Character, Civility, and Community in Infusing Culture and Diversity in Character Education" published monograph (Washington D.C.: Department of Education, 2008). Thomas Wren, "Philosophical Moorings," in *Handbook for Moral and Character Education*, Larry Nucci and Darcia Narvarez, eds. (New York, London: Routledge, 2008), 11–35.

2. Robert William Fogel, *The Fourth Great Awakening and the Future of Egalitarianism* (Chicago: University of Chicago Press, 2000).

3. See Michelle Goldberg, *Kingdom Coming: The Rise of Christian Nationalism* (New York: Norton, 2006); and George Lakoff, *Don't Think of an Elephant: Know Your Values and Frame the Debate* (White River Junction, Vt.: Chelsea Green, 2004).

4. Frank Rich, in an editorial in the *New York Times*, "From Those Wonderful Folks Who Gave Us 'Axis of Evil'" (July 16, 2006), writes: "Only if we remember that the core values of this White House are marketing and political expediency, not principle and substance, can we fully grasp its past errors and, more important, decipher the endgame to come. The Bush era has not been defined by big government or small government but by virtual government. Its enduring shrine will be a hollow Department of Homeland Security that finds more potential terrorist targets in Indiana than in New York."

5. "Nonspecificity" and "erasure" of traditions are the means by which public intellectuals foster and perpetuate a certain kind of moral vocabulary that promotes the disappearance of the detailed historical or empirical record. In some respects, it erases subject, deeds, and events while simultaneously discussing them. Nonspecificity promotes erasure. See Joy James, *Transcending the Talented Tenth: Black Leaders and American Intellectuals* (New York: Routledge, 1997), 40ff., esp. 54.

6. Toni Morrison, *Playing in the Dark: Whiteness and the Literary Imagination* (Cambridge: Harvard University Press, 1992), 63; see also 51–54.

7. Jim Wallis, *God's Politics: Why the Right Get It Wrong and the Left Doesn't Get It; A New Vision for Faith and Politics in America* (San Francisco: HarperCollins, 2006). See chap. 19, "Truth Telling about Race: America's Original Sin."

8. Langston Hughes, "American Heartbreak," from *The Collected Poems of Langston Hughes* by Langston Hughes, edited by Arnold Rampersad

with David Roessel, associate editor, copyright © 1994 by the Estate of Langston Hughes. Used by permission of Alfred A. Knopf, a division of Random House, Inc.

9. John H. McWhorter, *Losing the Race: Self-Sabotage in Black America* (New York: Free Press, 2000); Norman Kelley, *The Head Negro in Charge Syndrome: The Dead End of Black Politics* (New York: Nation Books, 2004); Robert C. Smith, *We Have No Leaders: African Americans in the Post Civil Rights Era* (New York: State University of New York Press, 1996); Chika Onyeani, *Capitalist Nigger: The Road to Success; A Spider Web Doctrine* (New York: Timbuktu, 2000); James, *Transcending the Talented Tenth; Leaders and American Intellectuals* (New York: Routledge, 1997); Juan Williams, *Enough: The Phony Leaders, Dead-End Movements, and Culture of Failure That Are Undermining Black America—and What We Can Do about It* (New York: Random House, 2006); Bill Cosby and Alvin F. Poussaint, *Come On People: On the Path from Victims to Victors* (Nashville: Thomas Nelson, 2007).

10. Walter Earl Fluker, ed., *The Stones That the Builders Rejected: The Development of Ethical Leadership from the Black Church Tradition* (Harrisburg, Pa.: Trinity Press International, 1998), 8–9; and Walter Earl Fluker and Catherine Tumber, eds., *A Strange Freedom: The Best of Howard Thurman on Religious Experience and Public Life* (Boston: Beacon, 1998), 8–11.

11. Lani Guinier, *The Miner's Canary: Enlisting Race, Resisting Power, Transforming Democracy* (Cambridge, Mass.: Harvard University Press, 2002).

12. Fluker, *Stones That the Builders Rejected.*

13. Manfred F. R. Kets de Vries, *The Leadership Mystique* (New York: Prentice Hall, 2006), 5.

14. Laurence Thomas, *Living Morally: A Psychology of Moral Character* (Philadelphia: Temple University Press, 1989), 17–26.

15. Howard Gardner, *Leading Minds: And Anatomy of Leadership* (New York: Basic, 1995).

16. He calls attention to a long tradition of philosophers who have made similar claims, among these being Socrates, Zeno, Aristippus, Diogenes, and more recently, Michel Foucault, F. M. Alexander, Wilhelm Reich, and Moshe Feldenkrais. Richard Shusterman, "Somaesthetics: A Disciplinary Proposal," *Journal of Aesthetics and Art Criticism* (1999), 57. The quotation from Thoreau is also in this article.

17. Howard Thurman, *With Head and Heart: The Autobiography of Howard Thurman* (San Francisco: Harcourt Brace Jovanovich, 1979), 60. Thurman shared this occasion with me in a conversation in Evanston, Ill., April 1978. The impact of Cross's advice, though not fully realized at that moment,

became in time a driving principle for decision-making in relation to social action for Thurman. Smith comments on the significance of this occasion and its relation to Thurman's baptism. See Luther E. Smith, *The Mystic as Prophet*, (Washington, D.C.: University Press of America, 1981), 24.

18. Thurman, *With Head and Heart*, 60.

19. See also Thurman's meditation "Life Abounds," where he discusses the self-healing of the body as part of the inherent logic of Life. Howard Thurman, *Meditations of the Heart* (Richmond, Ind.: Friends United, 1976), 105–6.

20. William James, *Talks to Teachers on Psychology: And to Students on Some of Life's Ideals* (New York: Henry Holt, 1921), 184.

21. I am deeply indebted to James Pawelski's excellent paper "Pragmatism, Habit Formation, and the Development of Character," University of Pennsylvania, March 7, 2005. Pawelski writes, "In making character a function of habit, James places himself in a tradition that goes back at least to Aristotle, who writes that 'character (*ēthos*) is the product of habit (*ethos*), and has indeed derived its name, with a slight variation of form, from that word'" (*Nicomachean Ethics* 2.1.1). I am deeply indebted . . . (Nichomachean Ethics 2.1.1). William James, *The Principles of Psychology*, vol. 1 (New York: Dover, 1950), 123-127.

22. Examples in African American life and history abound with this problematic variously referred to as "double consciousness" or "normative gaze" and the crippling labels of intellectual and social inferiority based on race, class and gender. See Cornel West's helpful discussion in *Prophesy Deliverance! An Afro-American Revolutionary Christianity* (Philadelphia: Westminster, 1982), chap. 2, "A Genealogy of Racism," pp. 47–65; and Patricia A. Turner, *Ceramic Uncles and Celluloid Mammies: Blacks and Their Influence on Culture* (New York: Anchor Books, 1994).

23. Howard Thurman, *Deep Is the Hunger* (New York: Harper & Brothers, 1951), 93.

24. Diane Dreher, *The Tao of Personal Leadership* (New York: Harper Business, 1996), 14.

25. Stephen L. Carter, *Integrity* (New York: Basic, 1996), 7.

26. Conversation with students at the Leadership Center at Morehouse College, Spring 2003.

27. See Thurman, "Who Are You?" audio cassette, n.d., Boston University Special Collections.

28. Howard Thurman, "Knowledge . . . Shall Vanish Away," in *The Inward Journey* (Friends United Press, 1971), 95-96. Reprinted with permission.

29. Thurman, *The Search for Common Ground* (New York: Harper & Row, 1971), 22. Parentheses added.

30. I will return to this theme in chapter 8.

31. "Innocence," says Thurman, "is the state of being which exists without knowledge and responsibility." It is that "which is essentially untried, untested, unchallenged. It is complete and whole within itself because it has known nothing else." Thurman, *Search*, 26–27.

32. Ibid., 27.

33. Daniel Goleman, Richard Boyatzis, and Anne McKee, *Primal Leadership: Realizing the Power of Emotional Intelligence* (Boston: Harvard Business School Press, 2002), 39.

34. Howard Thurman, H. I. Hester Lectureship, Golden Gate Baptist Theological Seminary, Mill Valley, Calif., February 8–12, 1971.

35. See Mendenhall Lectures 3, "Community and the Prophet's Dream," 1.

36. Thurman, *Search*, 34.

37. Emmanuel Levinas, *Difficult Freedom*, trans. Sean Hand (Baltimore: Johns Hopkins Press, 1990), 140.

38. Manfred F. R. Kets de Vries, *Leaders, Fools, and Impostors: Essays on the Psychology of Leadership* (San Francisco: Jossey-Bass, 1993), 29, 35.

39. Erich Fromm, *The Heart of Man: Its Genius for Good and Evil* (New York: Harper & Row, 1964), 39–40.

40. De Vries, *Leaders, Fools, and Impostors*. See chap. 4, "Dead Souls: Understanding Emotional Illiteracy," 61–88.

41. Goleman, Boyatzis, and McKee, *Primal Leadership*, 5, 19–21.

42. Rob Goffee and Gareth Jones, *Why Should Anyone Be Led by You? What It Takes to Be an Authentic Leader* (Boston: Harvard Business School Press, 2006).

43. Howard Thurman, "The Sound of the Genuine," baccalaureate address, Spelman College.

44. Luther Smith correctly observes that for Thurman, "the crucible of relationship" provides the hermenuetical key for ascertaining meaning in the various modes of existence in which one finds oneself. Luther E. Smith, "Intimate Mystery: Howard Thurman's Search for Ultimate Meaning (1900–1981)," *Ultimate Reality and Meaning: Interdisciplinary Studies in the Philosophy of Understanding* 11 (June 1988): 94–98. See also John H. Cartwright, "The Religious Ethics of Howard Thurman," *Journal of the Interdenominational Center* (Fall 1984–Spring 1985), 22–34; and Walter G. Muelder, "The Structure of Howard Thurman's Religious Social Ethics," in *Debate and Understanding*, ed. Ricardo A. Millet, special edition (Spring 1982), 7–13. In this perspective, epistemological and axiological questions are rooted in a moral anthropology that avoids the dichotomous portrayal of the self as an irreconcilable tension between nature and spirit. Rather,

for Thurman, the self is essentially relational and agential. Ratiocination is a secondary act. "The deed reveals meaning. Meaning does not exist as a disembodied force, but it becomes evident through relationships." Luther E. Smith, "Intimate Mystery," 97. All meaningful knowledge is for the sake of action, and all meaningful action is for the sake of loving relationship. John Macmurray, *The Self as Agent* (London: Faber and Faber, 1957), 15. Therefore, religious faith is not to be confused with dogmatic assertions fixed in creed and formal statements, but it has to do rather with "literal truth and the conviction it inspires." This truth is disclosed in creative encounter with a "Thou" in lived community with others.

45. Thich Nhat Hanh, *Living Buddha, Living Christ* (New York: Riverhead Books, 1995), 11.

46. Thurman, "The Idol of Togetherness," in Fluker and Tumber, *A Strange Freedom*, 21.

47. Walter Earl Fluker, "The Politics of Conversion and the Civilization of Friday," in *The Courage to Hope: From Black Suffering to Human Redemption* by Quinton Hosford Dixie and Cornel West (Boston: Beacon, 1999), 103–117.

48. Amos Wilder writes, "In any given situation, theology should relate itself not only to the philosophical ideas of the time but to its symbolic life and impulses. While theology properly takes the form of clearly thinking about God, the faith, the world, it has a basic substratum of imaginative grasp on reality and experience." Amos N. Wilder, *Theopoetic* (Philadelphia: Fortress Press, 1976), 25.

49. Ray L. Hart, *Unfinished Man and the Imagination: Toward an Ontology and a Rhetoric of Revelation* (New York: Herder and Herder, 1968).

50. Gerhard Ebeling, *God and Word* (Philadelphia: Fortress Press, 1967), 30.

51. James M. Gustafson, *Christ and the Moral Life* (Chicago and London: University of Chicago Press, 1968), 250.

52. Christopher Lasch, *The True and Only Heaven: Progress and Its Critics* (New York: Norton, 1991), 81.

53. Sidney Hook, *The Hero in History: A Study in Limitation and Possibility* (London: Seker and Warburg, 1945; new ed., New Brunswick, N.J.: Transaction, 1992).

54. Bernard M. Bass, *Bass and Stodgill's Handbook of Leadership: Theory, Research, and Managerial Applications,* 3rd ed. (New York: Free Press, 1990), 23.

55. King, *Where Do We Go from Here: Chaos or Community?* (Boston: Beacon, 1967), 172–91.

56. King, *Stride toward Freedom: The Montgomery Story* (New York: Harper & Row, 1958), 167.

57. King, *Where Do We Go from Here?* 98.

58. Ibid., 97–98.

59. Ibid., 99.

60. For Martin Luther King Jr., community is the ideal that serves as the goal of human existence and the norm for ethical judgment; it is the mutually cooperative and voluntary venture of persons in which they realize the solidarity of humanity by freely assuming responsibility for one another within the context of civil relations. Community provides the context for the sensuous articulation of the values of love, justice, and courage as dynamic and interrelated constructs. The search for community was the defining motif of Martin Luther King Jr.'s life and thought. From his early childhood until his death, there is a progression in his personal and intellectual understanding of the nature and goal of human existence, which he refers to as "the beloved community." The early development of the ideal of community in King reached its zenith in the March on Washington in 1963, but the following four and a half years proved to be a period in which his vision of community received its severest criticisms and challenges.

61. Walter Earl Fluker, *They Looked for a City: A Comparative Analysis of the Ideal of Community in Howard Thurman and Martin Luther King Jr.* (Lanham, Md.: University Press of America, 1988).

62. King, "A Christmas Sermon on Peace," in *A Testament of Hope: The Essential Writings of Martin Luther King, Jr.*, ed. James Melvin Washington (New York: Harper & Row, 1986), 257.

63. James Cone, *Martin and Malcolm and America: A Dream or a Nightmare* (Maryknoll, N.Y.: Orbis, 1991), 235.

64. Ibid.

65. King, "I See the Promised Land (3 April 1968)," in Washington, *A Testament of Hope*, 280.

66. Howard Thurman, *Meditations of the Heart* (Boston: Beacon, 1953, 1981), 134.

Chapter 4: Civility at the Intersection

1. Stephen L. Carter, *Civility: Manners, Morals, and the Etiquette of Democracy* (New York: Basic Books, 1998).

2. The Council on Civil Society, *A Call to Civil Society: Why Democracy Needs Moral Truths* (New York: Institute for American Values, 1998).

3. Edward Shils, *The Virtue of Civility: Selected Essays on Liberalism, Tradition, and Civil Society*, ed. Steven Grosby (Indianapolis: Liberty Fund, 1997).

4. For an excellent summary of the Aristotelian philosophical inheritance of civility and its modern theoretical history, see Lawrence Cahoone, "Civic Meetings, Cultural Meanings," in *Civility*, ed. Leroy S. Rouner (Notre Dame, Ind.: University of Notre Dame Press, 2000), 40–48.

5. James Schmidt, "Is Civility a Virtue?" in Rouner, *Civility*, 17–19.

6. Walter Earl Fluker, "Recognition, Respectability, and Loyalty," in Walter Earl Fluker, "Recognition, Respectability, and Loyalty: Black Churches and the Quest for Civility," in *New Day Begun: African American Churches and Civic Culture in Post-Civil Rights America* by R. Drew Smith (Durham, N.C.: Duke University Press, 2003), 113–41.

7. Amitai Etzioni's definition of civility is helpful. "The term civility has been used in different ways; most commonly it has referred to the need to deliberate in a civil manner about the issues society faces, and to sustain intermediary bodies that stand between the individual and the state." Amitai Etzioni, *The New Golden Rule* (New York: Basic, 1996), 95–96.

8. Robert D. Putnam, *Bowling Alone: The Collapse and Revival of American Community* (New York: Simon & Schuster, 2000). See especially Putnam's discussion on the significance of "social capital" as both a bonding and bridging social phenomenon and its relationship to civic infrastructures that build community. "Bonding" refers to the ways in which social capital tends to reinforce exclusive identities and homogenous groups. "Bridging" refers to ways in which social capital tends to produce broader and more inclusive group behavior and to encourage reciprocity (22–24).

9. Robert Wuthnow, *Christianity and Civil Society: The Contemporary Debate* (Harrisburg, Pa.: Trinity Press International, 1996).

10. Michael Walzer, "The Idea of Civil Society," *Dissent* (Spring 1991); Quoted in Wuthnow, *Christianity and Civil Society*, 298.

11. Putnam, *Bowling Alone*, 19.

12. Preston King and Heather Devere, eds., *The Challenge to Friendship in Modernity: Critical Review of International Social and Political Philosophy* (New York: Routledge, 2000).

13. See Jeffrey C. Goldfarb's excellent discussion in *Civility and Subversion: The Intellectual in Democratic Society* (Cambridge: Cambridge University Press, 1998), 1. Although the example he cites is the disruptive public speech of Malcolm X, the civility practiced by King and the modern civil rights movement represents the epitome of civility as disruptive speech and action. In this sense, King is rightly depicted as a bricoleur. See Jeffrey Stout, *Ethics after Babel: The Languages of Morals and Their Discontents* (Boston: Beacon, 1988).

14. King, "On Being a Good Neighbor," in *Strength to Love* (Philadelphia: Fortress Press, 1963), 32.

15. Ibid., 33.

16. Ibid.

17. King, "The Ethical Demands of Integration," in *A Testament of Hope: The Essential Writings of Martin Luther King, Jr.*, ed. James Melvin Washington (New York: Harper & Row, 1986), 124.

18. Howard Thurman, *A Strange Freedom: The Best of Howard Thurman on Religious Experience and Public Life*, ed. Walter Earl Fluker and Catherine Tumber (Boston: Beacon, 1998), 185.

19. Martin Luther King Jr., "A Knock at Midnight," in *Strength to Love* (Philadelphia: Fortress Press, 1963), 62–63; King, "Some Things We Must Do" address at Holt Street Baptist Church, December 5, 1957; King, " Letter from a Birmingham Jail" in *Why We Can't Wait* (New York: Harper and Row, 1963), 77-100; King, "A Time to Break Silence" in *A Testament of Hope: The Essential Writings of Martin Luther King Jr.*, ed. James Melvin Washington (San Francisco: Harper and Row, 1986), 231–244.

20. King and Devere, *Challenge to Friendship*.

21. Jean Paul Sartre, "Existentialism Is a Humanism," tr. Carol Macomber (New Haven, Conn.: Yale University Press, 2007), 17–72.

22. Manfred F. R. Kets de Vries, *Leaders, Fools, and Impostors: Essays on the Psychology of Leadership* (San Francisco: Jossey-Bass, 1993), 5–20.

23. Jean Paul Sartre, *No Exit and Three Other Plays* (New York: Vintage, 1955), 21.

24. David Gergen, *Eyewitness to Power: The Essence of Leadership—Nixon to Clinton* (Simon & Schuster, 2000); see esp. p. 80.

25. De Vries, *Leaders, Fools, and Impostors*, 20.

26. Anonymous student cited in *Death by Bread Alone: Texts and Reflections on Religious Experience* by Dorothee Soelle, trans. David L. Scheidt (Philadelphia: Fortress Press, 1978), 95–96. Used by permission.

27. Rainer Maria Rilke, from *The Notebooks of Malte Laurids Brigge* by Rainer Maria Rilke, translated by M. D. Herter Norton. Copyright 1949 by W. W. Norton & Company, renewed © 1977 by M. D. Herter Norton Crena de Iongh. Used by permission of W. W. Norton & Company, Inc.

28. Walter Earl Fluker, "Recognition, Respectability, and Loyalty: The Quest for Civility among Black Churches," in *New Day Begun: Black Churches, Public Influences, and American Civic Culture*, ed. R. Drew Smith (Durham, N.C.: Duke University Press, 2003).

29. Orlando Patterson, *Slavery and Social Death: A Comparative Study* (Cambridge, Mass.: Harvard University Press), 100.

30. Paul Laurence Dunbar, "We Wear the Mask," in *The Complete Poems of Paul Laurence Dunbar: With the Introduction to "Lyrics of Lowly Life,"* by Paul Laurence Dunbar (New York: Dodd, Mead, 1967), 71.

31. Gunnar Myrdal, *An American Dilemma: The Negro Problem and American Democracy* (New York: Harper & Brothers, 1944).

32. The subtitle of Myrdal's work, however, underscored the fundamental character of the issues at stake. He characterized the *dilemma* as *The Negro Problem and Democracy. The Negro Problem* (sometimes called *The Negro Question*) has been the staple ideological statement defining and representing the life and place of the African in American society since slavery. The Negro Problem, formulated by all sides of the male-dominated white power elite, was "What shall we do with the Negro?" The Problem, however, reached its most significant historical impasse during the last two decades of the nineteenth century and the first two decades of the twentieth. With increased African American political participation and economic development and the large population of blacks in the South during Reconstruction, these years witnessed a rise in racially motivated violence and legislative and judicial practices aimed at stripping agency from freed men and women and returning the country to a place that was safe for "white women." At the same time, former abolitionists, emigrationists, and mostly Northern white religious leaders, politicians, industrialists, and philanthropists worked diligently to solve the Negro Problem through education as a means of "civilizing" the child/savage generally depicted in bestial and minstrel images. Such was the social and political context that greeted the African American entrance into the twentieth century and informed the moral and civic practices of black intellectual elites and religious leaders. Ralph Luker, *The Social Gospel in Black and White* (Chapel Hill: University of North Carolina Press, 1991); Sidney M. Wilhelm, *Who Needs the Negro?* (New York: Anchor Books, 1971); Benjamin Quarles, *The Negro in the Making of America* (New York: Collier, 1964); Harold Cruse, *The Crisis of the Negro Intellectual: The Failure of Black Leadership* (New York: Morrow, 1967); Kevin K. Gaines, *Uplifting the Race: Black Leadership, Politics and Culture in the Twentieth Century* (Chapel Hill: University of North Carolina Press, 1996), 5; Darlene Clark Hine, "Rape and the Inner Lives of Black Women in the Middle West: Preliminary Thoughts on the Culture of Dissemblance," in *Unequal Sisters: A Multicultural Reader in U.S. Women's History*, ed. Ellen DuBois and Vicki L. Ruiz (New York: Routledge, 1990), 292–229; and Joy James, *Transcending the Talented Tenth: Black Leaders and American Intellectuals* (New York: Routledge, 1997). Patricia A. Turner, *Ceramic Uncles and Celluloid Mammies: Black Images and Their Influence on Culture* (New York: Anchor Books, 1994),

is an excellent resource for the significance of the black iconography and its impact on cultural and ideological sequences in black life and the larger society. Similarly, Spike Lee's film *Bamboozled* expresses some of the fundamental concerns of racial ideology and iconography and its impact on black life, culture, and the larger society. See Carl P. Henry, *Culture and African American Politics* (Indianapolis: Indiana University Press, 1990), 10–11. See Henry's critique of Cruse's dilemma-oriented polemic, which leaves unresolved the ideological premise that black elites must provide an adequate social theory based on living ingredients of African American history. The challenge for Cruse, as for other black elites, tends to be this unresolved problematic often couched in *dilemmalistic* language.

33. W. E. B. DuBois, *The Souls of Black Folk* (New York: Bantam, 1989), 45–46.

34. Kevin Gaines, *Uplifting the Race: Black Leadership, Politics, and Culture in the Twentieth Century* (Chapel Hill: University of North Carolina Press, 1996), 33. In his classic study *The Education of Blacks in the South, 1860–1935*, James D. Anderson contends that beyond the specific arguments regarding the utility and efficacy of industrial versus classical education among freed men and women, there was a larger, more significant ideological design promoted by race and capital. Anderson demonstrates the ways in which white patriarchy conspired with Negro leadership, most notably with Booker T. Washington, to maintain the subordinate status of black and white laborers through industrial education expressed most dramatically in the Hampton-Tuskegee Model. Critical to Anderson's analysis is the formation of an alliance of Northern white philanthropists, politicians, religious leaders, and industrialists who met in secretive meetings with the landed gentry of the South from 1899 to 1901 and who later forged a campaign for Southern education from 1901 to 1914 in order to ensure the perpetuation of hegemonic practices of the planters' class. At stake in this alliance was the resolution of two contending ideologies on the Negro Problem. One was the proposal offered by Northern and Southern religious and social leaders for universal education as a substitute for older and cruder methods of socialization and control. The resolution of this dilemma for those on all sides was universal education, but with an important caveat: freed people would benefit best from industrial education based on the Hampton Model. Key to the success of this campaign was collaboration with Negro leadership. "In pursuit of this goal, they collided with the South's landed upper-class whites and their allies, who depended for their wealth and power on large classes of illiterate, exploited agricultural laborers." James D. Anderson, *The Education of Blacks in the South, 1860–1935* (Chapel Hill: University of North Carolina Press, 1988), 80–81.

35. Norman E. Hodges, "Booker T. Washington: 'We Wear the Mask,'" in *Black Leaders and Ideologies in the South: Resistance and Nonviolence*, ed. Preston King and Walter Earl Fluker (Oxfordshire: Taylor and Francis, 2004), 76–110.

36. C. Eric Lincoln, *Race, Religion and the Continuing American Dilemma* (New York: Hill and Wang, 1984); and Victor Anderson, *Beyond Ontological Blackness: An Essay on African American Religious and Cultural Criticism* (New York: Continuum, 1995). See Cornel West's observations on "doubleness" in "Black Strivings in a Twilight Civilization," from *The Cornel West Reader* (New York: Basic, 1999), 87–118, specifically its relationship to despair, destruction, and death using DuBois's metaphor. Henry L. Gates and Cornel West, *The Future of the Race* (New York: Knopf, 1996); see also Robert Michael Franklin's discussion on "strenuous life" in *Liberating Voices: Human Fulfillment and Social Justice in African American Thought* (Minneapolis: Fortress Press, 1990). Most relevant to the purposes of the present discussion is the treatment afforded by cultural critics who ask the question of *dilemma* as it pertains to binary oppositions in black life that grow out of adaptation to a North Atlantic aesthetic. These studies seek to understand the ways in which attachment to the heroic ideal of the European aesthete prevents and further complicates progressive critiques and strategies for agency and peoplehood. Preoccupation with dilemma as a one-dimensional, causal phenomenon is unproductive and akin to riding two horses galloping in different directions, which is a strain on the anatomy. More progressive critiques look at the question of dilemma in respect to macro economic and political variables and their relationship to cultural meanings.

37. See Evelyn Brooks-Higginbotham's discussion on "the politics of respectability" as being the primary sociopolitical strategy for women of the Negro Club Movement. At stake for these black elites was the promotion of "manners and morals" as a campaign against pejorative images of black womanhood depicted as shameless, bestial, and sexually licentious. Evelyn Brooks-Higginbotham, *Righteous Discontent* (Cambridge, Mass.: Harvard University Press, 1993).

38. Gaines, *Uplifting the Race*, 35.

39. Ellis Cose, *The Rage of a Privileged Class: Why Are Middle-Class Blacks Angry? Why Should America Care?* (New York: HarperCollins, 1993). See Audrey Edwards and Craig K. Polite, *Children of the Dream: The Psychology of Black Success* (New York: Doubleday, 1992); see also "The Hidden Rage of Successful Blacks," *Newsweek*, November 15, 1993, 56–59, 61–63.

40. Price M. Cobbs and Judith L. Turnock, *Cracking the Corporate Code: From Survival to Mastery; Real Stories of African American Success* (Washington, D.C.: Executive Leadership Council, 2000), 4.

41. Howard Thurman, *Jesus and the Disinherited* (New York: Abingdon-Cokesbury, 1949), 72.

42. Ibid., 65.

43. Ibid., 73.

44. Thurman, *Deep Is the Hunger* (New York: Harper and Brothers, 1951), 80.

45. Howard Thurman, *The Creative Encounter: An Interpretation of Religion and the Social Witness* (New York: Harper, 1954), 57–65; Thurman, *Meditations of the Heart* (New York, Harper, 1953), 189; Thurman, "Meaning Is Inherent in Life" in *For the Inward Journey: The Writings of Howard Thurman*, by Howard Thurman (San Diego: Harcourt Brace Jovanovich, 1984), 14, 15.

46. Howard Thurman, "A Strange Freedom," in Fluker and Tumber, *A Strange Freedom*, vii.

47. Charles Olson, "These Days," taken from *Teaching with Fire: Poetry That Sustains the Courage to Teach*, ed. Sam M. Intrator and Megan Scribner (San Francisco: Jossey-Bass, 2003), 117.

48. Francis Fukuyama, *The End of History and the Last Man* (New York: Free, 1992), 141-339; see Walter Earl Fluker, *The Stones That the Builders Rejected: The Development of Ethical Leadership from the Black Church Tradition* (Harrisburg, Pa.: Trinity, 1998), 2. David Brooks suggests in an editorial in the *New York Times* that "All Politics Is Thymotic," March 19, 2006.

49. Martin Luther King Jr., "The Drum Major Instinct," in *A Knock at Midnight: Inspiration from Great Sermons of Reverend Martin Luther King, Jr.*, ed. Clayborne Carson and Peter Holloran (New York: Time Warner Books, 1998).

50. Goleman et al., *Primal Leadership: Realizing the Power of Emotional Intelligence* (Boston: Harvard Business School Prass, 2002), 24.

51. Olive Schriener, "The Sunlight Lay Across My Bed," in *A Track to the Water's Edge: The Olive Schreiner Reader*, Howard Thurman, ed. (New York: Harper and Row, 1973), 64–66.

52. Goleman et al., *Primal Leadership,* 36.

53. Jerry B. Harvey, *The Abilene Paradox and Other Meditations on Management* (San Francisco: Jossey-Bass, 1998).

54. Howard Thurman, *Meditations of the Heart* (Richmond, Ind.: Friends United, 1976), 104–5.

55. Sara Lawrence-Lightfoot, *Respect: An Exploration* (Cambridge, Mass.: Perseus, 2000), 9–10.

56. Rosalyn Terborg-Penn, *African American Women in the Struggle for the Vote, 1850–1920* (Bloomington: Indiana University Press, 1998); Karen A. Johnson, *Uplifting Women and the Race* (New York and London: Garland, 2000); Joy James, *Transcending the Talented Tenth;* Belinda Robnett, *How Long? How Long? African American Women in the Struggle for Civil Rights* (New York: Oxford University Press, 1997), 17–18.

57. Higginbotham, "The Politics of Respectability" in *Righteous Discontent* (Cambridge, Mass.: Harvard University Press, 1993). Frederick C. Harris, *Something Within: Religion in African American Activism* (New York and London: Oxford University Press, 2000), 40. James H. Evans, *We Shall Be Changed: Social Problems and Theological Renewal* (Minneapolis: Fortress Press, 1997), 17–43.

58. David Rubel, *Fannie Lou Hamer: From Sharecropping to Politics* (Englewood Cliffs, N.J.: Silver Burdett, 1990), 73. Kay Mills, *This Little Light of Mine: The Life of Fannie Lou Hamer* (New York: Dutton, 1993), 56–77. The role of the FBI in this bloody massacre was even more insidious. Kenneth O'Reilly, *Racial Matters: The F.B.I.'s Secret File on Black America, 1960–1972* (New York: Free, 1989), 1–7.

59. Quoted in Rosetta E. Ross, *Witnessing and Testifying: Black Women, Religion and Civil Rights* (Minneapolis: Fortress Press, 2003), 117n84.

60. Quoted in Lisa Frederiksen Bohannon, *Freedom Cannot Rest: Ella Baker and the Civil Rights Movement* (Greensboro, N.C.: Morgan Reynolds, 2005), 103; Eric R. Bruner, *And Gently He Shall Lead Them: Robert Parris Moses and the Civil Rights Movement* (New York and London: New York University Press, 1994), 27. See also Barbara Ransby, *Ella Baker and the Black Freedom Movement: A Radical Democratic Vision* (University of North Carolina Press, 2003); and Ross, *Witnessing and Testifying.*

61. Oswald W. S. McCall, *The Hand of God*, enl. ed. (Harper & Row, 1939, 1957), 19.

62. Barack Obama, keynote address, the Call to Renewal's "Building a Covenant for a New America" conference, Washington, D.C., June 28, 2006. See http://www.obama.senate.gov/speech/

63. Kwame Anthony Appiah, *Cosmopolitanism: Ethics in a World of Strangers* (New York: Norton, 2006).

64. Josiah Royce, *The Problem of Christianity* (Chicago: University of Chicago Press, 1968).

65. Howard Thurman, "Freedom Is a Discipline," in *Inward Journey.*

66. Appiah, *Cosmopolitanism*, 67.

67. Albert Schweitzer, *Reverence for Life* (New York: Harper & Row, 1969).

68. Ibid.

69. Jim Wallis, *God's Politics* (San Francisco: HarperSanFrancisco, 2005), 297–306.

70. See Michael J. Sandel, *Liberalism and the Limits of Justice*, 2nd ed. (New York: Cambridge University Press, 1998), 173.

71. Jane Steger, *Leaves from a Secret Journal* (Dublin, Ind.: Printit, 1978).

72. Fritjof Capra, *The Web of Life: A New Scientific Understanding of Living Systems* (New York: Anchor Books, 1996); Bill Devall and George Sessions, *Deep Ecology* (Salt Lake City: Gibbs Smith, 1985), 85–88.

73. Michael Lerner, *The Politics of Meaning: Restoring Hope and Possibility in an Age of Cynicism* (Reading, Mass.: Addison-Wesley, 1996).

74. Martin Luther King Jr., *Where Do We Go from Here: Chaos or Community?* (Boston: Beacon, 1967), 167.

75. Ibid., 190.

76. Thurman, *The Search for the Common Good*, 84–85.

77. See Howard Thurman, "The Fascist Masquerade," chap. 4 in *The Church and Organized Movements*, Randolph Crump Miller, ed. Interseminary Series (New York: Harper, 1946), 82–100; Howard Thurman, "Religion in a Time of Crisis," *Garrett Tower* 43, no. 4 (August 1943), 1–3. Thurman's view of the state bears close affinity with American Civil Religion ("transcendent universal religion of the nation") as espoused by Robert Bellah in both its positive and negative potentialities. See Bellah in *American Civil Religion*, Russell Richey and Donald G. Jones, eds. (New York: Harper & Row, 1974), 3–18; also, Robert Bellah, *The Broken Covenant* (New York: Seabury, 1975); "Evil in the American Ethos," Conference on the Legitimation of Evil, Grace Cathedral, San Francisco, February 22, 1970; and "Reflections on Reality in America," *Radical Religion* 1 (1974). See also Gail Gehrig, *American Civil Religion: An Assessment*, Society for the Scientific Study of Religion Monograph Series 3 (Society for the Scientific Study of Religion, 1981).

78. Thurman, *The Search for the Common Good*, 87.

79. Ibid., 87–88.

Chapter 5: Community at the Intersection

1. According to the authors of *Habits of the Heart*: "Americans have sought in the ideal of community a shared trust to anchor and complete the desire for a free and fulfilled self. This quest finds its public analogue in the desire to integrate economic pursuits and interrelationships in an

encompassing fabric of national institutional life. American culture has long been marked by acute ambivalence about the meshing of self-reliance and community, and the nation's history shows a similar ambivalence over the questions of how to combine individual autonomy and the interrelationships of a complex modern economy." Robert N. Bellah et al., *Habits of the Heart: Individualism and Commitment in American Life* (New York: Harper & Row, 1985), 256.

2. Patrice Guinard, *Alexis de Tocqueville: Visionary of Modernity*, with excerpts from his *Democracy in America*; trans. Matyas Becvarov (*Démocratie* 2.4.6) http://cura.Free.Fr/docum/10toc-en./html.

3. Ralph Waldo Emerson, "Self-Reliance," in *The American Tradition in Literature*, ed. Sculley Bradley, Richard Croom Beatty, and E. Hudson Long, 3rd ed. (New York: Norton, published by Grosset and Dunlap), 1131.

4. Ronald Takaki, *Iron Cages: Race and Culture in Nineteenth Century America* (New York: Oxford University Press, 1990), 11. While Takaki relies heavily on Max Weber's *Protestant Ethic and the Spirit of Capitalism*, it is helpful to compare his analysis with H. Mark Roelofs's concept of "the Protestant-Bourgeois Syndrome," where he argues that Martin Luther is preferred over John Calvin for the Protestant pole of this syndrome "because his type of radical, evangelical pietism was much more influential in the development of American religious feeling than was Calvin's more doctrinal theology." For the political, bourgeois pole, Thomas Hobbes is representative of the modern mind. Jonathan Edwards and Benjamin Franklin are their American counterparts. H. Mark Roelofs, *Ideology and Myth in American Politics: A Critique of a National Political Mind* (Boston: Little, Brown, 1976), 51. See also Richard Vetterli and Gary C. Bryner, *In Search of the Republic* (Totawa, N.J.: Rowman and Littlefield, 1987), 1–18; C. B. MacPherson, *The Political Theory of Individualism: Hobbes to Locke* (New York: Oxford University Press, 1962); and MacPherson, *The Life and Times of Liberal Democracy* (New York: Oxford University Press, 1977).

5. Jean Bethke Elshtain, *Democracy on Trial* (New York: Basic, 1995), 16.

6. See especially Bill George with Peter Sims, *True North: Discover Your Authentic Leadership* (San Francisco: Jossey-Bass/Wiley, 2007).

7. Michael Mandelbaum, *The Case for Goliath: How America Acts as the World's Government in the Twenty-first Century* (New York: Public Affairs, 2005); William Bennett, ed., *The Book of Virtues: A Treasury of Great Moral Stories* (New York: Simon & Schuster, 1993); and Bennett, *The Moral Compass: Stories for a Life's Journey* (New York: Simon & Schuster,

1995). For instance, in Bennett's case, one needs only to review his other books: *Counting by Race: Equality from the Founding Father's to Bakke, Our Children and Our Country: Improving America's Schools and Affirming the Common Culture* or *The De-valuing of America: The Fight for Our Culture and Our Children* in order to understand what constitutes "north" in his perspective.

8. Quoted in John Hope Franklin, *Mirror to America: The Autobiography of John Hope Franklin* (New York: Farrar, Strauss and Giroux, 2005), 272.

9. John F. Kennedy, *A Nation of Immigrants* (New York: Harper and Row, 1964).

10. Walter Earl Fluker, "Old Songs and Strong Arms: Remembering Daddy," in *Father Songs: Testimonies by African American Sons and Daughters*, ed. Gloria Wade-Gayles (Boston: Beacon, 1997).

11. Langston Hughes, "I, Too" from *The Collected Poems of Langston Hughes* by Langston Hughes, edited by Arnold Rampersad with David Roessel, associate editor, copyright © 1994 by the Estate of Langston Hughes. Used by permission of Alfred A. Knopf, a division of Random House, Inc.

12. See chap. 3, "Blessed Are the History Makers," in Walter Brueggemann, *Hope within History* (Atlanta: John Knox, 1987), 49ff.

13. Langston Hughes, "Let America Be America Again" from *The Collected Poems of Langston Hughes* by Langston Hughes, edited by Arnold Rampersad with David Roessel, associate editor, copyright © 1994 by the Estate of Langston Hughes. Used by permission of Alfred A. Knopf, a division of Random House, Inc.

14. Walter Earl Fluker, *They Looked for a City* (Lanham, Md.: University Press of America, 1989).

15. Two basic affirmations inform his perspective. One is that "life itself is alive." Thurman suggests that this most obvious characteristic of life, and one that is often overlooked, gives the initial clue to the nature of community. Attention to the processes at work in the living things around us reveals that there is a hard purposefulness, a determination to live in life itself. Thurman's point of departure is with nature. Nature is the paradigm he uses to interpret the dynamic, purposive character of life. See Howard Thurman, "I Will Not Give Up," in *Meditations of the Heart* (Boston: Beacon, 1953, 1981).

This "directiveness" that is at work in nature also manifests itself in the personal and social dimensions of human existence. This movement of life that is revealed in the natural order is synonymous with Thurman's use of "spirit" as defined by Luther Smith:

Spirit is the "breath of God" in creation, providing value and meaning to existence. Realizing and expressing itself in the material world, the work of the spirit is historical and political. It is the source for the definition of the individual, and the individual in relationship to the collective. As it discerns self, it discerns God and what it means to be a creature of God. . . . Spirituality is a way of life committed to understanding the nature and urgings of the spirit; the life organizes all its desires, energies, and resources so that they might be dominated by the spirit. Spirituality brings a harmony to living consistent with the peace and will of God.

Consequently, for Thurman, there is a fundamental structure of interrelatedness and interdependability inherent in all living things, including the social arrangements by which human beings relate to one another.

The second affirmation is that God is the creator of life and existence. For Thurman, God is not merely the creator of creatures, but is the "Bottomer of existence," that is, transcendent, all-inclusive, all-comprehending, and universal. God is related to life and existence as Mind in a way similar to the human mind in its relation to time-space existence. The Mind of God seeks to realize itself in time-space manifestations. Therefore, existence is understood as divine activity. Divine activity is the basis for the order that is observable in life and provides the framework for interpretation of the will of God. He argues that it is reasonable to assume, therefore, that

Wherever life is found, evidence of a creative intent must also exist in that which is being experienced, reacted to, observed or studied. One such sign, and the most crucial one, is the way life seeks always to realize itself in wholeness, harmony, and integration within the potential that characterizes that particular experience of life.

Thurman believed that the "creative intent" of the creator can be observed at all levels of life and existence, from tiny microscopic cells to human society. In respect to human society, social, political, and economic arrangements are expressions of this fundamental insight. "In human society," Thurman writes, "the experience of community, or realized potential, is rooted in life itself because the intuitive human urge for community reflects a characteristic of life." Society, however, finds its basis in the individual's need to be cared for and assured that she or he is not isolated from others.

16. Aristotle and Martin Ostwald, *Nicomachean Ethics* 3.6, Library of Liberal Arts, 75 (Indianapolis: Bobbs-Merrill, 1962).

17. "The man, then, who faces and who fears the right things and from the right motive, in the right way and from the right time, and who feels confidence under the corresponding conditions, is brave; for the brave man feels and acts according to the merits of the case and in whatever way the rule directs. Now the end of every activity is conformity to the corresponding state of character. This is true, therefore, of the brave man as well as of others. But courage is noble. Therefore the end also is noble; for each thing is defined by its end. Therefore it is for a noble end that the brave man endures and acts as courage directs." Aristotle, *Nicomachean Ethics* 3.7.

18. See Autobiography, part 2, chap. 8, http://www.Sscent.ucla.Edu/southasia/History/Gandhi/Pieter.Html.

19. Paul Tillich, *Systematic Theology*, vol. 1 (Chicago: University of Chicago Press, 1951), 91; 193–98. See also Paul Tillich, *The Courage to Be* (New Haven, Conn.: Yale University Press, 1952); Tillich, *The Dynamics of Faith* (New York: Harper, 1958).

20. Sages standing in God's holy fire
     As in the gold mosaic of a wall,
     Come from the holy fire, perne in a gyre,
     And be the singing-masters of my soul.
     Consume my heart away; sick with desire
     And fastened to a dying animal
     It knows not what it is; and gather me
     Into the artifice of eternity.
     —William Butler Yeats, "Sailing to Byzantium" (1927)

21. Howard Thurman, "I Need Courage" from *Meditations of the Heart* by Howard Thurman. Copyright © 1953, 1981 by Anne Thurman. Reprinted by permission of Beacon Press, Boston.

22. Thich Nhat Hanh, *Creating True Peace: Ending Violence in Yourself, Your Family, Your Community, and the World* (New York: Free, 2003), 18.

23. James Q. Wilson, *The Moral Sense* (New York: Free, 1993), 2.

24. Ibid., 122–23.

25. Ibid.; see the chapter titled "Fairness," 55–78.

26. Lani Guinier, *The Tyranny of the Majority: Fundamental Fairness in Representative Democracy*, foreword by Stephen L. Carter (New York: Free, 1995), 6.

27. The term "sympathetic understanding" exhibits Thurman's continuing debt to the "moral sense" teachings of Scottish common-sense philosophy (Smith, *The Theory of Moral Sentiments*, 1759), as filtered

through the moral teaching of nineteenth-century divinity schools, and the New-Kantian idealism of George Cross, Josiah Royce, and others.

28. "College and Color" was published in *The Student Challenge*, the official organ of the Student Fellowship for Student Life-Service, a national Christian student organization founded in 1922. It is Thurman's first nationally published work on matters of religion and race. Here he advocates a "Christian way in race relations" on American college campuses in which "sympathetic understanding" produces mutual respect. He also draws on the work of George Coe, a pioneer in the fields of psychology of religion and religious education, who was a major influence upon Thurman's intellectual development during his seminary years.

29. Jacob Needleman, *The American Soul: Rediscovering the Wisdom of the Founders* (New York: Jeremy P. Tarcher/Putnam, 2002), 10.

30. Howard Thurman, "College and Color," in The Papers of Howard Washington Thurman, Walter Earl Fluker, ed. (Greenville, S.C.: University of South Carolina Press, 2009)

31. Thurman, "College and Color."

32. The "technique of relaxation" for Thurman had specific religious connotations, following the study of mysticism he was undertaking in the late 1920s. Many of the writers in the early twentieth century who described the psychology of mysticism wrote of a preparatory stage akin to relaxation. George Coe, who was a major intellectual influence on Thurman, described the spiritual satisfactions of relaxation in *The Psychology of Religion*. See William James, *The Varieties of Religious Experience: A Study in Human Nature* (New York: Modern Library, 1936) chaps. 16, 17; Evelyn Underhill, *Mysticism* (New York: Dutton, 1910); George Coe, *The Psychology of Religion* (Chicago: University of Chicago Press, 1916), 138–40.

33. Howard Thurman, *Disciplines of the Spirit* (New York: Harper & Row, 1963), 120.

34. Ibid., 122.

35. Justice, according to Thurman, is normally understood as "the artificial equalization of unequals—the restoration of balance, of equilibrium, in a situation in which the balance has been upset." Thurman, *The Growing Edge* (New York: Harper, 1956), 79.

36. Ibid., 81–84.

37. I am using the term "compassion" as synonymous with "love." Thurman normally uses the term "love."

38. Thurman uses the word "mercy," but in this context the meaning is synonymous.

39. Howard Thurman, *Second Century Convocation*, Washington University, February 1955. The Howard Thurman Papers Collection, Boston University.

40. Ibid.

41. See the discussion on empathy and imagination above.

42. Thurman, *Growing Edge*, 27–28.

43. Howard Thurman, *For the Inward Journey: The Writings of Howard Thurman* (San Diego: Harcourt Brace Jovanovich, 1984); Thurman, *Mysticism and the Experience of Love* (Wallingford, Pa.: Pendle Hill, 1961).

44. Thurman, *Inward Journey*, 29.

45. See Smith, *Howard Thurman: The Mystic as Prophet* (Washington, D.C.: University Press of America, 1981), 46; see also in Smith, Thurman's treatment of "reconciliation," chap. 5, 104–27.

46. Ibid., 122.

47. D. R. Bhandari, "Plato's Concept of Justice: An Analysis," http://www.Bu.Edu/wcp/Papers/Anci/AnciBhan.Htm.

48. For instance, the tripartite hierarchy of reason, will, and appetite and corresponding doctrine of the state with rulers, soldiers/artisans, and workers is not quite what we have in mind when talk about democracy—and the question of justice as treating all equally and fairly with the rule of the wise formulated by Plato.

49. Thomas Wren reminds modern readers that indeed the prisoner to the shadows on the wall was *forced* into the light. "[T]he cosmic *telos* is the supplemental notion provided by external agents such as teachers, parents and society as a whole: recall that the prisoner was forced to begin his journey to the light." Thomas Wren, "Philosophical Moorings," in *Handbook for Moral and Character Education.* Edited by Larry Nucci and Darcia Narvaez (Mahwah, NJ: Erlbaum, 2008)15–16. Thurman strikes a similar note in his interpretation of Plato's Myth of Er in the *Republic*. The soul's *daimon*, according to Plato, selects an image or a pattern that we are supposed to live on earth but once we enter the realm of materiality we forget that image, but the *daimon* remembers and is therefore the soul-companion which guides us through *anamnesis* in recollecting the meaning of the soul's code. Howard Thurman, "The Inner Light" Audio Cassette, n.p., n.d., The Howard Thurman Educational Trust Fund, Morehouse College, Atlanta, Georgia. See also James Hillman, *The Soul's Code: In Search of Character and Calling* (New York: Random House, 1996)7–9.

50. Thurman, *The Creative Encounter* (New York: Harper, 1954), 67–71, 121.

51. Ibid., 81.

52. Warren Bennis and Robert Thomas, *Geeks and Geezers: How Era, Values, and Defining Moments Shape Leaders* (Boston: Harvard Business School Press, 2002), 108; see chap. 4, "Crucibles of Leadership," 87–120. Bennis and Thomas take into account the *era* in which the leader functions, his or her individual factors (experiences, organization of meaning), and leadership competencies (adaptive capacity, engagement of others to create shared meaning, voice, and integrity).

53. Dalai Lama, *Ethics for the New Millennium* (New York: Riverhead, 1999), 64.

54. Thich Nhat Hanh, *Living Buddha, Living Christ*, introduction by Elaine Pagels (New York: Riverhead, 1995), 11.

55. At his last speech, before an international conference on monasticism in Bangkok, Thailand, in 1968, it is reported that Merton referred to a traditional representation of the Buddha seated in the lotus position with one hand pointing to the earth and the other holding a begging bowl. This image is relevant for monasticism, Merton said. The begging bowl represents the ultimate theological belief in the interdependence of all living things. This concept is the most central to Mahayana Buddhism. The whole idea of compassion is based on a keen awareness of this mutual interdependence. http://www.Sheila-t-harty.com/Thomas%20Mertons%20Last%20Talk%20in%20Bangkok%201968.doc.

56. Walter Earl Fluker, "Airplane Trip from Myrtle Beach, South Carolina," reprinted from *From One Brother to Another: Voices of African American Men*, edited by William J. Key and Robert Johnson-Smith II, copyright © 1996 by Judson Press. Used by permission of Judson Press, 800-4-JUDSON, www.judsonpress.com.

57. Howard Thurman, "Keep Open the Door of Thy Heart," quoted in *A Strange Freedom* (Boston: Beacon, 1998), 301.

58. Reneé Girard, *The Scapegoat* (Baltimore: Johns Hopkins University Press, 1986); Theophus Harold Smith, *Conjuring Culture: Biblical Formations of Black America* (New York: Oxford University Press, 1994); Howard Thurman, *The Luminous Darkness; A Personal Interpretation of the Anatomy of Segregation and the Ground of Hope* (New York: Harper and Row, 1965).

59. See my discussion in *They Looked for a City*, chap. 3; see also Thurman, *With Head and Heart: The Autobiography of Howard Thurman* (San Diego: Harcourt Brace Jovanovich, 1981), 268.

60. Quoted by Thurman in *Disciplines*, 80; Thurman, *Inward Journey*, 16; see also Thurman, "The Circle of Life," cassette recording, no. 65–8, Howard Thurman Educational Trust Fund, San Francisco.

61. This notion has significant implications for Thurman's understanding of America and the redemptive suffering of black people. America is more than a historical project for Thurman; it is a divine-human experiment in the evolutionary processes of life. Despite the undue ravages and unmerited suffering of black Americans, Thurman's theodicy would suggest that their affliction has been a salvific element in an otherwise destructive destiny. This thesis is present in Howard Thurman, "America in Search of a Soul" in *Deep River: The Negro Spiritual Speaks of Life and Death* (Richmond, Ind.: Friends United, 1975) and "Freedom under God." See discussion of Thurman's understanding of the state under "The Triadic Character of Community: World," in *They Looked for a City*. Gandhi's request to hear the delegates of the Indian pilgrimage sing the Negro spiritual "Were You There When They Crucified My Lord?" carries this basic idea. Thurman quotes Gandhi as saying, "I feel that this song gets to the root of the experience of the entire human race under the spread of the healing wings of suffering." See Thurman, *With Head and Heart*, 134. Thurman also suggests that the black slave redeemed the religion his slave master profaned. Thurman, *Deep River*, 40.

62. See my discussion of the redemptive suffering of the individual for the collective destiny of the human race under "Means of Actualization: Nonviolence as Moral Imperative," in *They Looked for a City*.

63. Thurman, *Disciplines*, 83.

64. See the discussion below of the nature and function of nonviolence. Redemptive suffering and nonviolence are means of creating a climate of love. Redemptive suffering used in the second sense is synonymous with nonviolence. For both, the motivation, method, and goal is love or reconciliation. See Thurman, *Disciplines*, 104–27.

65. Thurman, *In Search of the Republic*, 26; see also p. 4.

66. Thurman, *Disciplines*, 83.

67. Elizabeth Yates, *Howard Thurman: Portrait of a Practical Dreamer* (New York: John Day, 1964), 233.

68. Thurman, *With Head and Heart*, 268–69; Thurman, "Habakkuk" in *The Interpreter's Bible*, vol. VI (New York: Abingdon-Cokesbury, 1956), 981.

69. Thurman, *Deep River*, 64.

70. King, "Pilgrimage to Nonviolence," in *Strength to Love*, 154.

71. The successful bus boycott in Montgomery, Alabama, culminated in the founding of the Southern Christian Leadership Conference (SCLC) on January 10, 1957. With SCLC, King became president of a large organization to coordinate nonviolent protest movements that were appearing in various parts of the South. The SCLC's activity centered

on two main foci: using nonviolent philosophy as a means of protest and securing the right of the ballot for every citizen, particularly black Southerners. "This Is SCLC" (leaflet of the Southern Christian Leadership Conference, rev. ed., 1964), in August Meier and Francis L. Broderick, *Negro Protest: Thought in the Twentieth Century* (Indianapolis: Bobbs-Merrill, 1965), 270; see also Garrow, *Bearing the Cross* (New York: Morrow, 1986), 83–126; and Adam Fairclough, *To Redeem the Soul of America: The Southern Christian Leadership Conference and Martin Luther King Jr.* (Athens, Ga., and London: University of Georgia Press, 1987), 11–35.

72. Martin Luther King Jr., "A Time to Break Silence" in *A Testament of Hope* (San Francisco: Harper & Row), 231–244.

73. Thurman collected all of Schreiner's available works and edited and published an anthology of her writings titled *A Track to the Water's Edge: The Olive Schreiner Reader* (New York: Harper & Row, 1973). See also Schreiner's "The Dawn of Civilization," in *The Nation and the Athenaeum*, March 26, 1921; "The Hunter," in *Track to the Water's Edge*, 84–95; and "Three Dreams in the Desert," in ibid., 53–56. These selections were favorites of Thurman from which he often quoted. See my discussion of the relationship between Thurman and Schreiner in *They Looked for a City*, chap. 1.

74. See especially Schreiner's "Three Dreams in the Desert," 53–56.

75. Ibid., 56.

Chapter 6: Staying Awake at the Intersection

1. King, *Where Do We Go from Here: Chaos or Community?* (New York: Harper & Row, 1967), 171.

2. Ronald A. Heifitz and Martin Linsky, *Leadership on the Line: Staying Alive through the Dangers of Leading* (Boston: Harvard Business School Press, 2002); Bill George with Peter Sims, *True North: Discover Your Authentic Leadership* (San Francisco: Jossey-Bass/Wiley, 2007); Warren Bennis and Robert Thomas, *Geeks and Geezers: How Era, Values, and Defining Moments Shape Leaders* (Boston: Harvard Business School Press, 2002), 101–6; Ronald Heifetz, *Leadership without Easy Answers* (Cambridge, Mass.: Belknap Press of Harvard University Press, 1994); Daniel Goleman, Richard Boyatzis, and Anne McKee, *Primal Leadership: Realizing the Power of Emotional Intelligence* (Boston: Harvard Business School Press, 2002); Manfred F. R. Kets de Vries, *Leaders, Fools, and Impostors: Essays on the Psychology of Leadership* (San Francisco: Jossey-Bass, 1993); Rob Goffee and Gareth Jones, *Why Should Anyone Be Led by You? What It Takes to Be an Authentic Leader* (Boston: Harvard Business School Press, 2006).

3. Ray L. Hart, *Unfinished Man and the Imagination* (New York: Herder and Herder, 1968).

4. Walter Earl Fluker, *The Stones That the Builders Rejected: The Development of Ethical Leadership from the Black Church Tradition* (Harrisburg, Pa.: Trinity, 1998); Hart, *Unfinished Man*, 1968.

5. Laurence Thomas, *Living Morally: A Psychology of Moral Character* (Philadelphia: Temple University Press, 1989), 17–26.

6. Robin S. Snell, "Studying Moral Ethos Using an Adapted Kohlbergian Model," in *Organization Studies*, Winter 2000, 267–95.

7. Robert Jackall, *Moral Mazes: The World of Corporate Managers* (Cambridge and New York: Oxford University Press, 1988), 101.

8. Marianne Williamson, ed., *Imagine What America Could Be in the Twenty-first Century: Visions of a Better Future from Leading American Thinkers* (Emmaus, Pa.: Daybreak/Global Renaissance Alliance, 2000). Peter Senge, "Systems," 167–78.

9. Howard Gardner, *Leading Minds: An Anatomy of Leadership* (New York: Basic, 1995).

10. See Peter J. Paris's excellent essay "Moral Development for African American Leadership," in *The Stones That the Builders Rejected*, 23–32; Alasdaire MacIntyre, *After Virtue: A Study in Moral Theory* (Notre Dame, Ind.: University of Notre Dame Press, 1981).

11. Aristotle, *Nicomachean Ethics* 1.1.1.

12. James Baldwin, "Nothing Personal," in *The Price of the Ticket: Collected Non-fiction, 1948–1945* (New York: St. Martin's/Marek, 1985), 393.

13. James O. Pawelski, "Character as Ethical Democracy: Definitions and Measures," unpublished paper, Vanderbilt University, September 1, 2003.

14. Stephen L. Carter, *Civility: Manners, Morals, and the Etiquette of Democracy* (New York: Basic, 1998).

15. Arthur Woodard, "May 31, 2006: Robben Island Tour Inspires Revelation," in Special Report: Journey to South Africa, *Morehouse Magazine*, Fall–Winter 2006, 45.

Chapter 7: Remembering, Retelling, and Reliving Our Stories

1. Robert A. Armour writes, "Actually no complete version of the stories has survived from ancient times, and the earliest version was written down by Plutarch, the Greek traveler and historian from the first century after Christ. For the next four hundred years, other western writers such as Diodorus Siculus, Firmicus Maternus, and Macrobius recounted the adventures of the two gods and added details of their own to the stories."

Armour, *Gods and Myths of Ancient Egypt* (Cairo: American University, 1986; 7th printing, 1993), 72.

2. Mircea Eliade, *Myth and Reality* (Colophon Books; New York: Harper, 1963), chap. 2, "Magic and Prestige of Origins," 21–38.

3. In an interview about her novel *Beloved*, Toni Morrison said, "There is no place you or I can go, to think about or not think about, to summon the presences of, or recollect the absences of slaves; nothing that reminds us of the ones who made the journey and of those who did not make it. There is no suitable memorial or plaque or wreath or wall or park or skyscraper lobby. There's no 300-foot tower. There is no small bench by the road." Mae G. Henderson, "Toni Morrison's *Beloved*: Remembering the Body as Historical Text," in *Comparative American Identities: Race, Sex, and Nationality in the Modern Text*, ed. Hortense J. Spillers (New York and London: Routledge, 1991), 71; "A Bench by the Road," *The World: The Journal of the Unitarian Universalist Association* 3 (January–February 1989): 4–5, 37–40. In a 1977 interview with Paula Giddens, Morrison explains, "The memory is long beyond the parameters of cognition. I don't want to sound too mystical about it, but I feel like a conduit, I really do. I'm fascinated about what it means to make people remember what I don't even know." Paula Giddings, "The Triumphant Song of Toni Morrison," *Encore*, December 12, 1977, 26–30, quoted in Carolyn C. Denard, "Toni Morrison," *Modern American Women Writers* (New York: Scribner's, 1991), 317. Morrison's narrative strategy is a "kind of literary archeology" in which she uses imaginative and cultural knowledge to retrieve and reconstruct the past of African Americans. Thus her works are sites of "dangerous memories," small benches by the road, memorials that invoke resistance and healing.

4. James Hillman, *The Soul's Code: In Search of Character and Calling* (New York: Random House, 1996), 4; see also chap. 1, "In a Nutshell: The Acorn Theory and the Redemption of Psychology," 3–40.

5. Ellen Van Velsor and Wilfred H. Draft, "A Lifelong Developmental Perspective on Leader Development," in *The Center for Creative Leadership Handbook of Leadership Development*, ed. C. D. McCauley and Ellen Van Velsor; 2nd ed. (San Francisco: Jossey-Bass, 2004), chap. 13.

6. Gil Baille, *Violence Unveiled: Humanity at the Crossroads* (New York: Crossroad, 1995), xv.

7. See Harold H. Oliver, *Relatedness: Essays in Metaphysics and Theology* (Macon, Ga.: Mercer, 1984).

8. Hugh Prather, from *Notes to Myself* by Hugh Prather, copyright © 1970 by Real People Press. Used by permission of Bantam Books, a division of Random House, Inc.

9. Howard Thurman, *With Head and Heart: The Autobiography of Howard Thurman* (New York: Harcourt Brace Jovanovich, 1979).

Chapter 8: Ethical Decision-Making at the Intersection Where Worlds Collide

1. Cultural critic Michael Eric Dyson suggests that Gaye's prophetic critique of the Vietnam War "might be viewed as the positive public expression of his religious beliefs: that God is love, that justice should prevail, and that human beings should treat each other with respect. His black-church Pentecostal roots and Christian ethics fueled his loving critique of the world. But Marvin's learning in the world allowed him to return the favor: his experience beyond the world allowed him to reshape his religious beliefs. *What's Going On* was outward looking; it cast a searching spiritual eye on social relations." Michael Eric Dyson, *Mercy, Mercy Me: The Art, Loves, and Demons of Marvin Gaye* (New York: Basic Civitas, 2004), 167, 1–2.

2. "Responsibility . . . proceeds in every moment of decision and choice to inquire: What is going on?" H. Richard Niebuhr, *The Responsible Self: An Essay in Christian Moral Philosophy*, introduction by James M. Gustafson (New York: Harper & Row, 1963, 1978), 60. See chap. 1, "The Meaning of Responsibility," 47–68.

3. See Darryl M. Trimiew, *Voices of the Silenced: The Responsible Self in a Marginalized Community* (Cleveland: Pilgrim, 1993).

4. Daniel Pink, *A Whole New Mind: Moving from the Information Age to the Conceptual Age* (New York: Riverhead Books, 2005), 125–51.

5. Michael Polanyi, *Personal Knowledge: Towards a Post-critical Philosophy* (London: Routledge, 1958, 1998); Polanyi, *The Tacit Dimension* (New York: Anchor Books, 1967); Malcolm Gladwell, *Blink: The Power of Thinking without Thinking* (Boston: Little, Brown, 2005).

6. Polanyi writes, "We must conclude that the paradigmatic case of scientific knowledge, in which all faculties that are necessary for finding and holding scientific knowledge are fully developed, is the knowledge of approaching discovery. To hold such knowledge is an act deeply committed to the conviction that there is something there to be discovered. It is personal, in the sense of involving the personality of him who holds it, and also in the sense of being, as a rule, solitary; but there is no trace in it of self-indulgence. The discoverer is filled with a compelling sense of responsibility for the pursuit of a hidden truth, which demands his services for revealing it. His act of knowing exercises a personal judgement in relating evidence to an external reality, an aspect of which he is seeking to apprehend." Polanyi, *Tacit Dimension*, 24–25, http://www.Infed.org/thinkers/polanyi.htm.

7. Thurman, *Deep Is the Hunger* (New York: Harper & Brothers, 1951; paperback, Richmond, Ind.: Friends United, 1975), 64.

8. http://www.gse.Harvard.edu/~t656_web/From 2000-2001_students/ Polanyi_Nina.htm.

9. W. Chan Kim and Renee Mauborgne, *Blue Ocean Strategy: How to Create Uncontested Market Space and Make the Competition Irrelevant* (Boston: Harvard Business School Press), 4.

10. Gladwell, *Blink*, 141.

11. Howard Thurman, "The Sound of the Genuine," baccalaureate address, Spelman College, May 4, 1980.

12. Howard Thurman, H. I. Hester Lectureship, Golden Gate Baptist Theological Seminary, Mill Valley, Calif., February 8–12, 1971.

13. "The Mensch of Malden Mills, CEO Aaron Feuerstein Puts Employees First," *Sixty Minutes*, July 6, 2003, http://www.CBSNews.com/ stories/2003/07/03/60minutes/main561656.shtml.

14. *Parade Magazine,* Sept. 8, 1996, 4–5.

15. Joseph L. Badarraco Jr., "The Discipline of Building Character," in *Harvard Business Review on Leadership* (Boston: Harvard Business Review Publishing, 1998), 89–113. Badarraco's "Guide to Defining Moments" (112–13) is concerned primarily with managers and leaders in corporate environments. Hence I have substituted "stockholders" with "stakeholder," and "company" with "community."

16. "Profile: Dr. Ben Carson," *Religion and Ethics Newsweekly*, January 11, 2008, episode 1119, http://www.pbs.org/wnet/religionandethics/ week1119/profile.html.

17. Ibid.

18. For a more extensive discussion of these four decision-making questions utilized by Carson in this case and others, see Ben Carson with Gregg Lewis, *Take the Risk: Learning to Identify, Choose, and Live with Acceptable Risk* (Grand Rapids: Zondervan, 2008), 11, 40, 106–24.

19. Ibid., 20, 25–26.

20. James M. Gustafson, *Christ and the Moral Life* (Chicago and London: University of Chicago Press, 1968), 250.

21. Dalai Lama, *Ethics for the New Millennium* (New York: Riverhead, 1999), 64.

22. According to most sources, including *Newsweek* and others, Katrina hit New Orleans early (5:00 a.m. to 7:00 a.m.) Monday, August 29. Federal troops and national assistance did not arrive until around 11:00 a.m. Wednesday, August 31.

INDEX

About the Author

Walter Earl Fluker is Executive Director of the Leadership Center at Morehouse College, Coca-Cola Professor of Leadership Studies, and since 1992 editor of the Howard Thurman Papers Project. He is also founder of VisionQuest International, a nonprofit organization committed to the development and practice of ethical leadership in national and global venues.

He is currently engaged in expanding a multifaceted international leadership project in South Africa in partnership with the Oprah Winfrey Foundations, the United States Department of State, and the African Presidential Archives and Research Center at Boston University.

Known as an expert in the theory and practice of ethical leadership, Fluker is a featured speaker, lecturer, and workshop leader at foundations, businesses, corporations, religious institutions, colleges and universities, as well as consultant to both national and international organizations. In his consulting practice, he works with professionals and emerging leaders in both the public and private domains.

Recently, he was appointed to the advisory board for the American Association of Colleges and Universities' new initiative: *Core Commitments: Educating Students for Personal and Social Responsibility* and to the Westminster Schools Board of Directors. He serves on the Board of Overseers at Boston University School of Theology, Garret-Evangelical Theological Seminary, and the Atlanta Speech School. Fluker has served as faculty for the Goldman Sachs Global Leaders Program and as distinguished speaker for the U.S. Embassy Speaker/Specialist Program in South Africa, Nigeria, India, and China. He was keynote speaker and special workshop facilitator at the 2007 Democratic Leadership Council's National Conversation and a member of the National Selection Committee for *U.S. News & World Report*'s "America's Best Leaders" for the past four years.

He has completed the first volume of the trilogy titled *The Papers of Howard Washington Thurman*, recently published by the University of South Carolina Press. His other publications include *They Looked for a City: A Comparative Analysis of the Ideal of Community in the Thought of Howard Thurman and Martin Luther King Jr.* and *The Stones That the*

Builders Rejected: Essays on Ethical Leadership from the Black Church Tradition; he is coeditor with Preston King of *Black Leaders and Ideologies in the South: Resistance and Nonviolence*; and coeditor with Catherine Tumber of *A Strange Freedom: The Best of Howard Thurman on Religious Experience and Public Life.*

His prior academic experience includes professorial and administrative positions at Vanderbilt University, Harvard College, Dillard University, and Colgate-Rochester Divinity School; and he has served as a visiting professor and scholar at Harvard University, the University of Cape Town (South Africa), Columbia Theological Seminary, and Princeton Theological Seminary. He earned a Ph.D. in Social Ethics from Boston University, a Master of Divinity degree from Garrett-Evangelical Seminary, and a bachelor's degree in philosophy and biblical studies from Trinity College.